Dispute Management in Heritage Conservation: The Case of *in situ* Museums

Kalliopi Fouseki

BAR International Series 2774

2015

First Published in 2015 by
British Archaeological Reports Ltd
United Kingdom

BAR International Series 2774

Dispute Management in Heritage Conservation: The Case of *in situ* Museums

ISBN: 978 1 4073 1439 6

Cover Image:

Acropolis Museum (photo: Kalliopi Fouseki, 10/08/2015)

Printed in England

All BAR titles are available from:

British Archaeological Reports Ltd
Oxford
United Kingdom
Phone +44 (0)1865 310431
Fax +44 (0)1865 316916
Email: info@barpublishing.com
www.barpublishing.com

Contents

Tables

Figures

Acknowledgments

This book is an enhanced version of my doctoral thesis that was completed at the University College London. It would have not been materialised without the tremendous support of my supervisors, Kathy Tubb and Tim Williams. The first stimuli for this research were cultivated during my MA in Cultural Heritage Studies at UCL. The encouragement of my then supervisor, Beverley Butler, was catalytic in instigating my doctoral research. I would also like to thank my invaluable friends who listened patiently any time I needed them. More importantly, I would like to thank my parents to whose memory I dedicate this book and my husband, Georgios Alexopoulos, who has been supporting me all these years at all levels.

CHAPTER ONE: INTRODUCTION

1.1 Introduction

One of the main foci in heritage management during the last four decades has been the integration of the so-called value-based approach into heritage management decision-making. This approach stresses the significance of assessing the divergent values that different parties assign to heritage sites at the early stages of a heritage management project (see for instance, Aplin 2002; Avrami et al. 2000; Darvill 1995; Deeben et al. 1999; De la Torre 2002; 2005; Demas 2002; Hall and McArthur 1996; Klamer and Zuidhof 1999; Mason and Avrami 2002; National Trust 2002; 2003; Pearson and Sullivan 1995; Skeates 2000; Tunbridge and Ashworth 1996). In this literature it is often argued that values are frequently conflicting and that such conflicts may deter the successful implementation of a project. However, despite the growing emphasis on the necessity to manage disputing values and recognise different power relationships, there is still a massive gap in current research with regards to the development of techniques for managing disputes that occur in the heritage sector as a result of conflicting values.

The shift in heritage management theory and practice from the emphasis on conservation and visitor management to the value-led approach took place gradually in the 1970s and reached a peak in the 1990s (Aplin 2002, 141). During this period special emphasis was placed on the recognition of values attributed to heritage by indigenous and minority groups as well as on the involvement of local communities in the heritage management process (Aplin 2002, 141). This emphasis is vividly reflected to the so called 'Burra Charter' heritage management process, among the widely used heritage management processes which has constituted the basis for several suggested heritage management plans (see the revised version at ICOMOS 2013; Truscott and Young 2000). However, the Burra charter, as well as similar heritage management processes (see Clark 1999; 2001; Kerr 1996), although acknowledging the importance of assessing the divergent interests, do not incorporate the development of specific dispute management strategies as an essential component of the process. Specific also heritage management plans for sites such as Stonehenge (English Heritage 2000) and of Hadrian's Wall (Bell 2013; Hadrian's wall Country 2002) (see other management plans in Hodder and Doughty 2007; Marta de la Torre 2005) emphasise the necessity to develop partnerships with the involved parties and actively involve local communities in the heritage management process. Despite these, there is a lack in developing strategies that can facilitate the achievement of the above aims. More recently, a didactic case study was produced by the Getty Conservation Institute (Myers et al. 2010) in collaboration with the Jordanian Department of Antiquities for use in academic programmes and courses. This study focuses on values-based approaches to heritage management and on the application of consensus building strategies. However, since this document is intended to be used for didactic purposes, it lacks the theorisation of the dissonant nature of values and heritage, and the development of appropriate tools.

It is the aim of this book to explore the development and integration of dispute management strategies within heritage management. It will do this through the investigation of disputes related to archaeological remains, discovered on rescue excavations, which are conserved *in situ* and are integrated into modern buildings (these cases are defined in the book as *in situ* museums). The main reason for selecting the case of *in situ* museums rather than examples where remains are preserved by record or reburial is because this case allows a holistic examination of dispute situations that occur before, during and after the discovery of archaeological remains. In other words, the examination of disputes related to the emergence of *in situ* museums permit the exploration of disputes related not only to the preservation and conservation but also to the presentation, interpretation and aesthetic integration of archaeological remains into a modern building. In addition, the case of *in situ* museums provides the chance to examine the extent to which the creation of an *in situ* museum can constitute a negotiated and compromise action or, occasionally, a source of dispute.

The case studies analysed in this book derive from a broad geographical area and chronological period in order to identify common disputing patterns. The identification of repeated patterns will form the basis for the development of the dispute management model. Although the intention is to compare examples across a diverse range of geographical regions, the case of the New Acropolis Museum (NAM) in Athens has been selected as the core case study of this book. My personal work experience as an archaeologist on the site of Makriyianni, where the museum building is located, has provided me with an in-depth knowledge of the history of the site. This also gave me the ability to assess the quality and accuracy of sources related to the NAM such as newspapers and personal communications.

1.2 Book outline

The core and ultimate aim of this book is to develop an operational dispute management model that can be incorporated into the overall heritage management process. Chapter 2 illustrates the methodological approaches that have been followed to develop this model and also outlines some of the difficulties and limitations encountered during the research. Chapter 3 provides the broader theoretical framework of the analysis and presents a descriptive dispute management model which constitutes the basis for analysing the disputes in the case studies and for creating the operational dispute management model in chapter 8. The formation of the descriptive dispute management model was based on an interdisciplinary assessment of theories examining the nature and management of dispute including sociological, economic, behavioural, psychological, geographical and organisation management theories.

This interdisciplinary examination allowed the identification of some of the main and common factors that lead to disputes. Among the several dispute factors those that apply mostly to the heritage sector have been selected. In this chapter I also demonstrate that the interdisciplinary approach adopted for conceptualising and developing a preliminary descriptive dispute management model should characterise the decision-making process and actions in the heritage sector as a whole. I will argue that although interdisciplinarity may constitute a potential source of dispute in itself it can also be a driving force for innovative projects. Innovation can occasionally play a significant role in avoiding and resolving external disputes as will be shown in the case of Jorvik Viking Centre, in York (UK), for example.

Chapter 4 will provide an overview of the case of *in situ* museums, a museum type which has not been thoroughly analysed and explored in heritage literature and museum theory. This chapter aims to conceptualize the case of *in situ* museums and to identify their distinctive characteristics which differentiate them from other museum types and which play a significant role in dispute genesis, escalation and resolution. Emphasis is placed on the extent to which innovation, change, ownership and aesthetics function as sources of dispute. These characteristics are analysed through broader theoretical perspectives using theories of organisational change, diffusion of innovation and aesthetics in order to understand why these factors lead to dispute as well as how they can possibly be used as a means for resolving a dispute. The conceptualisation of *in situ* museums makes it possible to identify further key elements that can be integrated into the dispute management model and which refer specifically to the case of *in situ* museums.

The following three chapters, 5, 6 and 7, present the case studies of the book which relate to disputes that emerged during the discovery of significant archaeological remains. The descriptive dispute management model suggested in chapter 3 is used in the case-study chapters as a tool for analyzing the disputes in the case studies. Chapter 5 presents examples of disputes that occurred during the construction of a private, development project. Chapter 6 examines cases of disputes that emerged from the discovery of archaeological sites during the implementation of a public project, mainly the rehabilitation of an open-space, and, finally, chapter 7

discusses the case of the New Acropolis Museum (NAM).

The analysis of case studies is divided into three main chapters based on the type of the development project that resulted in the discovery of the archaeological remains. This division is driven by the fact that public perceptions seem to be shaped, motivated and transformed both by the values that the public attributes to a contemporary project and the ones that it places on an archaeological site. Therefore, public attitudes towards the preservation or destruction of an archaeological site are interlinked with people's attitudes, perceptions and values towards contemporary projects during which an archaeological site is discovered. However, although I acknowledge the fact that public perceptions are usually an amalgam of perceptions towards the past and the present, I want to emphasise through the above division that, at least in the case of *in situ* museums, the perceptions towards the present and modern constitute the motivation force for shaping perceptions towards the past and antiquity.

The analysis of each case study begins with a brief historic review of the disputes which actually coincides with the first step of the descriptive dispute management model (chapter 3 and 8) the aim of which is the provision of a historic timeline. The analysis proceeds following the steps of the descriptive dispute management model suggested in chapter 3 (Figure 1). The aim of the analytical approach to the dispute situations in each case study is the identification of the constants and variables of a dispute situation. The term 'constants', a term often used in management science, refers in the book to the common behavioural patterns, actions and reactions of the involved parties in a dispute situation. The aim is to identify some common behavioural patterns and actions which remain similar in several case studies despite the geographical and chronological differences of the examples under examination. The 'variables' refer to those parameters that may contribute to changing the constants. The identification of variables and constants of a phenomenon or situation is an essential element in the formation of a decision-making model in management science (Prastakos 2002, 66). While management scientists decode the data they collect with numbers in order to develop quantitative models, my aim is to develop a qualitative model which can be used by heritage managers as the general framework that will inform their decision actions.

Chapter 5 examines the case of Wood Quay in Ireland and the example of the Rose Theatre in the UK in detail. These examples demonstrate that the public usually opposes the destruction of a nationally and internationally valued monument or site when it is threatened by the construction of a private building. Private buildings in these cases are interpreted and viewed as a metaphor of capitalism, consumption and homogenisation of the present threatening the nostalgia of the past. An interesting issue is how a site can be transformed from a locally important to a national one by public demand, in contrast to cases where the public reacts against monuments and sites that have already been acknowledged by the state as national monuments. This chapter also explores the interrelationship between collective, cultural, emotional, intangible benefits derived from the preservation of the past -mainly associated with the nostalgia of the past- and the tangible benefits, mainly economic, associated with the construction of a modern building. The case study of the Jorvik Viking Centre is used as a reference in order to demonstrate that innovative policy and preventive dispute management strategies can be beneficial for both the developers and the archaeologists. The extent to which the construction of an *in situ* museum has been used as a compromise solution is also explored. Other examples, such as the Aboa Vetus Museum in Finland and the Billingsgate Bathhouse in London are also used as a reference in order to illuminate some of the key issues that have been raised through the examination of the previous examples.

Chapter 6 analyses the example of the 'Archéoforum' in Belgium, the Administrative Square (*Πλατεία Διοικητηρίου*) in Greece and the Mitropolis Site Museum in Naxos, Greece, where significant archaeological remains were discovered during the rehabilitation of a square. Due to the inherent social benefits attached to the above projects, public reactions may occasionally be either positive or negative. The role of the construction of an *in situ* museum as a compromise solution is examined. The analysis of the above examples allows the exploration of the disputes that occur when collective and/or private socio-economic benefits derived from a public rehabilitation project clash with the cultural benefits derived from the preservation of an archaeological site. The latter can be collective and intangible when associated with symbolic meanings or private and tangible when associated with scientific research. For instance, an archaeological site of local significance may entail symbolic meanings for its local community, a value that cannot translate into tangible benefits. At the same time, the conservation of the site can be of scientific importance for archaeologists or historians and can lead to publication outcomes. The role of an open-public space in public minds and the negative impact that an archaeological site occupying an open-space has for a community are also examined. This challenges the role of an *in situ* museum when it functions as a compromise solution, and implies that an *in situ* museum should encompass the values that an open-public space has for the public including the enhancement of the quality of life understood in aesthetic, social and economic terms.

Chapter 7 discusses thoroughly the example of the New Acropolis Museum (NAM) in Athens. Although a museum project is a public project, and therefore, could have been analysed in the previous chapter, this example is examined in separately because of its

complexity. This case study provides a more holistic approach to the nature of dispute in heritage and its management since it reveals complex and multi-level disputes related to the discovery of archaeological remains during the construction of modern buildings. This chapter also demonstrates how the destruction or preservation of an archaeological site can be used for legitimising political or personal goals and objectives. Furthermore, positions (what the parties say) that hide needs (what must be done) or goals (what they really want to achieve) are clearly distinguished, a distinction which is thoroughly analysed in chapter 3.

Chapter 8 presents the operational dispute management model which is based on the descriptive model suggested in chapter 3 but enriched with guidelines and tactics based on the constants and variables that have been identified in the analysis of the case studies. The chapter also shows the integration of the model into the heritage management process.

1.3. Terminology

This section defines the term 'stakeholder' and distinguishes it from the term 'parties' which will be used throughout the book instead.

The concept of the 'stakeholder' was initially developed by R. Edward Freeman- Professor of Business Administration at the Darden School of Virginia - in the 1980s (Freeman 1984) and was further elaborated by Post et al. (2002). According to their definition the parties of a corporation are the individuals or groups of people who contribute, either voluntarily or involuntarily, to its wealth-creating capacity and activities, and, therefore, they are its potential beneficiaries and/or risk bearers (Post et al. 2002, 20-21). Although the stakeholder theory introduced by Freeman recognises the existence of several external parties including governmental parties, political groups, trade unions and communities, focus is placed on the owners of the company prioritising the needs and benefits of the company rather than the needs of the external parties.

In contrast to the business theorists, management scientists and decision-making theorists stressed mainly the importance of assessing the values and needs of external parties. Therefore, they use the term 'stakeholder' when they refer to either a person or an organisation that has a legitimate interest in a project or entity (Apostolakis and Pickett 1998; von Winterfeldt 2001). Similarly, in discussions on the decision-making process at non-profit organisations -such as heritage organisations- the term stakeholder tends to include everyone with an interest/stake in what the entity is.

The term stakeholders was introduced and used broadly in heritage management theory and practice in the 1990s. This term is being used by heritage managers when they refer to groups of people or individuals who have an interest or stake in how a heritage site is used, developed, interpreted or conserved, or 'who have the potential to cause impacts on the site or are themselves impacted by what happens at the site' (Demas 2002, 31).

Other terms being used include the term 'parties' (mainly used by negotiation theorists, see Lewicki et al. 1999), 'social entities' (mainly used by organisation management theorists such as Rahim 2001) and 'actors' (mainly used by sociologists, e.g. Callon 1986; Latour 1987; Latour 2005). The advantage of the above terms is that because of their generality they can apply to any individual or group of people, internal or external, who have an interest, value or need that either is gained or threatened by an action of a specific organisation. Regarding the fact that stakes and interests derive from deeper needs and wills, the term 'stakeholder' sounds quite restrictive. In addition, this term has immediate connotations with the business environment with which heritage cannot always be associated. Therefore, for the purpose of this book, the term 'parties' was viewed as more suitable than the term 'stakeholders'. Finally, the term 'actors' was not adopted since it is associated with a person or a group of people who take a specific action, while in some cases, the involved parties may not take any action at all.

1.4. Originality

This book provides a topical and innovative, interdisciplinary study that bridges negotiation and heritage management theories together in order to offer a sophisticated tool for managing disputes in the heritage sector. The interdisciplinary approach adopted in this book draws on economic, sociological and psychological theories concerning the nature of dispute and its management. This approach brings new dimensions to the theory of heritage management and has great potential for further research in the future. Finally, although the development of the model and its applicability is explored in the context of *in situ* museums, the same model can be used as a general framework for the development of a dispute management strategy in the heritage sector in general. Therefore, the aim is to provide a generic and flexible model which can be adapted in different situations.

CHAPTER TWO: METHODOLOGY

2.1. Introduction

The methodological approach adopted in the analysis is the triangulation approach according to which qualitative and quantitative methods and data are compared in order to see whether they corroborate one another (Silverman 2005a, 307; Silverman 2005b). The adoption of this method reduces the risk of invalidity and scientific inaccuracy which may result from the fact that each individual method has several drawbacks (Kirk and Miller 1986).

As Flick has pointed out qualitative research is inherently multi-method in focus (Flick 2002, 226-227). Although objective reality can never be captured, the adoption of a multi-method approach secures an in-depth understanding of the phenomenon in question (Denzin and Lincoln 2005, 5). Therefore the triangulation approach (Jick 2006), or according to Richardson and St. Pierre (2005, 959-978) the crystallisation approach (according to which the central image for qualitative inquiry should be the crystal rather than the triangle), allows the simultaneous exploration of different data sources which secures the validity of these data (see also Atkinson and Delamont 2005). In some cases, such as the NAM, a further reason which necessitated the adoption of the triangulation approach was the political sensitivity of the project, which often prevented interviewees from revealing information regarding their personal perceptions and attitudes. Luckily, 367 newspaper articles dating back to the 1980s, collected from the newspaper archive of the American School of Classical Studies and the websites of major Greek newspapers, have been examined.

2.2. Selection of the case studies

From a methodological point of view the book aims to fulfil two main epistemological questions. The first question is what can be learned about a single case study and the second is on what a case study can teach about a whole field (Stake 2005, 443). In view of these questions, the book analyses a series of single case studies in order to extract conclusions on the field of dispute management in the heritage sector.

Following Stake's classification of case studies, the book combines the method of *multiple or collective case study* with the use of an *intrinsic case study* (Stake 2005, 445). An intrinsic case study is of intrinsic interest in the sense that it has particularities which make it of interest of study (Stake 2005, 445). A multiple or collective case study is an *instrumental case study* - a case study the examination of which aims to provide insight into a specific issue and redraw a generalisation and theory - extended to several cases (Stake 2005, 446). In other words, several case studies

are studied jointly in order to investigate a phenomenon – in this case the phenomenon of dispute in the heritage sector.

The intrinsic case study in the book is the case of the New Acropolis Museum (NAM). The main reason for selecting the NAM as the core case study is the fact that it fulfils the criteria of *opportunity to learn* and *accessibility to data*. It also fulfils the basic requirements for *optimising understanding of a case study* which are the experiential knowledge and the study of the context and activities associated with this case study (Stake 2005, 444). Experiential knowledge has been provided by personal participation and working on the site as an archaeologist in 2000-2001.

The rest of the case studies are used to illuminate further issues related to the management of disputes that occur in the heritage sector. These are the Wood Quay site in Dublin (Republic of Ireland), the Rose Theatre in London (UK), the Administrative Square in Thessaloniki (Greece), the Archéoforum at Liège (Belgium) and the Mitropolis museum at Naxos (Greece). Other examples, such as the Jorvik Viking Centre in York (UK), the Aboa Vetus in Turku (Finland) and the Billingsgate Bathhouse in London (UK) will be used to a smaller extent in order to illustrate some of the recurrent key issues. The main criteria on which these case studies were selected were *accessibility* and the *opportunity to learn* (Stake 2005, 450-451). The notion of *accessibility* is closely related to the *opportunity to learn*. 'That may mean taking the one most accessible or the one we can spend the most time with' (Stake 2005, 451). This criterion is more important for a qualitative researcher than the criterion of representativity. As Stake mentions, sometimes it is better to learn a great deal from an atypical case than a little from a seemingly typical case (Stake 2005, 451). Therefore, the selection of the case studies for analysing the disputes was based on the availability of information regarding the disputes, a sensitive issue which the involved parties were often not willing to discuss. This has resulted in a phenomenological imbalance of information presented in each case study since some of the examples are described very analytically while others are presented very briefly. The inclusion though of the briefly presented examples was considered essential, since they raise disputed issues which do not occur in the examples that are thoroughly analysed. As Stake implies 'populations of cases can be represented poorly by single cases or samples of a very few cases, and such small samples of cases can provide questionable grounds for advancing grand generalisation' (Stake 2005, 460). Therefore the significance of using a case study as a method of inquiry relies not on the potential of gaining a representative and typical example but on testing a hypothesis and/or examining a 'single exception that shows the hypothetical to be false' (Stake 1978, 7).

A further selection criterion was the extent to which the case studies illuminated a wide range of issues in dispute, in order to allow a broad examination of disputes and their management in the heritage sector. I was also interested in covering as many as possible cases and stages of dispute, including disputes occurring before, during or after the creation of an *in situ* museum or cases of *in situ* museums which functioned either as an issue in dispute or as a compromise solution.

Additionally, an important criterion was the necessity to use examples from a *geographical and chronological range* in order to show that some types of dispute are common despite the different time period and geographical area in which they occurred. This examination will identify the repetitive patterns of behaviour, actions and reactions on the basis of which a generic dispute management model will be formed.

The case studies were selected among 118 examples that were catalogued in a searchable database on Access created by the author. The database contains the following information: the name of the country and city where the museum is located, the name and address of the museum, its opening date, the type of the museum structure, the reason why the construction of a museum was taken, the criteria on which the conservation of the archaeological remains was justified, the obstacles that occurred during the planning process, the type and date of the archaeological remains that are incorporated into the museum, the involved parties and scientists, types and levels of disputes, conservation, visitor access and financial problems, interpretation techniques, dispute management policy, references, (web references and literature) and photographs that have been taken by the author or have been used from bibliographic references and relevant web sites (Fouseki 2008). The creation of the database was based on information provided by the APPEAR Project (a European project for the 'Accessibility, Sustainable Conservation and Enhancement of Urban Subsoil Archaeological Remains'), bibliographic references including the proceedings of a conference held by the International Council of Archaeological Heritage Management (ICAHM 1996) on *in situ* conservation, the publication of Hartwig Schmidt analysing the shelters and the archaeological crypts in Europe (Schmidt 1988), the proceedings of two conferences held in Spain regarding the *in situ* conservation of archaeological remains in urban centres (Museu d' Història de la Ciutat 2000 ; Rascón Marqués and Méndez Madariaga 2003) and thorough research on the Internet. The database has been used as a basis for extracting data in order to classify the *in situ* museums into types and to explore how their main characteristics have evolved. Database forms were designed on Microsoft Access in order to organise information for each museum regarding the archaeological remains, their presentation techniques, type of museum structure, some selected images and bibliographic references.

2.3. Visual ethnography: personal and archival photographs

The issue of scientific validity reoccurs in the visual ethnography since 'the discourse on the validity or invalidity of photographs relies on a central irony of the photograph: it is both true and constructed' (Harper 2005, 749). A photograph is true because it reflects light falling on a surface (Harper 2005, 749). It is also constructed by the contexts in which it is viewed (Harper 2005, 749). In view of this, it is essential to examine the cultural phenomena that are grasped through their visual representations within the social settings in which such phenomena are generated and interpreted (Atkinson and Delamont 2005, 825).

I attempted to use photographs published by mass media including websites and newspapers, as a means to advance theories of the society and people's perceptions of the past (Harper 2005, 748; see also Fuery and Fuery 2003). I have also used photographs, taken during visits to the sites and the museums, aimed at either depicting the special characteristics of the museum or the interaction and behaviour of people within the museum. In the latter case, since the photographs are personal, they mainly connect my personal viewpoint with the argument being presented (Harper 2005, 748). The subjective and the personal point of view is an unavoidable element in any qualitative research; this does not undervalue the significance of the collected data, but it imposes the necessity to use a variety of data sources in order to ensure objectivity. Finally, photographs taken at the *in situ* museum of Naxos (Greece) and the Aboa Vetus Museum (Finland) were shown to individuals in order to examine their views on *in situ* presentation. These views were compared with views about objects displayed in other type of museums where objects are displayed in cases outside their physical context.

2.4. Personal experience

Personal experience has been identified by Denzin and Lincoln (2005, 5) as a useful qualitative research method. In the case of the New Acropolis Museum, my personal experience as an archaeologist working on the site in 2000-2001 provided me with invaluable in-depth view regarding the attitudes of my colleagues and cooperators including archaeologists, architects and designers and the ways in which they dealt with the problem. During this time I also witnessed the confrontations between the police officers sent by the local citizens and the archaeologists directing the excavations; the quarrels between the police officers who were sent by archaeologists to prevent local inhabitants from entering the archaeological site; and one local inhabitant, whose house had a brilliant view of the archaeological site, video-taping the excavation works. This experience provided me with the ability to assess the validity of other data collected from newspaper articles and by interviews.

2.5. Interviews

The scientific accuracy and validity of interview data has often been questioned and the subjectivity of data has often been emphasised, since interviewing is inextricably and unavoidably historically, politically, and contextually bound (Fontana and Frey 2005, 695). The interviewer is also a person, historically and contextually located, carrying unavoidable conscious and unconscious motives, desires, feelings, and biases (Sheurich 1995, 241). Interviewing forms also a social interaction context and therefore is influenced by this context (Fontana and Frey 2005, 703). Furthermore, the setting in which the interview takes place, the language and culture of the participants, the ways in which an interviewer presents him/herself and the necessity to gain trust affect to a great extent the outcome of the interview.

However, I believe that subjectivity, which is unavoidable, does not necessarily render data scientifically invalid. Qualitative data collected through interviews can provide researchers with valuable data in so far their accuracy is corroborated with data collected from other sources. In addition, subjectivity in the social science and humanistic field where the focal point is the 'man' and his/her perceptions, behaviours and attitudes is unavoidable. A degree of subjectivity inheres even in quantitative methods since the design of the questionnaire and the coding of the answers depends to a great extent on the analyst's point of view.

In the case of the New Acropolis Museum, as in most of the case studies, the majority of interviews included semi-structured, open-ended questions, which occasionally were transformed into unstructured interviews and discussions during the discussion process. The latter was necessary either because the discussant was not willing to answer a question or because he/she was so passionate about the topic it led him/her to deal with different issues, interesting but irrelevant to the main question asked.

Structured interviews were used in the case where I explored the perceptions of the Athenians towards the archaeological remains that are preserved in Athens. I conducted face-to-face interviews and also distributed self-administered questionnaires. The questionnaire was composed of the same pre-established questions with a limited set of response categories (Fontana and Frey 2005, 702). The face-to-face respondents received the same set of questions asked in the same order or sequence by the interviewer (Frey 2005, 702).

Unstructured interviews were conducted with archaeologists who had a personal experience of a dispute situation at some of the *in situ* museums that are examined in the book. Their comments are included

as personal communication but their anonymity has been retained.

I also sent a questionnaire electronically to some of the directors of the museums where disputes occurred. The questions were mainly open-ended. The main reason for sending this questionnaire was the necessity to cross-tabulate the information I collected from publications or personal communications with archaeologists working at *in situ* museums with their comments. Since directors were coming from various museums all over Europe, electronic interviewing (also a form of personal communication) was considered the best method in terms of time and cost. However, not surprisingly, only two out of eleven individuals answered the questionnaire including two persons whom I had met at two different conferences. The answers also were quite cryptic (see about cryptic answers in electronic interviews Markham 1998) since the issue of dispute is usually highly political and sensitive. Therefore some of the interviewees did not reveal a great amount of information despite the fact that the agreement was that I would retain their anonymity.

2.6. Virtual or online ethnography

Virtual or online ethnography refers to the examination of mainly discussions held in online networks and communities (digital communities). The ethnographer may either be purely an observer (unobtrusive observation) or actively participate as a member of the online community (participant observation) (Hine, 2000; Markham 1998).

In the case of the New Acropolis Museum (NAM) I used web forums in Greece on the Internet which revealed another perspective to the issue of the NAM. It was interesting to explore the spontaneous thoughts of the participants and therefore I decided to adopt unobtrusive observation in order to avoid directing the spontaneous discussion of the online members.

Although in virtual ethnography there is an inherent risk in making assumptions about the age, gender, ethnicity, educational level of a participant (Markham 1998, 806-807), I considered the data collected from the web forums to be quite important for highlighting aspects that were not obvious through other data sources, or for corroborating information derived from other sources.

2.7. Visitor book

I used the systematic analysis of the comments of visitors at the Mitropolis museum at Naxos (chapter 6). 388 visitor comments were categorised and coded. One of the aims was the examination of the extent to which visitors remembered specific objects or parts of the museum. In addition, I examined how they expressed the ways in which the museums enhanced their experience and reinforced a sense of place.

A main disadvantage of the visitor book is that many of the comments are very general, although this on its own constitutes a piece of information revealing how visitors react to a visitor book and/or whether they really gained something from their visit to the museum. In addition, information regarding the visitor profile, such as educational qualifications, age, occupational status, cannot be obtained. The advantages are that they express themselves spontaneously and write about those things that captured their attention. This can provide an insight into what was most memorable for them (on the usefulness of visitor books see also Sullivan 1984, 43-53). Despite the disadvantages, a visitor book can be used as an extra tool for assessing public perceptions. In the case of the Mitropolis museum of Naxos the visitor book proved to be quite useful since it supported the comments of inhabitants in the local newspaper *'Naxiologa'* that revealed a significant change in their perceptions regarding the museum.

2.8. Observation

Observation has often been characterised as 'the fundamental base of all research methods' in the social and behavioural sciences (Adler and Adler 1994, 389) and as the 'mainstay of ethnographic enterprise' (Werner and Schoepfle 1987, 257). In the case of the New Acropolis Museum participant and unobtrusive observation constituted a useful methodological technique for assessing the attitudes of the local inhabitants. In detail, I observed public demonstrations against the construction of the NAM recording thoroughly comments and reactions of the opponents. I also attended meetings and conferences of local citizens living in the area where the museum was eventually built. The data I collected did not actually provide me with much more information than I had already gained through other sources but the significance of the observation notes relies on cross-tabulating and checking the validity of information gained from alternative sources.

2.9. Newspaper articles

Newspaper articles are a valuable data source for heritage researchers in two main ways. Firstly, they often constitute the only available information source, especially in countries like Greece where cultural heritage literature is still developing. Although newspaper articles may provide mainly ideological interpretation of events 'employing a complex set of criteria and mechanisms' rather than facts (Yalouri 2000, 34), they are a very useful information source since they render the spirit of an age (Berelson 1952, 90; Skopetea 1988 in Yalouri 2001, 23) despite the fact

that newspaper articles may reflect strongly the subjective, and occasionally, politically motivated opinion of the journalists. This of course will depend on the type of newspaper, the reporters and journalist. In general, it has been acknowledged that journalists can often be 'professional politicians' and newspapers are 'political organisations' (Weber 1918). This implies that journalists may reflect a specific political, ideological belief which unavoidably affects the interpretation of a situation. At the same time, the articles reflect mainly their own subjective opinion to a subject, which, as mentioned above, has also been shaped by the political pressure. The case of NAM shows clearly that the ways in which different newspapers deal with this subject reflect the position of political party they represent. Secondly, newspapers reveal 'how the public, as an abstract entity, is perceived by authorities and journalists through official speeches and newspaper editorials' (Endere 2002, 23).

Despite the above drawbacks, media researchers have acknowledged that journalists and newspapers can reflect to some extent the taste and opinions of the wider public while, at the same time, leading and shaping them. The book does not aim to conduct a textual/content and discourse analysis which media researchers usually undertake in order to explore the background scenes and forces of journalists (Bertrand and Huges 2005, 185; Krippendorf 1980, 21). The aim is to explore the reflection of the public opinion through the newspapers, a task that can be achieved when combined with other sources.

2.10 Ethical considerations

It has been claimed that 'any method decision is an ethics decision' (Denzin and Lincoln 2005, 859). In this particular book, each selected method raised several ethical considerations regarding its use. One of the main ethical considerations that I came across was the occasional dilemma of whether I should reveal my identity as an archaeologist and former employee of the NAM, when discussing with the local inhabitants, or as a researcher studying the case of NAM when discussing with the managers of the museum. This raises the following ethical dilemma: What is ethically and scientifically right for a researcher? Is it ethical for a researcher to conceal his/her identity, in order to gain invaluable and more accurate data or should he/she sacrifice the accuracy of the data by revealing his/her identity?

A further ethical issue emerged from the ethical obligation to retain the anonymity of the interviewees. Therefore I refer to their opinions as anonymous personal communications.

2.11. Final comment: fitting methods to target groups

Each method was determined by the criterion of accessibility and fitness for purpose. Low cost and the convenience of fast communication determined the use of e-mail surveys for communicating with curators from several European countries. The case of the NAM required a combination of different methods since it is the core case study of the book. The visitor book at Naxos provided an in-depth insight into the changing perceptions of local inhabitants regarding the *in situ* museum as well as highlighting some of the basic distinctive characteristics of *in situ* museums that are usually praised by visitors. Newspaper articles proved to be a very useful source for most of the case studies since they provided various detailed information on the history of the dispute and the public impact of the site. Personal communication and interviews with the involved parties gave a further insight into the issue of dispute.

CHAPTER THREE: THE NATURE AND MANAGEMENT OF DISPUTES: TOWARDS A THEORETICAL FRAMEWORK

3.1. Introduction

This chapter presents a descriptive dispute management model which will be used throughout the book as a tool for describing and analysing disputes in the case studies. The model will be enriched with specific guidelines in chapter 8 which proposes an operational dispute management model for the heritage sector.

The creation of the descriptive dispute management model was based on the identification of key factors that contribute to the genesis, escalation and resolution of a dispute situation in the heritage sector and on the examination of the interrelationship of these key factors. As will be shown later in the book, occasionally the outcomes of a dispute situation do not only depend strictly on some isolated factors but on their interrelationship. The factors that lead, cultivate and possibly resolve a dispute situation in the heritage sector were identified through an interdisciplinary examination of the nature of dispute and its management. The adoption of an interdisciplinary approach was mainly imposed by the lack of dispute management theories in the heritage literature. The applicability of some of the key elements of each dispute management theory in the heritage context was then explored by examining the extent to which these elements fulfil basic principles of heritage management theory and practice, such as the emphasis on value-led management planning or involving the interested parties actively in the heritage management process.

The formation of the descriptive dispute management model is based on two basic principles. The first principle is that the effective resolution of a dispute situation is equal to its effective prediction and avoidance which I consider as one of the most important elements for managing dispute as will be proved later in the book. The second principle is that the adoption of an integrative approach (also known as problem-solving approach) is the most compatible approach to the participatory planning process that is emphasised in heritage management theory and practice (Allison 1999; Anyon 1991; Anyon et al. 2000; Carman 2002; Cernea 2001; Champion 2000; Creamer 1990; Greenberg 1997; Millar, 2007; Pwiti 1996; Seeden 1990; Start 1999). According to the integrative approach a heritage manager develops his/her dispute management strategy on the basis of mutual interests. The challenging task for a heritage/dispute manager is to persuade the involved parties that they actually share common interests. As will be stressed later, the question is how common interests can be identified or developed and how the involved parties can be persuaded that common interests actually exist.

Having formed the descriptive dispute management model the chapter proceeds with depicting how the suggested descriptive dispute management model is integrated into the heritage management. The schematic depiction of the dispute management model into the heritage management process allows the identification of similarities and differences between the two processes.

3.2. Conceptualisation of dispute and conflict

This section defines dispute, classifies its types and levels, and identifies its various sources as these have been analysed by various disciplines. Then, those elements that are applicable to the heritage sector are isolated and presented in a comprehensive descriptive dispute management model.

In general terms, the definition of dispute (or conflict) has evolved from the traditional meaning of an 'antagonistic state or action' to the meaning of a 'sharp disagreement or opposition of interests and ideas' (Lewicki et al. 1999, 16). Other theorists mention also the opposition of incompatible goals and/ or behaviours as a source of dispute and conflict (Deutsch 1991, 30; Fisher et al. 2005, 4; Litterer 1966, 180; Smith 1966, 511; Tedeschi et al. 1973, 232). A dominant element in the various definitions is the notion of interdependence according to which a dispute derives from the fact that the actions of an individual or group of people affects negatively the outcomes, gains, losses or benefits of another individual or group of people (Lewicki et al. 1999, 16; Pruitt and Rubin 1986; 4). This notion is mainly emphasised by economists and decision-makers although it can apply to other situations. In heritage literature the terms dissonance or dispute are more common than the term conflict (Howard 2003; Skeates 2000; Tunbridge and Ashworth 1996) probably because the term conflict is associated with more violent situations, especially with situations occurring in times of war (Boylan 1993; Chamberlain 2004; Layton et al. 2001). However, this term was recently used in a recently published journal issue on Museums and Conflict of the Museum Management and Curatorship (Lynch 2013). Dissonance is defined as 'a condition that refers to the discordance or lack of agreement and consistency as to the meaning of heritage' (Ashworth et al., 2005, 5). This definition implies that heritage may have multiple and often contradictory meanings and therefore heritage is unavoidably a 'contested concept' (Ashworth et al. 2005, 4).

Conflicts can be divided into violent and non-violent disputes. The book deals mainly with the latter since conflicts in the context of major political and social unrest such as wars, ethnic, racial and religious riots are generated by more deliberate, deep-rooted and systematic interventions and for reasons that have usually nothing to do with heritage *per se*. Non-violent conflicts or disputes can be latent, surface or active (Fisher et al. 2005, 6). Latent conflict refers to an underlying, invisible conflict which results when two or more parties have divergent interests in the production, allocation or exchange of scarce resources (Goldman and Rojot 2003, 17). The surface conflict has shallow or no roots and may be only a misunderstanding of goals that can be addressed by means of improved communication (Fisher et al. 2005, 6). Active or open conflict arises from the interactions of parties concerning specific, immediate problems (Fisher et al. 2005, 6). This type of conflict is visible and deep-rooted (Fisher et al. 2005, 6). While the active conflicts are obvious and easily identified, a heritage/dispute manager needs to be equipped with the appropriate skills in order to identify latent and surface conflicts that often lead to active conflicts. These skills relate mainly to communication and psychological techniques which will be presented in chapter 8. These techniques can facilitate the assessment of indicators of latent and existing dispute situations.

Fisher et al. provide a generic framework as a means to identify the various dispute types. According to this framework, when the goals and the behaviour of two or more parties or groups of people are compatible, usually there is no dispute. In the case of incompatible goals and compatible behaviour there is a latent dispute (Fisher et al. 2005, 6).

For instance, during my experience as an archaeologist on rescue excavations I found that in the case of an archaeological discovery during the construction of a modern building, usually the landowner tends to be friendly with the responsible excavators although their goals may deeply contradict with the ones of the archaeologists. For example, the landowner may deeply wish for the completion of the excavations while the archaeologists may desire their continuation. This incompatibility of goals is a potential source of dispute and entails a latent dispute which, depending on the circumstances, may lead to an actual conflict. These circumstances and parameters will be identified during the analysis of the case studies and will be summarised in chapter 8. Fisher et al. (2005, 6) claim that when the goals are compatible but the behaviour incompatible there is a surface dispute. During my experience as an archaeologist and as a fieldworker, I have met people who have negative attitudes towards archaeologists. These negative perceptions often result from the existing bureaucratic procedures of the Greek Archaeological Service in land expropriation processes or refusals to grant construction permits. Therefore, although the goal of an excavator may be compatible with that of a landowner (for example, completion of excavations and permission for construction) the incompatible behaviours (for example, aggressive behaviour of landowner and friendly behaviour of archaeologist) may lead to surface disputes. Finally, when both the goals and the behaviour are incompatible there is an open dispute (Fisher et al. 2005, 6). The interrelationship of goals, behaviours, values, interests, positions and perceptions are presented below in the book.

The book divides disputes into two main categories, namely, internal and external disputes. Internal disputes refer to disputes that occur between two or more individuals or groups of people who belong to the same heritage organisation. External disputes occur between two or more parties and/or groups of people who do not belong to the same organisation. Internal and external disputes may be inter-personal, inter-group or intra-group. Inter-personal disputes occur between two or more individuals (Rahim 2001, 23). Inter-group disputes occur between two or more groups and finally intra-group disputes occur between two or more persons who belong to the same group (Rahim 2001, 24). In addition, external disputes may be inter-organisational when two or more organisations are in dispute.

Intra-personal disputes -disputes 'in which a person is motivated to engage in two or more mutually exclusive activities' (Murray 1968, 220)- are not examined in the book since the study of this type of dispute requires psychological experiments and in-depth information which could not be gained for this project. This, however, does not undervalue the potential significance of this type of dispute.

3.3. Understanding the nature of dispute

Understanding the nature of dispute is a difficult but essential task when dealing with its management. In this case, understanding the nature of a dispute situation is equal to identifying its deeper sources and driving forces which, according to each case, may differ significantly.

Almost every academic discipline has its theoretical approach towards understanding disputes. Economists and decision-making theorists tend to explain dispute genesis and management by using quantitative, mathematical models the aim of which is the development of an optimal strategy that will lead to the maximisation of the profit as explained below. Psychologists and behaviourists explore intrapersonal and interpersonal disputes focusing on the importance of individual perceptions. Sociologists investigate inter-group disputes including familial, racial, religious and social class disputes. They usually examine the motivation and cognitive processes associated with a dispute, seeking the roots of social disputes in some form of aggressive drive or need, common to the human beings (Stroebe et al. 1988). Political scientists who are interested in the examination of international relations examine disputes between nations, political parties and ideologies (Nightingale 1974, 141). Organisation theorists explore disputes related to the function and management of an organisation emphasising not only the negative (dysfunctional outcomes) but also the positive outcomes (functional outcomes) of dispute (Cosier and Dalton 1990; Litterer 1966; Rahim 2001). Heritage management theorists emphasise the contradictory interrelationship of perceptions, values and goals of individuals and groups of people as these are shaped by the past and its uses in the present (Lynch 2013; Skeates 2000; Tunbridge and Ashworth 1996).

Therefore, reviewing the dispute literature as a whole is almost an impossible task. In addition, no theory is comprehensive and each is characterised by gaps regarding the understanding and management of dispute. Therefore it is essential to adopt an interdisciplinary approach which allows the fusion of different theories and consequently the filling of gaps of each theory separately in the development of a dispute management model. Since the case studies derive from the heritage sector, it is essential to select those elements that apply to heritage.

Conflict theories can be classified into two broad theoretical approaches: behaviourist or micro-theories and classical or macro-theories (Dougherty and Pfaltzgraff 1981). Behavioural or micro- theories analyse the individual (rather than group) conflicts that occur mainly at an unconscious level in order to understand unstated motivational factors, whereas classical or macro-theories examine the conflict interaction of groups including national, institutional, ethnic, class, and ideological groups at conscious level (Dougherty and Pfaltzgraff 1981).

Although the book deals with inter or intra-group disputes and conflicts, and therefore focuses on the macro-level theories, this chapter examines briefly the micro-theories since intra-personal disputes and unconscious factors play a significant role in the escalation of conflict.

Behavioural approaches to dispute explore the extent to which human beings possess either biological or psychological characteristics that would predispose them towards aggression and dispute. They also aim to examine the relationship between the individual and his/her existence in his/her environment (Cairns 1994; Turner et al. 1987).

Among the various behavioural theories – including animal behaviour theory, the instinct or innate theories of aggression and the frustration-aggression theory – the social identity theory is the most important in this case since it recognises that 'individuals are different in groups and that it is this difference which produces recognizable forms of group action' (Cairns 1994, 9). Individuals employ social categories such as nationality, ethnicity and/or gender in order to simplify their social world and as a means of self-reference. These categories are internalised and may constitute an important aspect of the individual's social identity (Nightingale 1974, 141). Collective behaviour occurs when a number of individuals perceive themselves in terms of the same social category at the same moment in time (Turner et al. 1987). In view of this, it would be interesting to examine what type of social categories do

groups of people who oppose or support the *in situ* conservation of an archaeological site employ in order to shape a common, collective identity which empowers them to legitimise their claims. The analysis of the case studies proves that when groups are homogenised by asserting a common social identity they become powerful and aggressive.

Despite the fact that social identity theory attempts to explore the interrelationship between an individual or groups of people and the environment, the majority of behavioural/micro-theories focus on the unconscious, individual level. Therefore, it is essential to co-examine them with theories that analyse dispute on group, conscious levels such as the classical/macro-theories of dispute.

One of the key assumptions of these theories is that disputes stem from group competition and the pursuit of power and resources (Fisher et al. 1991). The methods that classical theorists use in order to explore inter-group disputes is based on observations of group phenomena for single events in order to determine the importance and relationships of many variables using historical or case study approaches. A similar approach is adopted in the book the aim of which is to identify the interrelationship of variables and constants in the examination of case studies dating back to the 1970s in disagreements and disputes over heritage and its preservation.

The main theories that deal with the balance of power and its role in dispute genesis, escalation and management are the decision-making and game theories developed mainly by economists. These theories originated in the twentieth century in the rational actor model, a model developed by economists with the aim of explaining human economic behaviour (Osborne 2002; von Neumann and Morgenstern 1947). Their assumption was that people make rational choices and decisions based on informed choices and weighing of opportunities (Oikonomou and Georgiou 2000, 277). The main idea is that rational 'players' are involved in a 'game' the rules of which are known to all the players. The ultimate aim of each 'player' is to maximise his gain and win the game and therefore it is essential for all the players to develop an optimal strategy in order to achieve the maximum gain (Osborne 2002; von Neumann and Morgenstern 1947). A game is usually described as a matrix of payoffs (results), which depicts the results of the 'game' for each combination of strategies of each player (Oikonomou and Georgiou 2000, 277).

One of the main disadvantages of game theory is the assumption that there are no intrinsic biases to the decision-making process and the ignorance of the fact that individuals or groups of people involved in the process bring their own perceptions and mental models into such a situation (Lyles and Thomas 1988). Therefore, although game theory may be useful within a financial context, in real-life situations the applicability of this theory is limited. Moreover, the distributive nature of negotiation transaction that game theory emphasises is not compatible with the heritage management principles that emphasise participatory planning and involvement of interested parties. Despite the disadvantages, game theory introduces a logical sequential approach that facilitates the deductive decision-making process by determining the goals or objectives, evaluating the potential alternatives and choosing the optimal one.

Thomas Schelling acknowledged the weaknesses of the rational decision-making theory and suggested a more sophisticated game theory (Schelling 1960). His model introduced the importance of irrationality into strategic thought. One of the most important contributions of Schelling is his hypothesis of the interdependency of dispute, competition and cooperation among actors (Schelling 1960). According to this hypothesis, each dispute situation contains elements of cooperation and cooperative engagements often engender an element of dispute.

The notion of irrationality is strongly reflected in the 'garbage can model' developed by decision-makers (Cohen et al. 1972; Lovata 1987). This model emphasises the notion of accidentality according to which decision-making is largely the product of a stream of solutions, problems and situations that are randomly associated (Cohen et al. 1972; Lovata 1987). An opportunity to make a decision is described as a 'garbage can' into which many types of problems and solutions are dropped independently by decision-makers as these problems and solutions are generated. Although the garbage can model provides a real-world representation of the non-rational manner in which decisions are often made within an organisation, this model cannot constitute the most effective means of decision-making. The reason for this lies in the fact that the alignment of the problems, solutions and individuals often occurs either after the opportunity to make a decision regarding a problem has passed or before the problem has been discovered (Cohen et al. 1972).

A heritage manager who represents a heritage organisation is usually involved directly in a dispute situation. Therefore, it is imperative to examine the organisation management approach to dispute.

Organisation management theorists have classified disputes on the basis of the antecedent conditions that lead to disputes -including goals, values, tasks, interests, beliefs and ideas- into the following categories: the affective dispute, substantive dispute, dispute of interest, dispute of values, goal disputes, realistic versus non realistic disputes, institutionalised versus non-institutionalised disputes, retributive dispute, misattributed dispute, and displaced dispute (Rahim 2001, 21; Whitfield 1994, 18).

Affective dispute occurs when two interacting social entities, while trying to solve a problem together, become aware that their feelings and emotions regarding some or all of the issues are incompatible (Rahim 2001, 21). This dispute is also known as psychological dispute (Ross and Ross 1989, 139), relationship dispute (Jehn 1997a) and emotional dispute (Pelled et al. 1999, 2). Substantive dispute occurs when two or more organisational members disagree on their task or content issues (Jehn 1997b, 288; Rahim 2001, 21). This dispute is also known as task dispute (Jehn 1997a; Pelled et al. 1999), cognitive dispute (Amason 1996) and issue dispute (Hammer and Organ 1978, 343). Dispute of interest is defined as an inconsistency between two parties in their preferences for the allocation of a scarce resource (Druckman and Zechmeister 1973, 450; Druckman et al. 1988). Dispute of values occurs when two social entities differ in their values or ideologies on certain issues (Rahim 2001, 22). This dispute is also known as ideological dispute (Rahim 2001, 22). Goal disputes occur when a preferred outcome or an end-state of two social entities is inconsistent (Rahim 2001, 22). Realistic dispute refers to the incompatibilities that have rational content while non realistic dispute occurs as a result of a party's need to release tension and express hostility, ignorance or error (Ross and Ross 1989, 139). These types correspond to Haiman's intrinsic and extrinsic disputes (Haiman 1951, 181) and to Mack's and Snyder's real and induced disputes (Mack and Snyder 1957, 220). Institutionalised disputes which are characterised by explicit rules, predictable behaviour and continuity may contradict with non-institutionalised disputes that lack the above three characteristics (Rahim 2001, 22). Retributive dispute is characterised by a situation where each party determines its gain by incurring costs to the other party (Saaty 1990, 49). Misattributed dispute relates to the incorrect assignment of causes (behaviours, parties, issues) to dispute (Rahim 2001, 23). Displaced dispute occurs when the disputing parties either direct their frustrations or hostilities to social entities that are not involved in dispute or argue over secondary issues (Rahim 2001, 23).

The main disadvantage of the organisational approach to dispute is the narrow focus on inter-personal, intra-organisational dispute as opposed to the previous dispute theories which deal with external and inter-group disputes. Therefore, it is essential to collate all the above theories in order to provide a holistic approach to the examination of the nature of heritage sector disputes and their sources.

Finally, other potential sources of dispute may include the extent to which material interests are fulfilled (realistic theory) (Campbell 1967), inequality and injustice expressed by competing social, cultural and economic frameworks (dispute transformation theory) and the difference in cultural communication styles and the content of message. Cultural miss-communication relates to contradictory transmissions, a failure in transmission, obsolete transmission and undesirable transmission (Tunbridge and Ashworth 1996, 27).

3.4. Dispute in heritage management theory

Although heritage management theory has recently emphasised the necessity to assess and manage the divergent values that different individuals or groups of people attach to heritage and its contemporary uses (Feilden and Jokilehto 1998, 18; Pearson and Sullivan 1999, 33), it lacks suggestions for specific ways in which the divergent values and the derived disputes can be managed. This was recently attempted to be addressed by the Getty Conservation Institute and its case study on assessing and managing conflicting values (Myers et al. 2010). Heritage management theorists and practitioners suggest the active involvement of various parties with an interest in a heritage site so that different values, positions and interests can be freely expressed and accommodated.

However, incorporating and representing the various interests is not an easy task. The active engagement of the involved parties can be particularly useful for understanding differences and diversities but not always for avoiding or resolving disputes and tensions. Although understanding disputes is an essential step in managing disputes, more skills, techniques and tactics are required for their effective avoidance and resolution.

The aim of this section is to provide an introduction to the nature of dispute in the heritage sector. This will constitute the broader framework within which the nature and management of dispute at *in situ* museums will be examined.

Some researchers have endeavoured to explain heritage dissonance arising from the contradictory interrelationship between heritage consumption and heritage production (Howard 2003; Tunbridge and Ashworth 1996). Although this commodified approach explains to some extent the divergent values that arise from the contradictory set of production and consumption, the limited attachment of these connotations do not provide a holistic overview of dispute in heritage. However, the aim of this section is not to present an overview of all the potential divergent uses, values or interests that different groups of people or individuals attach to heritage but to provide a general framework for a systematic analysis of the driving forces that cultivate disputes and conflicts related to heritage. This framework will constitute an important tool for analysing the disputes in the case studies.

In the heritage sector some of the most common disputes occur because of a contradiction between the benefits of the past (cultural benefits) and the benefits of the present (social and economic benefits) (Lowenthal 1985); between the collective ownership of a common past and the private ownership of a more recent and personal heritage at local, national or international level (Carman 2005); between local, national and international identities shaped by the sense of place and the associations with the past (Ashworth and Graham 2005); between visitor accessibility, tourism and conservation of an archaeological site; between religious values or uses and scientific values and uses (Stovel et al. 2005); between contemporary uses of archaeological sites by living communities and conservation-visitor-scientific accessibility (Blain and Wallis 2007); and between human and cultural rights (O'Keefe 2000). Disputes are also inherent in the political abuses of the past/heritage for political power (Breglia 2006; Smith 2004), in the notion of change (Teutonico and Matero 2003) and in the notion of innovation as will be thoroughly analysed in chapter 4.

The contradictory interrelationship between the benefits of preserving the past and the benefits of destroying the past in favour of present development and modernisation is an issue that is examined in depth in chapter 5. This section provides a general framework in which the issue of the contradiction of benefits and burdens of the past is also discussed in chapter 5.

David Lowenthal identifies the following categories of benefits of the past: 'familiarity and recognition; reaffirmation and validation; individual and group identity; guidance; enrichment; and escape' (Lowenthal 1985, 38). Among these benefits, the benefit of guidance which refers to the ability of the past to teach and guide an individual in the present is not related strongly to the case studies and therefore is not analysed in this book.

The benefits and burdens of the past for the present are explored from two main perspectives. Firstly, the role of these benefits in dispute genesis, escalation and management will be examined. Secondly, the extent to which an *in situ* museum can fulfil the above benefits as a means for dispute resolution will be analysed. A comparison between the benefits of the past for the present and the benefits of the present development is undertaken.

The first benefit of the past identified by Lowenthal is the benefit of familiarity which is defined as the ability of the past to let 'our minds make sense of the present...Objects that lack any familiar elements or configurations remain incomprehensible' (Lowenthal 1985, 39). Regarding the fact that archaeological sites and objects are often incomprehensible due to their fragmentary state and lack of interpretation, disputing attitudes may arise when this 'unfamiliar and incomprehensible past' contradicts with the familiar and comprehensible present represented for example by the construction of a modern public building. This implies that rendering the past familiar through its preservation and integration into the present, as in the case of *in situ* museums, may make it possible for disputes to be resolved. However, at the same time, as will be shown in the case studies, the public may oppose the destruction of archaeological remains endangered by the construction of modern structures. These sites, despite their fragmentary state which renders them incomprehensible and unfamiliar, acquire their familiarity through their associations with a glorious and national symbolic past as will be clearly shown in the case of the Rose Theatre and Wood Quay (chapter 5). This implies that it is not only the 'object of the past' that raises feelings of familiarity or unfamiliarity but also the symbolic associations with this past. I also think that, at least in the case of *in situ* museums, what renders the archaeological past familiar in people's senses is the link of the past with the present. Lowenthal rightly states 'The past we depend on to make sense of the present is, however, mostly recent…it stems mainly from our own few years of experience. The further back in time, the fewer the traces that survive, the more they have altered, and the less they anchor us to contemporary reality' (Lowenthal 1985, 40) unless this past is associated with national symbolisms. The notion of familiarity might constitute a basis for achieving harmony when people feel equally familiar with their personal and impersonal past as well as with the ways in which these pasts are managed. Contrarily, when people are dominated by feelings of familiarity and unfamiliarity of different pasts, then disputes and tensions may occur.

A second benefit of the past for the present identified by Lowenthal is the ability of the past to validate 'present attitudes and actions by affirming their resemblance to former ones' (Lowenthal 1985, 40). He continues by saying that the past validates the present by preserving and by restoring (Lowenthal 1985, 40). 'Preservation invokes the continuance of practices that supposedly date from time immemorial' (Lowenthal 1985, 40) while restoring allows a remote past to legitimate and fortify the present order 'against subsequent mishap or corruption' (Lowenthal 1985, 41). What are the implications of this contention both in terms of dispute genesis and its management and in terms of the role of *in situ* museums in dispute genesis and management? How can archaeological, fragmentary remains evoke continuance of practices? As mentioned above, demands to preserve an archaeological site associated with a glorious and national past evoke the continuance of glory in the present (this will be clearly shown in the cases of the Rose Theatre, Wood Quay and NAM). Therefore the destruction of a glorious past raises dispute. On the contrary, an *in situ* museum that protects and presents the glorious past to the public may function as a compromise to this claim.

The association of an archaeological site with a national past which reaffirms and validates the present and which renders the present and the past familiar is also interlinked with the ability of the past to reinforce current identity (Lowenthal 1985, 41) both at personal and community or national level. As a result, if the national past reinforces community and national

identity then its destruction is perceived as a threat to the feeling of security and continuity.

According to the benefit of enrichment, the past enriches the present and 'imbues life with longevity' (Lowenthal 1985, 48). The notion of enrichment can be understood in different and possibly contradictory ways (see chapters 5, 6 and 7).

The last benefit mentioned by Lowenthal is that of 'escape' according to which the 'past offers alternatives to an unacceptable present' (Lowenthal 1985, 49). This applies mainly in cases where modern development threatens the past which reinforces the feeling of nostalgia.

A further source of dispute in the heritage sector is a contradiction between preservation and visitor access. The preservation of the past and its tourist and/or economic exploitation as a means of economic development and revitalisation may juxtapose with local communities' attitudes and perceptions who view tourists as invaders and threateners to their local heritage (see chapter 6). Tourism development also may cause internal disputes between those who support visitor access and interpretation and those who are concerned with conservation and preservation issues.

Contests and disputes are also caused in cases where sites are being used by religious groups or are associated with religious uses. For example, in the case of Stonehenge (Blain and Wallis 2007) and of Ancient Olympia in Greece (Supreme Council of Ethnikoi Hellenes 2007) 'new religion followers' have attempted to reuse the sites for ritual activities.

Other archaeological sites may become the focus of disputes either among professionals or among the public when they become the context for staging the revival of ancient activities. For instance, in the case of Ancient Olympia disputes have occurred between archaeologists and the General Secretariat for the Organisation of the Olympic Games when the latter decided to re-use the ancient stadium for hosting one of the Athens 2004 sports events (*Ethnos* 08/12/2003; *Eleftherotypia* 20/04/2006).

Disputes may also occur at heritage sites that are being used by living communities where issues of conservation and authenticity in restoration are raised. A typical example is the area of Mount Athos, a World Heritage Site, which has functioned uninterruptedly as a living monastic community since the Byzantine period. The cultural heritage needs protection but is a living space for these communities (Alexopoulos 2007). Symbolic or sacred values are also attached by indigenous groups who resist visitor accessibility as in the case of the Aborigines in Australia (Daes, 1997).

Disputes may also be caused when public goods (such as heritage) are in clash with private goods (such as private properties). The ownership of public goods, as opposed to private, is usually collective and in these cases disputes are usually more intensive as the social identity theory has implied.

The issue of collective or private ownership of a personal or impersonal past and present is often intermixed with the issue and the contradiction between human and cultural rights. Archaeological heritage managers act as the guardians of items representing a 'public good' and of items preserved 'in the public interest' (Cleere 1989, 10). What is not clear is where this 'public interest' originates and why it is given such an emphasis in archaeological heritage management (Carman 2005, 46). Although ethically the 'past' belongs to all (Merriman 2000, 1) this does not always imply that all humans have an interest in the preservation of archaeological remains. In Greece, according to the Constitutional law (art.24) the natural and cultural environment is recognised as a right for everyone (Siouti 2004, 81) and therefore its protection is considered to be a priority and obligation of the state. The protection of the cultural environment is considered to serve the 'public good' and 'common benefit' (Siouti 2004, 83). The question that arises is whether this is perceived as a 'public good' by the public especially when this disputes with the rights of the individual.

Both social identity and human needs theories stress the fact that individuals are different in groups and that it is this difference which produces recognisable forms of group action (Turner et al. 1987). Individuals, as members of their identity groups, will strive for their personal needs within their environment (Burton 1990, 36-48). The situation becomes more complicated when collective identities that are shaped at local level clash with national or international identities. Scale itself is a potent source of dissonance since any one scale has the potential to undermine other levels of heritage (Graham et al. 2000, 181).

A difference between collective and personal identities shaped by collective and personal heritage respectively can also constitute a source of dispute as well as a deviation between a personal and impersonal past. Each individual assembles his own heritage from his own life experiences, 'within a unique life space containing reference points of memory and providing anchors of personal values and stability, which are not identical to those of anyone else' (Tunbridge and Ashworth 1996, 70). Personal heritage relates intimately to a sense of place, and an emotional and symbolic attachment. Personal and/or collective identities and heritages impose personal and/or collective ownerships and accesses which can again contradict each other.

As Graham has stated, heritage 'is inherently a spatial phenomenon since the relationship between a heritage object, building, association or idea and its place may be important in a number of ways' (Graham et al. 2000, 4). Consequently, identities and perceptions of heritage and its association with a specific place can be multiple and contradictory.

Personal identities may dispute with collective ones, and often, collective identities are more powerful than those of individuals. Although, a group of people with collective identities may not necessarily share a personal past, what may link them in case of dispute is the fact that each individual of this group shares a similar personal past, all of which are threatened by the preservation of an impersonal one. Alternatively, they share a common impersonal past with which they feel familiar and which is threatened by the domination of a personal present reflecting benefits to specific individuals.

The idea of identity is strongly associated with the idea of belonging, which implies a psychological and emotional use of heritage (Aplin 2002, 10) and with the idea of collective or private ownership, which implies a more utilitarian use of heritage. Identities can also be cultural, emotional or political depending on the values and beliefs attached to heritage and the place where it is located. In view of this, identities are 'multi-faceted' and 'inter-dispute-faceted'. In particular, where national identities are formed, the potential for dispute always exists either in cases where there is more than one national heritage or in cases where emotions of national pride are strongly cultivated and any exploitation or use of the past that goes against national symbols is perceived to be desecration (Butler 2001). In view of this, people might feel familiar with a 'glorious' past that reinforces their, usually, collective national identity and therefore any action that endangers this feeling, for example interventions to national, symbolic monuments, might cause disputes and tensions. On the other hand, there is the possibility that a nation state might wish to create a collective, national identity, familiarising people with a 'glorious' past (Butler 2001). This might contradict the personal past of individuals or groups of people either because they have other historic identities or because the preservation of this 'collective', national, familiar past requires the 'destruction' of their personal past and private property. The creation of a collective, familiar, national past leads to the formation of a national identity, which is either in harmony or in dissonance with other aspects of identity.

Contestation can also be understood only if 'the dynamic sense of place is mirrored in heritage landscapes which carry a multiplicity of meanings and significations, and cannot be interpreted simply as hegemonic representations foisted on a supine population by an ideology in which meaning has been appropriated by dominant social groups' (Graham et al. 2000, 76). Another source of dispute is the fact that identity formation, as values, is a dynamic process. The notion of dynamic, constant and changeable (see above) inheres dispute, tension and contestation.

At intra-organisational level the main issues in dispute relate to the ethics regarding conservation, preservation, excavation and interpretation, ethics and authenticity of material and/or historic and cultural aspects and context of a site (Vitelli et al. 2006; Zimmerman et al. 2003) and aesthetics. Debates, tensions and disputes regarding the aesthetics of heritage have mainly been raised by experts and academics including conservators, archaeologists and architects who deal with the presentation of heritage resources. In view of this, a long-term debate regarding the ways in which 'workaday objects or religious icons or objects with a clear function' should be exhibited as works of art emphasising the aesthetics has been raised (Howard 2003, 28). The issue of aesthetics is discussed more analytically in chapter 4.

3.5. Dispute management: towards a theoretical framework

This section presents a descriptive dispute management model which will constitute the basis for the analysis of the case studies. The development of this model was based on an interdisciplinary examination of sociological, psychological, behavioural, decision-making, economic, organisation, heritage, communication, negotiation and other dispute management theories some of the key elements of which were examined in the previous section. Unlike heritage theorists and sociologists, psychologists have provided some analytical tools that facilitate the diagnosis of a dispute situation. Economists and decision-makers also have attempted to suggest mathematical models which are intended to enable dispute resolution through mathematical relations. Organisation managers and dispute management theorists have suggested the organisation of workshops and forums as a way to involve groups of people in discussions and dialogues. However, specific guidelines as to how the above strategies can be implemented are still lacking. This book aims to fill this gap in the case of the heritage sector by providing heritage managers with guidelines related to the avoidance and/or resolution and management of disputes in the case of *in situ* conservation of archaeological remains in urban centres (see chapter 8).

Three main forms of dispute management have been identified: dispute settlement, dispute transformation and dispute resolution (Hamad Ahmad 2005; Reimann 2005, 7). Dispute settlement strategies aim to end a direct violence, without necessarily coping with the basic causes of the dispute (Reimann 2005, 8). The outcome usually entails a loss for one side and a gain for the other while emphasis is given to third-party intervention such as mediation and facilitation (Galtung 2000). While dispute settlement does not deal with the basic causes of dispute, dispute transformation aims to transform 'relationships, interests, discourses and the society or parties to the dispute themselves' (Reimann 2005, 8). However,

dispute transformation does not guarantee the resolution of a dispute situation. Therefore, specific dispute resolution strategies have been developed aimed at reducing, eliminating or terminating a dispute (Rahim 2001, 75). The aim is to achieve a satisfying solution for the involved parties, which meets the needs and interests of all the parties concerned (Fisher et al. 1991). This can be achieved through improvement of communication between the parties in dispute and the development of a mutual understanding of the interests of all the parties.

Dispute management differs from dispute resolution in that, unlike dispute resolution, it does not necessarily imply avoidance, reduction or termination of dispute. In organisation theory it involves 'designing effective strategies to minimise the dysfunctions of dispute and enhancing the constructive functions of dispute in order to enhance learning and effectiveness of an organisation' (Rahim 2001, 76). This raises a further issue for exploration, namely, how the driving forces to dispute can be used as a means for achieving harmony. In other words, how can the functional outcomes of a dispute be used for its management and resolution? More holistic examinations of dispute management identify the following steps: dispute prevention, dispute initiation, escalation of dispute, ensuing complications, dispute settlement, dispute management, dispute resolution and dispute transformation (Fisher et al. 2005, 7; Hamad Ahmad 2005). The analysis of the case studies will follow, for reasons of clarity and visual effectiveness, three main steps including dispute genesis, escalation and resolution.

Five main dispute management strategies have been identified by negotiation theorists including mediation, arbitration, litigation, negotiation and engagement (or participatory planning or local involvement) (Crawley and Graham 2002). A mediator attempts to improve the process of decision-making and to assist the parties in reaching their own resolution. Mediation is mainly used in industrial, business, neighbour or family disputes, as an alternative to judicial litigation and arbitration. It is a service offered both commercially and by voluntary organisations, often within a specialised field (Office of the Deputy Prime Minister 2003, 21). There are various forms of mediation. These include facilitative mediation, where the mediator assists the parties' own efforts to formulate a settlement; evaluative mediation, where the mediator introduces a third-party view over the merits of the case; and conciliation, in which the mediator takes a more active role in putting forward terms of settlement (Lovan et al. 2004). Although mediation is an important approach to securing consensus, it cannot provide the whole basis for dialogue and consultation in the preparation and implementation of plans (Lovan et al. 2004). The aim of stakeholder dialogue is to achieve the kind of agreements that would render the need for mediation of a dispute unnecessary (Lovan et al. 2004).

In contrast to mediation, an arbitrator is given the authority to impose a resolution on the disputing parties (Fisher et al. 2005, 96; Goldman and Rojot 2003, 265). Litigation is the judicial resolution of a dispute. Although litigation has constituted one of the most common dispute resolution methods (Nafziger 2004, 3), experienced litigators have often adopted more informal dispute resolution methods, such as arbitration.

While mediation, arbitration and litigation include the involvement of a third neutral party, negotiation constitutes a direct verbal communication process among the interested parties who endeavour to resolve a dispute among themselves (Nicholson 1970, 67; Morley and Stephenson 1977, 15; Tribe 1993, 1). Negotiation is a process of reaching consensus by exchanging information, bargaining and compromise that goes on between two or more parties with some shared and some disputing interests. Negotiation is likely to be part of the process of mediation, but can also happen outside any formal mediation and without the assistance of a neutral person (Office of the Deputy Prime Minister 2003, 23). Negotiation unfortunately is not a 'concept that figures strongly in conventional notions of public participation' (Office of the Deputy Prime Minister 2003, 22) and consequently in heritage management. Therefore, it is essential to develop negotiation strategies that can be integrated into the overall heritage management process which emphasises dialogue with parties and interested parties.

Negotiation theorists have determined four main types of negotiation: competitive or distributive negotiation, accommodative negotiation, avoidance and integrative or problem solving negotiation (the last two terms will be used interchangeably). These types correspond to the types of dispute management approaches that each party adopts when they resolve the disputes themselves. Competitive or distributive negotiation refers to the situation where the more one party gains the more the other party loses - known also as win-lose situation (Lewicki et al. 1999, 106; Tribe 1993, 3). Accommodative negotiation refers to the existing solutions that both parties select in order to build, preserve, or enhance a good relationship with each other. This happens when the negotiator is more interested in strengthening the relationship with the other party rather than in the outcome (Lewicki et al. 1999, 106). Avoidance refers to the likelihood of avoiding negotiation especially when an enhanced relationship is not important. Finally, integrative (or collaborative or problem solving) negotiation takes place when the involved parties in negotiation seek to identify one another's interests and see their resolution as a mutual problem (Fisher et al. 1991, 11). Another term used by Fisher et al. (1991) for this type of negotiation is 'principled negotiation' or 'negotiation on merits'. The main principles of integrative negotiation are to separate people from the problem, to focus on interests and not positions, to generate a variety of possibilities before deciding what to do and

invent options for mutual gain, and to insist that the result be based on some objective standard (Fisher et al. 1991,11). By examining the weight or value given by the parties to their different needs and objectives, one side can increase its options in a negotiation without necessarily reducing those for the other side (Tribe 1993, 6).

Negotiation is usually perceived as one of the formal dispute management processes. However, negotiation can take more informal forms such as *track two diplomacy*. Track two diplomacy is an unofficial, informal interaction between members of adversary groups or nations that aims to develop strategies, influence public opinion, and organise human and material resources in ways that might help resolve their dispute (Montville 1991, 162). The parties in dispute explore together means of defining their dispute and suggest alternatives for resolving the dispute. This dispute management strategy is time-consuming and also costly.

Finally, engagement means entering into a deliberate process of dialogue with others, actively seeking and listening to their views and exchanging ideas, information and opinions, while being inclusive and sensitive to power imbalances (Office of the Deputy Prime Minister 2003, 23). Unlike mediation or negotiation, engagement can occur without there being a dispute to resolve. Engagement is a means to identify and clarify disputes by listening to diverse interests; negotiation or mediation may then follow (Office of the Deputy Prime Minister 2003, 23).

This book emphasises the development of a negotiation process along with the engagement, since heritage managers have to act quickly, while lacking financial resources and time. The advantages are that negotiation is inexpensive and 'maintains relationships' (Whitfield 1994, 117). Alternative dispute methods, such as mediation and arbitration or litigation, will also be discussed throughout the book, since, as will be seen in the analysis of the case studies, arbitration and litigation have often been used as an alternative dispute resolution method by the involved parties. Engagement, participatory planning and local involvement are a useful strategy for avoiding or preventing potential disputes. However, they are not enough. What is needed is constant negotiation. The aim of the suggested dispute management model is used for this purpose.

3.6. Steps in a dispute management process

The formation of the suggested descriptive dispute management model has been based on thorough research on existing dispute management theories developed by economists, decision-makers, sociologists, psychologists, behaviourists and organisation managers.

Each step of the process will be described in detail stating clearly which elements of which theories have been used and how these elements apply in the heritage context. Furthermore, specific tools that can be used for the achievement of the goal of each step will be presented.

The first step of the model is to predict and prevent a dispute, if possible (Figure 1). Preventing the genesis and escalation of a dispute requires the ability to identify 'clues and signals clearly and then intervening before the situation becomes more violent' (Fisher et al. 2005, 104). The aim of the book is to identify these 'clues and signals' of a potential dispute. These will be summarised in the operational dispute management model suggested in chapter 8. Identifying these 'clues and signals' requires also specific skills and tactics which will again be analysed in chapter 8.

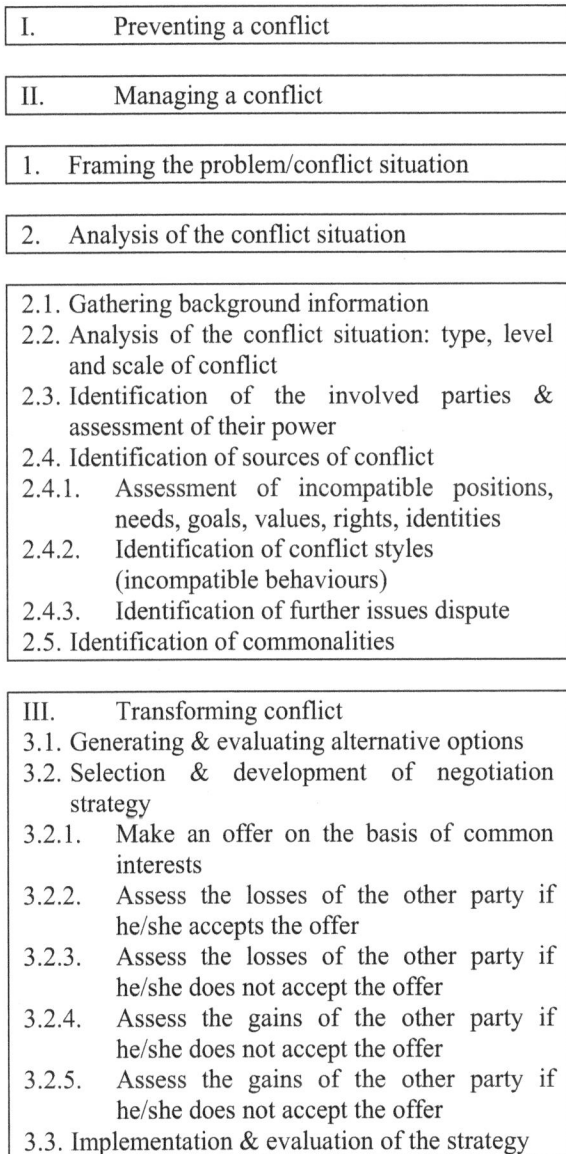

I.	Preventing a conflict

II.	Managing a conflict

1.	Framing the problem/conflict situation

2.	Analysis of the conflict situation

2.1. Gathering background information
2.2. Analysis of the conflict situation: type, level and scale of conflict
2.3. Identification of the involved parties & assessment of their power
2.4. Identification of sources of conflict
2.4.1. Assessment of incompatible positions, needs, goals, values, rights, identities
2.4.2. Identification of conflict styles (incompatible behaviours)
2.4.3. Identification of further issues dispute
2.5. Identification of commonalities

III. Transforming conflict
3.1. Generating & evaluating alternative options
3.2. Selection & development of negotiation strategy
3.2.1. Make an offer on the basis of common interests
3.2.2. Assess the losses of the other party if he/she accepts the offer
3.2.3. Assess the losses of the other party if he/she does not accept the offer
3.2.4. Assess the gains of the other party if he/she does not accept the offer
3.2.5. Assess the gains of the other party if he/she does not accept the offer
3.3. Implementation & evaluation of the strategy

Figure 1 - Dispute Management Process.

The second main phase of the model is to manage the dispute once this occurs. In order to achieve this,

negotiation theorists point out the significance of understanding how the involved parties define a problem or a dispute situation (this is known as 'framing'). Therefore, understanding the ways in which each party frames a dispute situation determines to a great extent the negotiation/dispute management style that the party will need to adopt and consequently the dispute management strategy that the party will eventually develop.

Frames have been approached as *cognitive heuristics*, as *categories of experiences* and as an *issue in development* (Lewicki et al. 1999, 29). The researchers who view frames as *cognitive heuristics* imply that a decision-maker employs a set of rules for simplifying complex situations (known as cognitive heuristics) in order to make a decision which is not necessarily the optimal one but an acceptable and reasonable one (decision theorists call it a 'satisficing solution' = satisfy+suffice). The tendency of decision-makers and negotiators to simplify complex situations derives mainly from the fact that there are limitations when decision-makers have to select among the alternatives. These limitations might refer to limited time, the mental capacity of managers and limited information and resources. As a result, decision makers are occupied by the notion of bounded rationality which closely relates to the notion of non-certainty according to which 'the consequences of actions are not certain but rather depend on another agent's actions and/or external events with unknown probabilities' (Intriligator 1982, 308; Tversky and Kahneman 1981).

Cognitive heuristics are also defined as *cognitive biases* since they affect a negotiator's process in evaluating outcomes and alternatives (Lewicki et al. 1999, 32). Despite the static character of the cognitive heuristics according to which they are restricted to explaining the perceived outcome ignoring the available information and events that follow, identifying them during a negotiation process is a significant step. However, their identification is a difficult task as will be explained below.

Some of the main cognitive heuristics that have been identified by negotiation and behavioural theorists include perceptions of losses and gains achieved by a specific outcome; a decision maker's orientation to making risky judgements (risk seeking versus risk aversion); anchoring (how a particular reference point for a decision affects that decision); over-confidence (a tendency to overestimate the likelihood of success); availability of information and isolation effects (how parties prioritise information and exclude that which they see as less relevant) (Tversky and Kahneman 1981).

The 'loss aversion' heuristic and the 'regret aversion' heuristic are two of the most important heuristics for negotiation transactions. According to the 'loss aversion' heuristic the majority of people are more willing to take risks in order to minimise or avoid prospective loss than to take risks in order to achieve a prospective gain (Goldman and Rojot 2003, 157; Kahneman and Tversky 1995, 54-56). This means that in a negotiation transaction, the typical negotiator is likely to accept an offer as long as he/she perceives that this offer is greater than his/her reservation prices (the maximum or minimum that a negotiator is willing to pay) (Goldman and Rojot 2003, 163). According to the 'regret aversion' heuristic people will pay a premium to avoid making a wrong decision. This explains why, as will be shown in the analysis of the case studies, negotiation transactions end up being taken to the court. It seems that regret aversion is maximised when a party is at the point of having to take concrete steps in pursuing an alternative to the proposed negotiation settlement (Guthrie 1999, 83-84).

Frames have also been viewed *as categories of experience* that parties bring to a particular situation (Lewicki et al. 1999, 33). Researchers who examine frames as categories of experiences have suggested seven dominant frames that parties may use in a dispute situation (Lewicki et al. 1999, 33). These are substantive frames (parties have a particular disposition about the key issues); loss-gain frames (how the parties view the risks associated with particular outcomes - this is similar to the 'loss aversion heuristic'); characterization frames (how the party views the other - this will depend on the experience with the other party and on the information about the other party's history or reputation) (see below probability of performance); outcome frames (this refers to the degree to which a party has a specific outcome that she/he wants to achieve); aspiration frames (predispositions that a party has towards satisfying a broader set of needs in negotiation); process frames (how the parties will go about resolving their dispute; negotiators who have a strong process frame are less likely than others to be concerned about the specific negotiation issues but more concerned about who is at the table, how the deliberations will proceed, or how can certain issues be handled) and evidentiary frames (facts and supporting evidence that parties present to support data or evidence that argues for or against a particular outcome or loss-gain frame).

Finally, frames are examined as an *issue development*. This approach employs a communication perspective and focuses on the patterns of change (transformation) that occur as parties communicate with each other in a disputing context (Lewicki et al. 1999, 36; Putnam and Holmer 1992, 138). The notion of transformation in the case studies will be mainly explored in terms of how the actions and reactions of each party shifted from a contending style to a compromising one or vice versa. The parties begin to develop a shared or common definition of the issues related to problem and a process for resolving them (Putnam and Holmer 1992).

Having identified the frames of each involved party, the next step is the in-depth understanding of a dispute situation. Understanding a dispute situation requires first gathering background information on pre-existing disputes or debates. Secondly, it requires a detailed description of the reasons why disputes occurred, among whom disputes occurred and when. Ideally, this step should be achieved through the participation of different parties since interpretations of a dispute situation may differ among several parties. The book describes analytically the 'what' and 'why' of dispute occurrence, escalation and resolution in the case studies using the suggested descriptive model and dispute analytical tools that have been suggested by dispute management theorists.

Firstly, gathering background information on pre-existing disputes or debates in the past as well as on the relationships of the involved parties in the past is a significant step. Fisher et al. (2005, 21) suggest the use of a 'timeline' - a graphic that shows events plotted against time. In the analysis of case studies a timeline is used in the section of each case study that examines the history of disputes.

The depiction of the linear history of a dispute using the timeline allows the isolation of the key phases and stages through which a dispute has escalated. Consequently this allows the identification of those factors that contributed to dispute escalation. The main stages through which a dispute usually goes through includes pre-dispute, confrontation, crisis, outcome and post-dispute stages (Fisher et al. 2005, 19). A dispute may rapidly evolve from a pre-dispute stage to a crisis stage and vice versa.

During the pre-dispute stage a latent dispute may exist which is invisible. As mentioned above a latent dispute occurs when behaviours are compatible and goals are incompatible. During the confrontation stage the dispute becomes more open. Occasional fighting may break out between the sides, which may include a low level of violence (Fisher et al. 2005, 19). At the crisis stage communication has probably ceased and public statements tend to be in the form of accusations made against the other sides (Fisher et al. 2005, 19). The outcomes derived from a crisis include defeat of a side, negotiation, mediation, arbitration. Usually at this stage there is a decrease in confrontation and the possibility of a settlement (Fisher et al. 2005, 19). At a post-dispute stage the dispute ends, tensions decrease. However, if the problems arising from incompatible goals have not been adequately addressed there is the risk of another pre-dispute situation (Fisher et al. 2005, 19).

The analysis of the case studies follows three main stages: dispute genesis, escalation, alternated by de-escalation, and resolution. These stages may include the above described sub-stages.

The identification of the involved parties and the assessment of their power is an essential step not only in dispute management but also in the overall decision-making process, as well as in the heritage management process.

Disputes mainly arise from incompatible positions, needs, goals, values, rights and identities, behaviours/dispute styles and further existing issues in dispute.

The sources of dispute will depend on the particularities of each situation and case. However, disputes generally occur due to the incompatibility of goals, interests, behaviours, aspirations, positions or needs. The incompatibility may not exist in reality and may be simply perceived as existing by the parties. Therefore, disputes are mainly the result of the perceived incompatibility and divergence.

A distinction should be made among incompatible and interdependent values, interests, needs, positions, perceptions, attitudes/behaviours and goals. All these constitute potential driving forces and although they may be intermixed and interlinked, they may equally differ. Therefore, it is essential to distinguish them. Perceptions relate to the beliefs that a person has. Needs derive from desires and goals that a person thinks it must achieve. Interests relate to specific goals that people want to achieve. Values are associated with the reasons why an individual or group of people want to achieve an aim (why do I want to achieve) and goals with specific targets that lead to specific outcomes. Positions refer to the open statements of the parties. Behaviours/attitudes relate to the ways on which people act or claim.

In the context of this book perceptions are defined as the processes that individuals follow in order to interpret and construct their beliefs on the importance of the past and/or the present. In the case of an *in situ* project it is essential to assess perceptions towards the project or the archaeological site that is discovered before the initiation of the project by using qualitative methods. During the implementation of the project it is important to maintain a constant dialogue. In addition, it is essential to assess the perceptions towards the party and the offer.

One useful technique for assessing and modifying perceptions is the transactional analysis. This method allows the analysis of conscious and sub-conscious stimulus response patterns of human interactions so that people can better understand what they are doing when they interact with others and how to change what they are doing if change is required (Goldman and Rojot 2003, 132). In view of this, transactional analysis can provide negotiators with a tool for understanding human behaviour and how it is formed by emotions and bounded rationality as well as for altering perceptions (Goldman and Rojot 2003, 154; Harris 1969; James and Jongeward 1971).

The three main aspects of Transactional Analysis (TA) are structural analysis, transactional analysis proper, and life positions. Structural or personality analysis is the study of ego states, where ego states are defined as 'coherent systems of thought and feeling manifested by corresponding patterns of behavior' (Berne 1972, 11). Human beings interact with each other in terms of three psychological states which exist in an individual: Parent, Adult and Child state. The Parent ego state reflects the attitudes, values and behaviour of authority figures, especially parents. This state may include prejudicial, critical, manipulative or nurturing attitudes and behaviour (Rahim 2001, 137). The nurturing parent is the part of the personality that is sympathetic and offers protective love for others while the critical parent is the side of personality that causes most individuals to avoid the use of crude language in the presence of young children or members of an older generation (Goldman and Rojot 2003, 133). The Adult ego state represents the rational part of personality. It is based on reason, collecting and processing information for problem solving, and discussion on the basis of evidence and information. It assumes that human beings are equal, important and reasonable (Goldman and Rojot 2003, 138). The Child ego state reflects the experiences and conditions of early childhood. In this state, the individual thinks, feels and behaves just as she or he did as a child (Goldman and Rojot 2003, 138). The Child ego state is divided into the natural child, the adaptive child, and the little professor. The natural child is the curious, impulsive, feeling, self-centred, demanding, affectionate, playful part of the structure of personality. The adaptive child seeks to please others, to get along, to gain acceptance, to survive. The little professor is the shrewd, intuitive, creative, fantasising, and improvising part of personality (Goldman and Rojot 2003, 133).

According to transactional analysis proper there are three types of transaction: complementary transaction, uncomplimentary transaction, and ulterior transaction. Complementary transaction occurs when the ego states are parallel; that is, a message sent from one ego state (e.g. Parent) receives an expected response from the appropriate ego state of the other party (e.g. Child). Uncomplimentary or crossed transaction occurs when a message from one ego state receives a response from a different ego state than expected. As a result dispute may occur. Ulterior transaction occurs when the overt stimulus indicates a transaction at one level (adult-adult) but the underlying intent of it may place the transaction at another level (parent-child).

According to life positions if an individual is communicating from one ego state it can correspond to one of these four positions:

From parent to child: I'm ok-you're not ok
From child to parent: I'm not ok-You're ok
From adult to adult: I'm ok-You're ok
From child to child: I'm not ok-you're not ok

Goldman and Rojot suggest that the style of a 'nurturing parent' is beneficial for negotiations that aim to meet mutual goals but not ideal for financial negotiations. The 'critical parent style' may be good for fostering the development of effective strategies but can cultivate a competitive negotiation style that is not always beneficial. The 'adult ego state' is preferable in cases where tactical and strategic choices are needed and when alternative proposals are weighed within an integrative negotiation (Goldman and Rojot 2003, 133).

The second basic proposition of TA is that the ego state in command at a particular time governs the response to a stimulus (Goldman and Rojot 2003, 135). Understanding which ego state is in control is greatly facilitated by the descriptive nature of the everyday language used in labelling the different parts in the structure of personality. For instance, negotiators who adopt a 'child ego state' tend to have a relaxed, informal posture with high pitched voice tone. The 'critical parent ego state', on the other hand, adopts a more formal posture with loud, authoritative voice using words that indicate judgment or control. The 'nurturing parent' tends to be open leaning forward. The voice is sympathetic and softer and the words used are those of encouragement and of comfort. Finally, the adult ego state tends to be moderately relaxed in posture with clear, unaffected voice tone using words that are organised, explanatory, descriptive or interrogatory (Goldman and Rojot 2003, 133).

Various disciplines define and classify needs into various types. From a psychological point of view, Maslow (a psychologist who developed the theory of 'Hierarchy of Needs' in 1943) classified needs into deficiency and growth needs. Deficiency needs are those needs that do not cause any particular feelings if they are met. However, if they are not met, then the individual feels anxious (Maslow 1943). Deficiency needs include physiological, social, esteem, cognitive, safety and aesthetic needs while growth needs include self-actualisation (the instinctual need of an individual to achieve the best he/she can) and self-transcedence needs (Maslow 1943, Table 1).

SCIENTIFIC APPROACH	TYPE OF NEED
Psychological approach (Maslow 1943)	Deficiency needs ❑ Physiological e.g. eating, sleeping ❑ Safety ❑ Love/belonging/social ❑ Esteem (the need of humans to be respected, self-respect and respect others) ❑ Cognitive (the human need to learn and explore) ❑ Aesthetic (human needs of something aesthetically pleasing)
	Growth needs ❑ Self-actualisation (a human's need to achieve the best he/she can) ❑ Self-transcedence (spiritual needs)
Negotiation approach (based strongly on psychology) (Goldman and Rojot 2003, 56-57)	Functional needs ❑ Economic ❑ Physical Emotional needs (feelings of:) ❑ Love ❑ Amusement (obtaining mental and physical stimulation) ❑ Personal achievement (satisfying self-directed goals) ❑ Social status (= a means for confirming identity) ❑ Security (maintaining good relationships with family, friends, colleagues) Conscious needs Unconscious needs
Human needs theory (Burton 1990)	❑ Security ❑ Recognition ❑ Development ❑ Identity

Table 1 - Classification of needs.

Although Maslow's hierarchy of needs has been either criticised and/or even reformed (Alderfer 1980) his classification provides a starting point for understanding human needs. Goldman and Rojot combine physical and economic needs into a broader category which they call *functional needs*. Other needs that Goldman and Rojot recognise include emotional, conscious and subconscious needs. They classify emotional needs into security, love, amusement, personal achievement and social status (Goldman and Rojot 2003, 57). The need for security has also been identified by Burton in his *human needs theory*. According to his theory, 'the human participants in dispute situations are compulsively struggling in their respective institutional environments at all social levels to satisfy primordial and universal needs - needs such as security, identity, recognition, and development. They strive increasingly to gain the control of their environment that is necessary to ensure the satisfaction of these needs. This struggle cannot be curbed; it is primordial' (Burton 1991, 82-83).

Burton further states: 'Now we know that there are fundamental universal values or human needs that must be met if societies are to be stable. That this is so thereby provides a non-ideological basis for the establishment of institutions and policies. Unless identity needs are met in multi-ethnic societies, unless in every social system there is distributive justice, a sense of control, and prospects for the pursuit of all other human societal developmental needs, instability and dispute are inevitable' (Burton 1991, 21).

Furthermore, Burton suggests that it is essential to shift from the power of politics towards the 'reality of an individual power' in order to stress that individuals, as members of their identity groups, will strive for their needs within their environment (Burton 1991, 84).

The above needs coincide with the heritage management theory in dispute in the following way. Lowenthal's analysis of the benefits and burdens of the past and present is actually an analysis of the needs that the preservation of the present and/or past fulfils. The familiarity and ability of the past to validate the continuance of glory cultivates the feeling and need of continuity, security and belonging. The ability of the past to enrich aesthetically the present fulfils the need of human beings to live within an aesthetic environment. The ability of the past to teach the present fulfils educational and cognitive needs.

In the case of *in situ* museums, it is essential to examine what needs are fulfilled by the claim to construct a public building or rehabilitate an open-space or construct a private house and then how these needs contradict with the needs fulfilled by the preservation of the past. Physiological and safety needs are mainly fulfilled by the construction of a modern private or public building. In addition, economic needs are also an important type of need that can be fulfilled either by a modern development project or by the enhancement and exploitation of an archaeological site.

Needs can also be common, both compatible and incompatible, and disputing. Common needs exist when opposing parties mutually benefit from a dispute resolution (Goldman and Rojot 2003, 49). Compatible needs are found when one side, though not gaining any particular benefit for itself, can accommodate the other's special needs without sacrificing anything that it needs (Goldman and Rojot 2003, 49). Disputing needs exist when one side is the other side's loss with respect to a particular need (Goldman and Rojot 2003, 49). Incompatible needs are involved in a transaction if one side's needs can be met only at the expense of not meeting some need of the other side (Goldman and Rojot 2003, 49). The aim of the dispute manager/negotiator is to identify the common needs. The analysis of the case studies attempts to identify some of the individual and collective needs that are inherent in the claim of preserving or destroying cultural heritage.

In contrast to needs and interests, goals are 'specific, focused, realistic targets that one can specifically plan to achieve' (Lewicki et al. 1999, 41). In addition, while needs and interests may motivate goals they may also be unrealistic and very general.

The identification of goals includes the statement of desired goals, the determination of the priority among those goals, the identification of potential multi-goal packages and the evaluation of the possible trade-offs (Lewicki et al. 1999, 41).

Interests are the underlying concerns, needs, desires, or fears that motivate a negotiator to take a particular position (Fisher et al. 2005). They can be divided into the following types: substantive interests, process interests, relationship interests, interests in principle. Substantive interests relate to the focal issues under negotiation (Fisher et al. 2005, 115). Process interests are related to the way a dispute is settled (Fisher et al. 2005, 115). Relationship interests indicate that one or both parties value their relationship with each other and do not want to take actions that will damage it (Fisher et al. 2005, 115).

It is imperative to distinguish between positions, needs and interests. Each party usually presents a position publicly. However, underlying interests may be hidden behind the positions and deeper needs that each party wants to satisfy. In view of this, there is a clear distinction between needs, interests and positions the identification of which requires constant dialogue and communication. For example, as the NAM example illustrates, the local citizens have a need for keeping their flats which had to be expropriated (chapter 7). Their interest is therefore to prevent the construction of the museum on Makriyianni plot and keep their flats. But because of the crisis in which they are involved what they express publicly is their stance, which is against the destruction of the archaeological remains discovered during the construction of the museum.

There is an extensive literature on values and several authors as well as legislation documents have attempted to classify them into broader types including aesthetic, social, spiritual and financial. My own definition to the notion of values is that values in heritage encompass the goals, interests and needs and the criteria of significance. I want also to encompass the values (significance) that the past has for the present as well as the significance of the present when it is opposed by the past. Accordingly, the following types of values can be distinguished: political, economic, social, scientific, ethical and historical or archaeological (research) (de la Torre 2005; Klamer and Zuidhof 1999). Further values will be discussed throughout the book during the analysis of the case studies.

The aim of this step is to identify the orientation that each party takes towards a dispute. Dispute management theorists have developed a framework, called the dual concerns model, which identifies four basic types of approaches that parties usually take towards a dispute (Rahim 1983; Thomas 1992). The approaches are shaped on the basis of the value, emphasis and concern they place on their own outcomes and/or the outcomes of the other party.

According to the dual concerns model the possible main strategies that a party in dispute may adopt are: yielding, problem-solving, compromising, inaction and contending. The strategy that each person or group of people will select will depend on the concern about their own outcomes and the concern about the other's outcomes (Lewicki et al. 1999, 19). The stronger the concern of an individual or a group of people for their own outcomes, the more likely people will pursue contending strategies. Contrarily, the weaker their concern about their own outcomes, the more likely they will pursue inaction (Lewicki et al. 1999, 21). Similarly, the stronger their concern for encouraging or helping the other party to achieve his/her outcomes, the more likely people will adopt problem solving or yielding strategies. The weaker their concern for the other's party outcomes, the more likely they will adopt contending or inaction (Lewicki et al. 1999, 21).

In other words, a party pursuing the contending strategy is interested in achieving his/her own outcomes and shows little concern for the other party's outcomes. In contrast, a party that adopts a yielding (also called accommodating) strategy is mainly interested in how the outcomes of the other party will be achieved rather than his/her outcomes and goals. Inaction (or avoiding) is adopted by those parties that show little concern for both their own outcomes and the other's outcomes. Problem-solving (also called collaborative or integrative negotiation) is pursued by those parties who have high concern for both their own outcomes and the other's outcomes. Some researchers acknowledge compromise as a fifth strategy located in the middle of the model in order to indicate a moderate effort to pursue 'one's own outcomes and a moderate effort to help the other party achieve his or her outcomes' (Lewicki et al. 1999, 22). However, since the boundaries between compromise and problem solving dispute style are very close (Pruitt and Rubin 1986, 29), the term integrative style in this book will refer to either a compromise or a problem-solving style.

Further issues in dispute that occurred in the past or the present complicate a dispute situation. This can be revealed clearly in the case of NAM (chapter 7) as well as in the rest of the case studies.

The next step is to identify commonalities. During this step, a heritage/dispute manager attempts to identify the underlying common interests among the parties involved in a dispute situation. This again requires constant communication and dialogue with the involved parties, which may prove difficult in cases where a heritage manager is directly involved in the

dispute. Therefore, it is essential to identify not only the actual but also the potential common interests among the parties from the early stage of a project and before the occurrence of a dispute situation.

After managing disputes, the final phase of the proposed model revolves around the transformation of the dispute through a) generating and evaluating alternative options, b) selecting and developing a negotiation strategy and c) implementing and evaluating the strategy.

Alternative solutions can be generated by inventing options which usually include the redefinition of the problem by either adding resources or by establishing more than one issue in dispute. The parties then agree to trade off among these issues so that one party achieves a highly preferred outcome on the first issue and the other person on the second issue (Lewicki et al. 1999, 119). Other options include allowance of one person to obtain his/her objective and pay off the other person for accommodating his/her interests (Lewicki et al. 1999, 119), minimization of the other party's cost and suffering (Lewicki et al. 1999, 120), invention of new options that bridge the needs of the involved parties (Lewicki et al. 1999, 120).

The notion of alternatives has mainly been developed by economists who deal with decision-making theory and bargaining (negotiation theory). Economic models are mainly mathematical models that explain the behaviour and actions of the involved parties through mathematical interrelationships. The assumption is that decision-makers consistently assess the advantages and disadvantages of any alternatives according to their goals and their objectives. They then evaluate the consequences of selecting or not selecting each alternative in order to select the alternative that provides the maximum utility (optimal choice) (Cheshire and Feroz 1989, 119-130; Lyles and Thomas 1988; 131-145). In contrast, sociological theories and models aim to find the solution that solves the problem (Lyles and Thomas 1988, 131-145).

The evaluation of the alternatives includes narrowing the range of solution options, evaluating solutions on the basis of quality and acceptability (Vroom and Yetton 1973), agreement on the criteria in advance of evaluating options (Fisher et al. 1991).

The selection and development of alternatives will depend strongly on the costs and benefits that derive for each party from the proposed offer.

Some behavioural scientists suggest that integrative or problem-solving negotiation is the most appropriate dispute management strategy (Likert and Likert 1976). However, others have indicated that the appropriateness of a dispute management strategy is strongly dependent on the situation implying that a distributive negotiation can equally be effective (Rahim and Bonoma 1979). Despite the recognition of some positive aspects of distributive negotiations, focus will be given to the development of an integrative negotiation process (collaborative or problem-solving) that is compatible with heritage management principles emphasising participatory planning and involvement of parties.

The steps of a negotiation process coincide with the steps of a dispute management process. The new elements are the 'consideration of the best alternative' and the 'assessment of the costs and benefits' derived from each alternative option and offer. Goldman and Rojot suggest the cost-benefit bargaining power model which encompasses the above key elements as well as highlighting their interrelationship based on the costs and the benefits that derive from each offer.

Their model presents how the negotiation power of a negotiator increases or decreases depending on adjustments to the key elements of the model. The bargaining power in their model refers to the ability of a negotiator to influence the outcome of a negotiation transaction as regards his/her own goals (Goldman and Rojot 2003, 43). The main concept is that the increase or decrease of a negotiator's bargaining power depends on the costs and the benefits that derive for a disputing party from disagreeing with the offered terms as compared with the cost and benefits derived from agreeing with them.

The key elements of their model coincide with the key elements that have been identified in the theoretical analysis of the previous sections, although they refer to them in different terms (Table 2).

KEY ELEMENT	GOLDMAN'S and ROJOT'S ELEMENTS
Needs (heritage theory, economic theory and human needs theory)	Offer to Meet the Other's Needs (OMON)
Alternative/options (economic theory)	Best Alternative to the Proposed Agreement (BAPA)
Cognitive heuristics (sociological/behaviour-al/psychological theory)	Perception (P)
Bounded rationality (sociological/behaviour-al/psychological theory)	Predictive Accuracy (PA)
Notion of trust (Lewicki et al. 1999, 131-134)	Probability of Performance (POP)

Table 2 - *Key elements of Goldman and Rojot's theoretical model in relation to the key elements identified in the theoretical analysis.*

In detail, the elements of their model are:

a) Offer to Meet the Other's Need (**OMON**): This element refers to a negotiator's willingness to meet the needs of the other party (Goldman and Rojot 2003, 49). It corresponds to the key element of goals/objectives of the involved parties which are motivated by their needs and interests (economic/rational model and value-led approach of heritage).

b) Best Alternatives to the Proposed Agreement (**BAPA**): This element refers to someone's perception of his best alternatives to the proposed agreement (Goldman and Rojot 2003, 58). It corresponds to the alternatives/options that the involved parties generate during a negotiation transaction (economic/rational model).

c) Perception (**P**): This refers to the involved parties' critical estimates or subjective judgment of reality. This element corresponds to the cognitive biases/heuristics derived from the subjective perceptions with which the involved parties act (sociological /psychological/ behavioural approach).

d) Predictive Accuracy (**PA**): This element refers to a party's certainty or uncertainty regarding the net value of what is proposed or of the alternatives to that proposal (Goldman and Rojot 2003, 69). This element corresponds to the notion of bounded rationality and cognitive biases that derive from the certainty or uncertainty of decision-makers regarding the limited available information (political model). Goldman and Rojot include three more elements in their model that also affect the outcome of a negotiation transaction. These are:

e) Probability of Performance (**POP**): This element refers to the perceptions that a party has towards the negotiator regarding the likelihood that the negotiator will in fact do what he/she promises (Goldman and Rojot 2003, 65). This element corresponds to the notion of trust. People usually trust someone they perceive as similar to them or as holding a positive attitude, those who depend on them and those who initiate cooperative, trusting behaviour. Finally people are more likely to trust those who make concessions (Lewicki et al. 1999, 132).

f) Accuracy of Data (**DA**): This element refers to a party's estimation of the actual cost required which might differ from the real actual cost.

g) Cost (loss) of Impending Negotiations (**COIN**) and Accrued Cost (**AC**): The first refers to the estimated cost required in getting involved in a negotiation transaction and the second element refers to the actual cost required for getting involved in a negotiation transaction (Goldman and Rojot 2003, 66).

The term cost has a broader meaning and refers to money, time and effort.

Goldman and Rojot claim that the negotiation power of each involved party depends on the interrelationship of two or more of the above elements rather than the elements themselves. In detail, they suggest that the main negotiator can have a great influence on the other parties and affect the negotiation transaction in a positive way, if s/he is willing to meet the needs of the other parties (**OMON**). However, this according to Goldman and Rojot, is not sufficient. It also requires a great probability of performance (**POP**), which means that the heritage manager must not only offer to meet the other's needs but must also persuade the involved parties that s/he will indeed deliver on the promises made (Goldman and Rojot 2003, 74). This implies that heritage organisations, which are responsible for the management of the archaeological heritage and rescue excavations and that function bureaucratically and authoritatively, as in the case of Greece, cultivate a generally negative climate causing a lack of trust on behalf of the citizens. In such a situation, if the director of a Local Ephorate (Directorate) of Antiquities would be willing to meet the goals of the other interested parties, negative presumptions could lead to failure of negotiations. This, therefore, raises a further difficulty for the heritage manager who must persuade other parties of his/her trustworthiness.

Furthermore, Goldman and Rojot suggest that a negotiator can expect a positive outcome from a negotiation transaction in cases where the involved parties consider that the estimated cost (in terms of time, effort and money) for any other option or solution is likely to be higher than the one that the heritage manager offers (**AC and DA**) (Goldman and Rojot 2003,65). In other words, the more the heritage manager has persuaded the involved parties that she/he will meet their needs together with the general profile of the citizens that she/he has and of the required cost to achieve the agreement, the more likely is that the negotiation transaction will be without problems. However, this will depend on the alternatives of the other parties (**BAPA**), or better on the perceptions of the other parties regarding their alternatives. When the parties perceive that the estimated cost or loss of entering the negotiation transaction (**COIN**) is less than the cost required for agreeing to the terms offered by the heritage manager, then the negotiation transaction will not be solved immediately. However, this will depend on the extent to which the disputing parties are certain of the estimated cost and the success of the best alternatives and options (Predictive Accuracy, **PA**). As a result, the negotiation transaction will depend strongly on the subjective perceptions and the cognitive biases with which the involved parties act, regarding especially the estimated cost and the best alternatives they have.

To sum up, the positive outcome of a negotiation transaction will also depend on the extent to which the initiating negotiator endeavours to achieve the goals or meet the needs of the other party. It will also depend on the extent to which the involved parties in the negotiation perceive that their alternatives are better or worse than the offer on the table, the perceptions of the involved parties about the required cost in getting involved in the negotiation process when this is compared with their expected outcome/gains for getting involved and the extent to which the involved parties trust or perceive the initiating negotiator to be a reliable person. Therefore, a heritage manager has to assess constantly the perceptions and beliefs of the involved parties regarding the estimated cost and the alternatives, their values, interests, goals, objectives, aspirations and motivations and, to alter the negative perceptions, as necessary.

The interrelationship of the above elements has constituted a guide in the analysis of the case studies (chapters 5-7). This has allowed the extraction of conclusions and further guidelines regarding the tactics that heritage managers can adopt in order to achieve an agreement. The analysis of the case studies has made it possible to identify further interrelationship pairs of dispute elements.

3.7. Integrating the dispute management model into the heritage management process

As mentioned above, the dissonant character of heritage derives from disputing values attached to the heritage resource by various groups of people or individuals (Tunbridge and Ashworth 1996, 5). The heritage management process suggested by the Burra Charter gives special emphasis to the assessment of the significance of the site that includes a thorough analysis of the values attributed to heritage (Sullivan 1997, 16). This section suggests a heritage management planning process that is based on the Burra Charter management process (Truscott and Young 2000) and the model suggested by Demas (2002, 28) (Table 3). The aim is to demonstrate how the suggested descriptive dispute management model fits into the broader heritage management process. Although the steps are presented for visual reasons in sequence, they should be undertaken regularly and simultaneously depending on the situation.

PHASE 1:
IDENTIFICATION AND DESCRIPTION OF THE SITE

a) Statement of the aims and the expectations of the planning process

During this stage, parties and the responsible heritage organisation should be encouraged to declare their motivations for engaging in the process as well as their expectations. This constitutes the first step for establishing a common ground and for determining the differences in expectations that might lead to future disputes (Demas 2002, 30).

b) Documentation and description of the site

This stage offers the opportunity to identify gaps in knowledge about the history and the physical condition of the site. Detailed information can be gathered through inventories, surveys, historical and archaeological records, graphic archives and interviews with local inhabitants (Sullivan 1997, 17).

c) Identification of the parties

One of the first tasks of the planning process is to identify all the parties, and ascertain their power positions and aspirations (Hall and McArthur 1996, 27; Sullivan 1997, 18). This is an essential step as well as an ongoing process that will broaden the understanding of the value of the place and determine potential opportunities and constraints (Sullivan 1997, 18). In the case of *in situ* museums, information provided by the APPEAR project, websites, bibliographic references, personal interviews regarding the involved parties and initiators of the creation of an *in situ* project have demonstrated the main involved parties. These include: archaeologists, local communities or societies, local political authorities, developers, conservators, engineers, designers, architects, exhibition developers, lawyers, historians, town planners, geologists, climatologists, topographers, universities, expert technicians from UNESCO, experts in technology and informatics and experts in the creation of audio-visual material.

HERITAGE MANAGEMENT PROCESS

1. IDENTIFICATION AND DESCRIPTION OF THE SITE
a) Statement of the aims and expectations of the planning process
b) Documentation and description of the site: oral, physical and documentary information
The history of the site
Associations with the site
Physical condition of the site
Management context of the site

c) Identification of the parties
Identification of the parties
Determination of their interests, values, perceptions, priorities and goals
Review of others' past behaviour
Estimation of their relative power
Assessment of how well a heritage organisation meets their needs (economic, symbolic etc)
Evaluation of the effectiveness of parties' managing strategies

2. ASSESSMENT OF THE SITE

---

a) Assessment of the physical condition of the site (resource analysis)
b) Assessment of the significance of the site (aspiration analysis)
c) Assessment of the management context of the site (environmental analysis)
Legal context
Financial context
Power base context
Current infrastructure
Regional and local development
Staff resources
Structure organization
Monitoring/maintenance systems

3. DEVELOPMENT OF POLICY
a) Establishment of the purpose and the policies
b) Set of objectives
Day-to-day decisions
Mid-term decisions
Long-term decisions
c) Development of strategies
Management (e.g. dispute management)
Conservation strategies & visitor access
Control of research/excavation
Internal and external infrastructure development
Ongoing consultation with parties or involvement of parties

Table 3 - Heritage Management Process.

PHASE 2: ASSESSMENT OF THE SITE

This phase constitutes the strategic analysis of a heritage management organisation (what is the situation an organisation faces) (Richardson and Richardson 1989). Strategic analysis combines an aspiration analysis (assessment of the significance of the site), a resource analysis (assessment of the physical condition of the site) and an environmental analysis (assessment of the management context).

a) Aspiration analysis (assessment of the significance of the site)

This analysis identifies the aspirations and interests of the major parties in the heritage site and assists management to formulate strategic objectives in the light of other's desires and interests. In view of this, heritage managers identify why the site is important and by whom it is valued (Demas 2002, 34). The values that can be placed on archaeological sites might be historical, archaeological, artistic, natural, social, spiritual, symbolic or economic (Demas 2002, 35). Frequently, the above values coexist and dispute with each other, and therefore, a heritage manager needs to find a balance among them in order to avoid disputes. This step coincides with step *2.4.* of the descriptive dispute management process.

b) Resource analysis (assessment of the physical condition of the site)

During this stage heritage managers document and assess the physical state of a site or a structure as well as the threats to a site (Demas 2002, 39; Hall and McArthur 1996, 26).

c) Environmental analysis (assessment of the management context of the site)

The assessment of the management context of a site looks at all the relevant factors that might affect its future conservation and management and identifies the existing opportunities and constraints (Demas 2002, 41). Environmental analysis assists planners and managers to anticipate short and long-term changes in the operational environment. It includes macro-environmental, market and competitor analysis as components of the organisational environment (Hall and McArthur 1996, 26). Macro-environmental analysis examines political, social, economic and technological factors that affect an organisation and the site for which it is responsible. Market analysis identifies who the visitors are. Competitor analysis identifies what other experiences can be substituted for the ones offered at a particular heritage site in terms of factors such as price, accessibility, promotion and marketing, packaging and the experience itself (Hall and McArthur 1996, 26). A useful way of understanding the management environment at a site is to analyse the strengths, weaknesses, opportunities and threats of the management environment (SWOT analysis) (Demas 2002, 42; Sullivan 1997, 22). The importance of a SWOT analysis has been emphasized in Step 3 of the general dispute management process.

PHASE 3: DEVELOPMENT OF POLICY

In general, a management policy refers to the overall statement, aim or vision of an organisation, identifying what it sees to be its core role, overall objectives and intended future position (Hall and McArthur 1996, 24).

a) Establishment of the purpose and policies

At this stage, heritage managers identify or revisit the purpose of a heritage organisation or the purposes for which a site is being conserved and managed as well as the values of the site that are going to be preserved. Policies or guiding principles are the critical link between the assessments of values, condition and management context on the one hand, and the objectives and strategies on the other (Demas 2002, 43).

b) Set of objectives

The objectives are clear targets, with measurable results, whose completion can be verified, and

constitute the means to translate policies into actions (Demas 2002, 46; Hall and McArthur 1996, 24).

c) Development of strategies

The development of strategies constitutes the means to achieve a desired end (Hall and McArthur 1996, 22). Strategies comprise management action programme stating how identified strategic objectives will be achieved. The process of developing strategies is called strategic planning (Hall and McArthur 1996, 22). The strategies relating to heritage sites or organisations include maintenance strategies, conservation strategies (managing the resource), visitor management strategies, control of research, including the establishment of policy regarding research activities (namely excavations) that will be allowed on site, infrastructure development, on-going consultation with or involvement of particular relevant groups, financial management strategies and dispute management strategies (Pearson and Sullivan 1995, 211-213; Sullivan 1997, 17). This step coincides with *Step 4* of the general dispute management process.

PHASE 4: PREPARATION OF THE MANAGEMENT PLAN

The management plan is the end product of forward planning. It explains why the site is important and what is planned to preserve that importance (Demas 2002, 49). Management plans can include day-to-day decisions if they serve short-term objectives; operating and action plans, if they serve mid- term objectives; and strategic plans, if they serve long-term objectives (Hall and Mc Arthur 1996, 23).

3.8. Summary

This chapter began with a theoretical discourse on the nature of dispute in heritage management and other disciplines. The advantages and disadvantages of dispute theories were initially defined highlighting at the same time the necessity to provide a holistic approach to the understanding of the nature of dispute. Starting from the behavioural/micro-theories that mainly analyse the intra-personal dispute explained by subconscious motivational factors it is essential to move on to inter-group disputes which are more observable. Classical/macro-theories of dispute with emphasis on decision-making and game theories are useful in providing an insight into the understanding of the notion of power and its role in the genesis and escalation of dispute. The notion also of interdependence is crucial and has facilitated the development of a dispute management strategy as will be shown in the next sections. According to this notion the actions of one player affect the actions of another (Oikonomou and Georgiou 2000, 276).

Having analysed the nature of dispute the chapter preceded with the development of a descriptive dispute management model which is incorporated into the broader heritage management process. Some of the steps of the heritage management process and the negotiation and dispute management process overlap. In detail, the first step of the heritage management planning process that refers to the statement of the aims and expectations of the planning process coincides with the first step of the dispute management process that refers to framing the problem. The identification of parties and their values (third step in the heritage management planning process) corresponds to the second step of the dispute management process (sub-step 2.3). In view of this, the initial understanding of parties (or involved parties) and their values/goals/interests and objectives is vital for both heritage managers and negotiators/dispute managers. Finally, the selection and the development of a dispute management strategy constitute part of the third step of the heritage management process that analyses the development of strategies.

CHAPTER FOUR: DISPUTE MANAGEMENT AT *IN SITU* MUSEUMS

4.1. Introduction

This chapter conceptualises the case of *in situ* museums -a museum type that has not been examined extensively in museum and heritage literature -and identifies their distinctive characteristics that render them different from other museum types. The chapter explores the role of these characteristics in dispute genesis, escalation and resolution. Emphasis is given to the notions of ownership, change, innovation and aesthetics which have been identified by the author as the main driving forces that lead to disputes at *in situ* museums. Additionally, the extent to which these notions can function simultaneously as potential factors of dispute resolution and dispute transformation is also examined.

4.2. Conceptualisation of *in situ* museums

The term *in situ* museum in this book refers to a museum building that preserves, enhances and presents *in situ* conserved archaeological remains to the public. The archaeological remains comprise mainly immovable architectural remains and often movable artefacts, replicas or originals, the latter being displayed either in showcases located in the proximity of the immovable remains or *in situ* exactly as they were discovered during the excavations. Conforming to the standard definition of museums, an *in situ* museum – like any museum- is a 'permanent institution in the service of society and its development, open to the public, which acquires, conserves, researches, communicates and exhibits the tangible and intangible heritage of humanity and its environment for the purposes of education, study and enjoyment (ICOM 2001, art.3).

How then do *in situ* museums differ from sheltered sites and enclosures (for an analysis on shelters and protective enclosures see Aslan 1999)? Firstly, while shelters and enclosures are aimed at functioning as 'preventive conservation measures for immediate effect by keeping water away from the archaeological site' (Aslan 1997) *in situ* museums provide a long-term preventive protection. As a result, there are often examples in which a shelter preceded the construction of an *in situ* museum as in the case of Vergina and the Mitropolis museum at Naxos in Greece. Secondly, the term *in situ* museum encompasses cases in which the enclosing building was constructed or designed before and not only after the discovery of the archaeological site. In other words, the initially planned function of the building which finally enclosed the remains was often different from that of providing protection to the site, simply because the archaeological discovery had not been predicted.

In situ museums may be underground, semi-underground or ground-level structures displaying only *in situ* conserved architectural remains or co-displaying immovable architectural remains with movable replicas or authentic objects. Occasionally, the architectural remains have been slightly moved from their initial location for conservation reasons. In some cases reconstructed replicas of immovable and movable remains and objects are used for interpretative reasons. Out of the 118 *in situ* museums that are included in the database the majority (109=92%) belong to the underground museum type, also referred to as archaeological crypts by Schmidt (1988). Eight examples belong to the ground-level museum type (7%) while only one belongs to the type of semi-underground museum structure.

Underground *in situ* museums are usually located beneath ecclesiastical buildings such as churches, cathedrals, abbeys, under squares or parking lots, within basements of private (banks, restaurants, hotels and shops) or public buildings (such as hospitals, libraries), within existing museum structures and art galleries and, finally, within train stations. Most of the underground *in situ* museums are located in the basements of modern private or public buildings (30% =34 examples). The second most frequent type of underground *in situ* museum appears in the basements of museums or art galleries (26% = 28 examples) (Figure 2). This reveals that the original function of a building as a museum or art centre facilitates the later integration of *in situ* conserved archaeological remains compared to other buildings. The type of underground *in situ* museums in the basements of ecclesiastical buildings is also quite frequent (20% = 22 examples). The remains are usually related to previous construction phases housing similar religious activity. *In situ* museums located beneath squares (9% = 10 examples) constitute a less frequent type since difficulties in the conservation of remains within limited spaces do not usually allow visitor accessibility. The least frequent type is the type of *in situ* museum located in the basement of car parks (3%= 3 examples), within train stations (7% =7 examples) and basements of historic buildings (3% = 3 examples). As mentioned above, immovable remains and movable objects may be original or replicas often left or replaced in their initial location of discovery. This may occasionally raise ethical concerns among professionals who deal with interpretation in a museum context. One of the ethical issues may relate to the extent to which it is legitimate to use replicas or move objects and remains in order to create a stimulating display for the public. A further issue relates to the extent to which reconstruction should dominate over the authentic surviving material. This issue will mainly be discussed in the case of the Jorvik Viking Centre. These ethical questions can be often used as arguments for or against the construction of such museums.

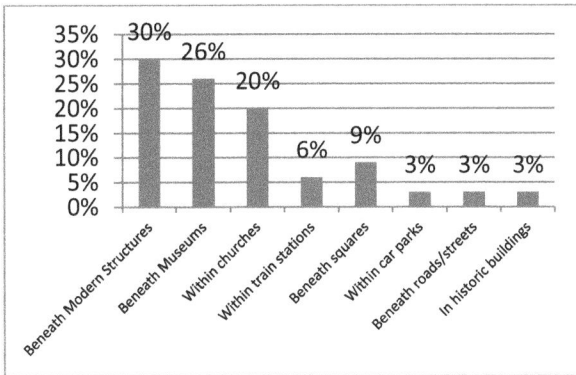

Figure 2 - Typology of archaeological crypts.

4.3. Sources of dispute at *in situ* museums

This chapter will argue that within the context of *in situ* museums issues of ownership and change are the main issues of dispute. Two main types of ownership have been distinguished by the author in the case of *in situ* museums. The first type refers to the ownership of private property on which cultural property has been discovered, such as the land or the building into which the archaeological remains are eventually integrated. The second type refers to the ownership of cultural property, in this case, the archaeological remains that are accidentally discovered. In both cases the owner can be a private entity (a person, a group of people or an organisation) or a public entity (the state, government, local community). Both may have rights of ownership in the same object, including the archaeological remains. However, the interests are different and therefore disputes occur. The ownership of land or a building, depending on the legislation of each country, may or may not affect the ownership of the archaeological remains. In the case of state ownership of a private plot or building, the accidentally found remains belong automatically to the state, in many countries, which is the main custodian and manager of the remains. The state also occasionally, at least in Greece, has the right to expropriate a private land and 'purchase' the remains along with the land.

In several cases, the state remains a co-owner of the archaeological remains expropriating only the part of the land that is occupied by the remains. Where archaeological remains are incorporated into a building that belongs to a private entity, despite the state restrictions regarding the intervention with the remains, the owner's exploitation of the archaeological site might dispute with the ethics and principles of the archaeologists. In view of this, disputes arise from the goals concerning the use of the privately or publicly owned heritage.

Given the fact that the owner may develop powerful emotional and symbolic bonds with his/her private property (emotional ownership) disputes can be more intense when these bonds are threatened by the presence of an archaeological site. In view of this, the

question is how an *in situ* museum can be made to function as a compromise in balancing private and public interests and emotions.

In addition to disputes related to issues of ownership, change and its management is a potential source of dispute. According to structuration theory, places are in a continuous state of becoming (Pred 1984, 24). Similarly, a heritage place is in a continuous state of becoming and therefore change is inevitable. Regarding the fact that 'organisational dispute, politics and change are intertwined' (Jones et al. 1998, 517) and that 'the effective management of change demands recognition of the interdependence of planned change and dispute' (Thomas and Bennis 1972, 7) it is essential to determine the inherent change trends in the case of *in situ* museums and analyse their potential for cultivating disputing reactions or for resolving them.

The main changing trends in the case of *in situ* museums become clear when examining their development. Generally, at *in situ* museums a gradual evolution from the simple protection and invisibility of the *in situ* conserved remains to visibility, accessibility and enhancement can be noticed. Disputing trends are intrinsic in each of the evolutionary stages since accessibility may contradict conservation and interpretation may clash with conservation or visitor access.

Emphasis in this examination is placed on Greece, since the core case study on which the creation of the operational dispute management model is based is the New Acropolis Museum in Athens. However, other European case studies are also explored. The European perspective not only provides a broader context generalising the validity and applicability of the suggested model but is also essential since international heritage management policies have unavoidably affected the relevant Greek policy. Despite the differences in administration and legislation among the various countries, some common principles on heritage protection have been agreed upon at international and European level shortly after the Second World War [see the UNESCO Hague Convention for the Protection of Cultural Property in the Event of Armed Dispute – an international treaty between the High Contracting Parties (UNESCO 1954) and the European Cultural Convention (Council of Europe 1954) respectively].

I have divided the development of *in situ* conservation and *in situ* presentation in Greece into five chronological periods (Fouseki 2008). This division as well as the exploration of the practice of *in situ* conservation and presentation has been based on extensive data collected in summer 2004. The data derive from archaeological newsletters dating back to the 1880s. The aim of the analysis below is not only to provide a complete picture of the *in situ* conservation policy in Greece, in parallel with relevant developments in other European countries, but also to identify the inherent changing and, occasionally, disputing, trends in the evolution of practices and concepts regarding the *in situ* conservation of archaeological remains discovered during construction works.

The first period extends from the years 1829-34 when the newly founded Greek state gained independence from the Ottoman Empire until roughly the first decade of the twentieth century. During these years the Greek Archaeological Service was gradually established as main custodian of the archaeological and cultural heritage of the country despite the enormous socio-political and economic problems. This period saw the introduction of the first legislative measures and the development of central and peripheral directorates for the protection and management of cultural heritage as well as the establishment of museums all over the country.

The second period coincides with the significant expansion of the Greek borders and the major socio-economical changes caused by various wars including: the Balkan Wars (1912-3), the Greek-Turkish War (1919-22), the Second World War (1940-44) and the Greek Civil War (1944-5 and 1946-9). In particular, the so-called 'Asia Minor Catastrophy' (1922) and the ensuing population exchanges between Greece and Turkey brought a significant number of refuges to the Greek state. As a consequence, the increasing needs for housing and the relevant urban expansion brought the construction of numerous blocks of flats which in turn resulted in the discovery of significant archaeological remains. Due to the severe financial difficulties and the several problems of the existing heritage protection policies these remains were often not preserved.

The third period, covering the 1950s, is characterised by intensive post-war construction in urban centres, which often revealed extensive archaeological remains. During this period the *in situ* conservation of significant archaeological remains in the basements of modern buildings gradually replaced the reburial of ancient remains, previously the most common practice for rescuing archaeology.

During the fourth period (1960s-1980s) the Greek Archaeological Service developed more systematic conservation measures for archaeological remains preserved *in situ* and at the same time attempted to render them accessible to the public according to the international principles on heritage management. Despite the 'dark ages' of the military dictatorship (1967-1974), during which the destruction of archaeological sites discovered as a result of the intensive construction of blocks of flats was legitimised by the Construction Law *(Οικοδομικός Νόμος)* many archaeological remains were conserved in the basements and some of them were visible or accessible to the public. Finally, the fifth period extends from the early 1990s until the present and is characterised by the attempts of the Hellenic Ministry of Culture to enhance

and present the archaeological remains to the broader public according to contemporary museological practice.

In the early 19th century while the New Greek state was being formed, the first voices calling for the necessity to preserve archaeological heritage in Greece were raised by the scholar Adamantios Korais. He was one of the first to express his concern for the looting of antiquities in 1807 and suggested specific measures that the Greek church could have overseen (Kokkou 1977, 28; Petrakos 1982, 17). The protection of antiquities from looting remained the main concern also of the newly founded Greek state (1830) and this is reflected in the Greek legislation adopted in the following years (Protopsaltis 1967, 39; Skouris and Trova 2003, 10).

Despite these early attempts to protect archaeological heritage in Greece, no detailed legislation emphasised the protection of archaeological remains during construction works since construction activity was very limited at that period. On the contrary, many significant monuments were being destroyed in order to provide building material for the erection of public buildings (Kokkou 1977, 55). It was only in 1830 that a legal framework was established for the protection of archaeological heritage endangered by construction works (Petrakos 1982, 113-7; Protopsaltis 1967, 142). A special decree was issued by Andreas Moustoxidis, director of the first national archaeological museum in Aegina, according to which any structure/remains discovered on a private plot should be examined before any official building permission be given to the owner (Protopsaltis 1967, 142).

Meanwhile, in other parts of Europe, the use of protective structures constructed over or around the archaeological remains was common. To some extent these buildings constituted the earliest origins of *in situ* museums, although the aim of these structures was strictly the conservation of the remains rather than their enhancement and presentation. These structures were designed mainly for the protection of Roman mosaics and baths, which were considered particularly important in the nineteenth century. Two of the earliest and most characteristic protective structures were built in Germany and Switzerland respectively aiming mainly at protecting the archaeological remains from the weather conditions. A protective structure was built in Hüfingen, Germany, (1821) over and around the remains of a Roman site (Schmidt 1988, 107) and a similar structure in *neoclassical* style was built (1831) over the remains of a Roman house with *in situ* conserved mosaics in Zofingen, Switzerland (Schmidt 1988, 109).

After the introduction of the first detailed archaeological law for Greece (FEK 22, 16/5/1834) in 1834 by George Ludwig von Maurer, a consultant to King Otto of Greece, the main means of *in situ* preservation was that of reburial. This law referred to issues of discovery, ownership and conservation of archaeological collections and was strongly influenced by the archaeological legislation of Italy at that period (Petrakos 1982, 20; Skouris and Trova 2003, 11). According to this law, Greek antiquities, discovered on state property, belonged to the Greek state and for the Greek nation, while the ownership of antiquities discovered on private plots was equally shared among the state and the private owners (FEK 22, 16/5/1834). At the same time, the establishment of the Greek Archaeological Service in 1833 and the founding of the Archaeological Society of Athens in 1837 (Kokkou 1977, 72, 99) contributed to a more systematic protection of the archaeological heritage. Gradually the cultural heritage under protection included also Byzantine antiquities and non-monumental remains and not only classical monumental buildings and artefacts which initially constituted the main priority in Greece since they were associated with a glorious past that was used to revive the present (FEK 158, 27/7/1899; Yalouri 2001, 36).

Despite protective measures for the archaeological remains discovered accidentally on plots in Greece, *in situ* conservation was still a rare practice due to the difficult financial situation of the new state that was incapable of compensating private owners for the expropriation of their lands. The rescue of any discovered archaeological remains was mainly dependent on the willingness of the private owner to declare the discovery to the local museum (PAE 1873-74, 24). Even in cases where the archaeological service required the interruption of construction works, the government could not afford to compensate the owner (PAE 1873-74, 24). As a result, reburial was the most common practice for the protection of accidentally found remains, including even structures that were perceived by archaeologists as particularly important. The reburial of a monumental public building of classical times, probably a stoa, and a Roman building, discovered in 1910 during the construction of a road in Piraeus were typical examples of the situation (PAE 1873-74, 145-148). Although reburial was the cheapest and easiest way to preserve archaeological remains discovered during construction works, two exceptional examples exist from these years.

The first example is the case of the 'Zappeion Megaron' in Athens that was constructed through the initiative of Evangelos Zappas in 1873 during a series of efforts for reviving the ancient Olympic Games in the city (PAE 1874, 37-47). During the construction of the 'Zappeion' a Roman bathhouse was discovered and despite the initial plans for reburial the ancient remains were finally conserved *in situ* after the intervention of the Archaeological Society (PAE 1874, 37-47). The second example is the *in situ* conservation of a public gallery dating back to the Hellenistic period, discovered in 1886 during the construction of a private house in Piraeus. The gallery was conserved *in situ* in the basement of the new house (PAE 1886, 17-18).

Political instability in Greece led to further financial difficulties, which were further complicated by the Balkan wars (1912-13) and the Greek-Turkish War (1919-22) that interrupted any progress and plans to systematise further excavations (Veleni 1993, 92). In the 1920s, the construction of blocks of flats in big cities for housing the Greek refugees from Asia Minor revealed extensive archaeological sites that were usually reburied or even destroyed. Again, the severe financial situation and the lack of archaeologists made the *in situ* conservation of even significant archaeological remains impossible (PAE 1961, 207-214; Veleni 1993, 84).

In the late 1920s, the legal obligation of private owners to finance rescue excavations (Legislative law, 30.12.1927 'Guidelines for conducting excavations' [FEK 6/A'/21.1.1928] and Codification of the law 5351/1932 'About Antiquities' [FEK 275/A'/24.8.1932]) resulted in the adoption of *in situ* conservation of archaeological remains in the basement of blocks of flats as a compromise between the archaeologists and the property owners (PAE 1935, 159-195; Veleni 1993, 95). However, reburials continued to constitute the most usual practice (Veleni 1993, 97). The protection of archaeological remains discovered during the construction of modern buildings, which was established by law, did not suffice. The required public participation did not exist in Greece. Protecting antiquities in big cities was an inhibitory factor to modernisation (Veleni 1993, 95).

The years between the Second World War (1940-44) and Greek Civil War (1944-45 and 1946-49) were again characterised by political instability and serious socio-economic changes. This prevented the systematic protection of antiquities endangered by the construction of public works. While in Greece the attempts by the state to protect effectively the archaeological heritage discovered during development projects remained unsuccessful, in Europe the first *in situ* museum was founded. This was the *in situ* museum of Liège in Belgium which was built in 1910 after the discovery of important remains of a Roman hypocaust during the installation of a gas main (Monjoie, 2005; Renson 2004, 13). The archaeological site was conserved beneath a square and was accessible to the public. Some panels with brief texts were installed identifying the different parts of the site (Renson 2004, 15).

Despite these early examples of *in situ* conservation it was only in the post-war urbanisation that the significant majority of *in situ* archaeological remains were conserved in the basements of modern structures.

This period is characterised by post-war redevelopment in both Greece and the rest of Europe that involved intensive construction during which archaeological remains were often discovered. The establishment of various international organisations aimed at shaping a common policy regarding the management of the archaeological heritage in the aftermath of the difficulties that followed the destructive consequences of the war (see UNESCO 1954 and Council of Europe 1954).

During the late 1950s, in Greece, the development of tourism led to the construction of hotels and tourism infrastructure on several islands of the Aegean, a process which brought about the discovery of important archaeological remains many of which were conserved *in situ* in the basements of modern buildings. The tendency to incorporate archaeological remains into modern buildings coincided with the 1956 Recommendation on International Principles Applicable to Archaeological Excavation, adopted by UNESCO (1956). This recommendation emphasised the *in situ* conservation of monuments and the educational significance of archaeology.

At a European level, several types of *in situ* museums, similar to the one that had been inaugurated in Liège, emerged. Such examples included the *in situ* museum in Cologne, Germany, that encloses the Roman Praetorium, which was discovered in 1946 by the Roman and Germanic department of the Wallraf-Richartz Museum. The museum was built in 1954 beneath the Townhall and the presentation of the remains was enriched through model replicas and informative panels (Schmidt 1988, 138-139). A similar *in situ* museum in the form of an archaeological crypt was built in 1957/8 in Oberriexingen, Germany (Schmidt 1988, 141). The museum covers a Roman wine cellar with movable objects displayed *in situ*. (www.unituebingen.de/uni/ymu/sqhm/xingen/frames.ht m).

While in Greece the *in situ* conserved remains were totally inaccessible and invisible, in Europe a tendency to render them both visible and accessible prevailed, as demonstrated by the Piazza Armerina in Sicily. The latter is an example of a glass museum that encloses mosaics dating to the Roman period (Schmidt 1988, 101-105). The museum was built in 1958 based on the designs of architect Franco Minissi (Minissi 1961). This museum reveals a special concern to cater for the visitor and his/her ability to view the mosaics in the best possible way without walking on them.

The *in situ* conservation of archaeological remains in the basement of blocks of flats was also a common practice in both Greece and Europe. An indicative example of the effort to promote public accessibility, which seemed to be totally lacking in Greek cases, is the Roman Docks in Marseille, which were uncovered during the construction of post-war apartments and conserved and presented *in situ* in the basements of the erected building (Ville de Marseille, www.mairie-marseille.fr/vivre/culture/musée/docks.htm).

From the 1960s until the 1980s both at national and international level, *in situ* conservation was gradually

developed to include *in situ* presentation, as illustrated in Figure 3.

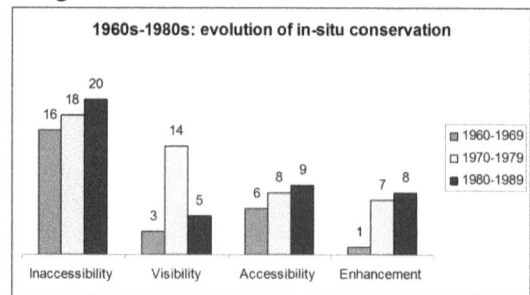

Figure 3 - In situ conservation in Greece (1960s - 1980s).

This Figure is based on the analysis of data collected from archaeological newsletters and newspapers regarding the *in situ* conservation policy. 267 archaeological sites are mentioned as having been preserved *in situ* and incorporated into modern buildings.

In Greece, the rapid urban development that had started gradually in the late 1950s, continued unremittingly during the 1960s and the 1970s revealing archaeological sites that were finally conserved *in situ* in the basements of blocks of flats. The main reason for *in situ* conservation was to secure the accessibility of the archaeologists to the ancient remains rather than to make the sites accessible to a broader public, although at international level the necessity to render the sites and museums accessible to everyone had already been recognised by the *UNESCO Recommendation Concerning the Most Effective Means of Rendering Museums Accessible to Everyone* (UNESCO 1960).

While at an international level, the UNESCO 'Recommendation Concerning the Conservation of Cultural Property Endangered by Public or Private Works' (UNESCO 1968) emphasised the protection of archaeological remains discovered on rescue excavations, the Greek Construction Law in 1968 permitted the destruction of antiquities discovered during the construction of blocks of flats (FEK 279, 28-11-1968, art.8; Petrakos 1982, 26; Veleni 1993, 98;). This coincided with the period of military dictatorship in Greece (1967-1974) when neoclassical buildings were demolished in order to make room for blocks of flats during intensive urban construction. In other countries, *in situ* museums were gradually enriched with presentation techniques, and the initial protective structures were being transformed into proper museum buildings. In 1960, an *in situ* museum was constructed in Turkey, at Side, over the ancient walls of the Thermae (Schmidt 1988, 97). This museum not only conserved the remains *in situ* but it also presented the archaeological finds, displayed in showcases. A similar example is the case of the Roman house in Sargans, Switzerland, that includes mainly a protective glass structure covering the ancient remains. The structure was built in 1968 and shows clearly that it was aimed not only at conserving and protecting the remains but also at rendering them visually accessible to pedestrians (Schmidt 1988, 117).

The 'General Construction Law' which was introduced during the military dictatorship in Greece (1967-74) enabled developers to undertake the construction of public works ignoring the presence of antiquities (FEK 279, 28-11-1968, art.8; Petrakos 1982, 26; Veleni 1993, 98). Rescuing archaeological remains discovered during the construction of modern buildings was also made an impossible task due to the small number of archaeologists serving in the Archaeological Service. The monuments selected for restoration and conservation were those that were internationally famous and therefore increased an honourable profile of Greece (Mouliou 1996). It was believed that the same profile could also be raised through the development of modern projects. However, the *in situ* conservation of the majority of the archaeological remains discovered during the construction of modern buildings was considered as an interruption to progress and modernisation.

In Europe, the new concept of *integrated conservation* was introduced by the 1975 Amsterdam Declaration of the Congress on the European Architectural Heritage (Council of Europe 1975). This concept refers to the need for developing integrated conservation policies for the protection of the architectural and archaeological heritage within the system of land-use planning, and the regulation of new buildings or other development areas of cultural importance (Pickard 2001, 8). Within this framework, *in situ* museums grew rapidly. The immovable architectural remains were presented in association with movable objects displayed in showcases or *in situ*. Interpretative panels, model replicas of the site and maps enriched the presentation as in the case of the York Minster Undercroft, built in 1972. The latter has the form of an archaeological crypt with *in situ* conserved remains dating to the Roman period (Schmidt 1988, 151). The site was recently renovated in the 1990s and enriched with interpretative panels, models and multimedia (Figs. 11 and 12). The panels (as in the case of the Aboa Vetus Museum which will be analysed in chapter 5) were addressing the visitor directly (Figure 4).

You are looking down at the actual culvert, built by the Romans in the first or second century and which still drains the water from this area. The photograph was taken just after it was excavated, River Ouse, following a gradual slope downwards. The excellent engineering skills of the Romans enabled them to move water over enormous distances using gravity alone.

Figure 4 - Part of a text panel displayed in the Undercroft Museum

During the 1960s and 1970s, protective shelters or structures that were built over the archaeological remains were enriched with interpretative material. For example, the Roman palace at Fishbourne, UK, is covered by a protective structure built in 1970, which aims to present and enhance the remains with the use of models and panels, and visitor facilities such as a restaurant and a shop (Schmidt 1988, 127). Even archaeological remains conserved beneath churches or cathedrals were imbued with a visitor-friendly approach such as the Duomo in Florence, Italy, that presents the *in situ* conserved remains of the second cathedral (Santa Reparata) dating to Early Christian Times (5th-6th century AD) in an innovative way which includes the use of multimedia. The excavations took place in the 1960s and the site opened in 1974 (Firenze by Net, www.mega.it/ita/gui/monu/buc.htm).

Similarly, the *in situ* museum of Nyon in Switzerland integrates the remains of a Roman basilica discovered during the construction of a modern building. The museum displays movable objects both in showcases and *in situ*, a new type of presentation that gradually dominated in the following years (Schmidt 1988, 147).

These latest changes in museological interpretation and presentation of the *in situ* conserved remains in Europe affected also the ways in which *in situ* remains in Greece were presented to the public. In 1978 an exceptional intervention took place in Serres, Northern Greece, where the local Ephorate of Antiquities conserved parts of the Byzantine fortification of the ancient city in the basement of a block of flats catering for both the conservation of the remains and their aesthetic enhancement (AD 1978, 316). The local Ephorate of Byzantine Antiquities undertook the appropriate conservation works and reconstructed a small part of the fortification. The construction of a supporting wall at the north side of the basement aimed to form three levels from which visitors could gain a view of the remains. The use of different colours for different parts of the basement was perceived by architects as an appropriate way to provide an aesthetic setting for the remains.

The intensive construction of blocks of flats and the development of tourist infrastructure in Greece continued during the 1980s. A new Construction Law was introduced in 1985 that forced town planners to request permission from the Archaeological Service before initiating a project (Law 1577/1985, FEK 210 A'/ 18-12-1985) and allowed the *in situ* conservation of archaeological remains and their integration into modern buildings. Although the issue of accessibility was not addressed in any way by the main policy, there were some attempts to render archaeological remains physically accessible to the public or at least visible through the use of transparent materials (Christodoulakos 1993, 472). Such examples include the remains of a monumental Hellenistic water pipe preserved in the basement of a hotel on the island of Rhodes (Dreliosi and Filemonos 1993, 439) and the remains of a Minoan lustral basin preserved *in situ* beneath two blocks of flats in Chania, Crete, in which case the basement is also accessible by way of a staircase accessed from the street (Christodoulakos 1993, 472-3).

These examples reveal a change in the management of archaeological remains that were found during the construction of modern buildings in Greece. The tendency to make the underground remains visible to a broader audience can be interpreted as an attempt to render archaeological heritage a common heritage for everyone. Occasionally, this was also used as a way of convincing the local community about the significance of their local archaeology thereby ensuring the collaboration of landowners whenever significant remains were recovered during the construction on their properties. Within this framework, even archaeological remains located in churches were enriched with interpretative material and efforts for their presentation. Such an example was the archaeological crypt of St Dimitrios in Thessaloniki. The remains were discovered during excavation works in 1918 and have been conserved since the 1980s in the basement of the church forming an archaeological crypt enhanced through the display of movable objects in showcases (Loverdou-Tsigarida 1988).

At European level *in situ* museums followed the general museological trends that propagated innovative ways of interpretation and presentation combining the display of movable objects and immovable remains. The archaeological crypt next to the Notre-Dame in Paris, that was constructed in 1980 and recently renovated, is an early example of an *in situ* museum in the form of an archaeological crypt that preserves *in situ* remains interpreted according to contemporary museological standards including the use of multimedia and videos.

The Museum of Medieval History in Stockholm, Sweden, built in 1986, not only preserves the *in situ* remains of the medieval settlement but also recreates a medieval atmosphere through the reconstruction of medieval houses and the display of movable objects (Weidhagen-Hallerdt 1993). In this case, an effort has been made to inform the public about the original uses of the displayed objects.

This case study is, to some extent, similar to the Jorvik Viking Centre in York, UK, built in 1982-1984. A theme park, enriched by the reconstruction of Viking houses and various educational activities was created in an attempt to finance the *in situ* conservation of the Viking settlement discovered during the construction of a shopping centre (Addyman-Gaynor 1984; Addyman 1990).

In situ remains were also displayed in the subways and metro stations, a solution that became common practice in Greece in the 1990s. One of the examples of this period is the *in situ* conservation and presentation of the so-called Eastern Gate in Sofia, Bulgaria, which was conserved and enhanced in the 1980s in a subway next to the Party House (Krustanov 1981).

4.4 1990s-21st century: From *in situ* presentation to *in situ* enhancement

The creation of *in situ* museums was established as a common practice in Greece during the 1990s as a result of the development of infrastructure and the undertaking of major public works combined with changes in international heritage management principles regarding the enhancement of archaeological heritage. Both the 'Charter for the Protection and Management of the Archaeological Heritage' (ICOMOS 1990) and the 'European Convention for the Protection of the Archaeological Heritage of Europe' (Council of Europe 1992) stressed the significance of *in situ* conservation and accessibility to the public, emphasising also the importance of the originality of the context of the surroundings (ICOMOS 1990). The 'developer pays' principle emerged in several European countries such as the UK, where it was expressed in the Planning Policy Guidance (PPG) 16 (1990), the Czech Republic (Ŝtulc 2001, 57) and France (Longuet and Vincent 2001, 104). This principle and the respective legislation and/or guidelines supporting it were partly the result of strong public reaction opposing the destruction of national monuments that were discovered during the construction of modern buildings. Examples include the Rose Theatre in London (UK) and the Wood Quay in Dublin (Ireland). However, as will be demonstrated in the following chapters, the relevant legislation always seems to have 'loopholes' that can be manipulated by powerful involved parties in order to legitimise their actions. In Greece such kind of principles became dominant in later years.

From a presentation and interpretation point of view, innovative ways of displaying *in situ* conserved remains in the urban centres were adopted in big cities. Such innovations in the enhancement of urban archaeological remains were not limited to cases of extensive archaeological sites but also to small-scale archaeological remains discovered beneath the streets and in the basements of private buildings. An indicative example is the Bruxella 1238 museum in Brussels which opened in 1992. This museum incorporates immovable archaeological remains and movable objects inside a transparent glass structure and is open to the public once a month (Figure 5).

Figure 5 - Bruxella 1238, Brussels, Belgium. (Photograph: Kalliopi Fouseki, 05/10/2005).

The tendency to recreate a context and a sense of place that occurred in the 1980s in the Medieval Museum in Stockholm and the Jorvik Viking Centre in the UK can be observed in the case of the Mitropolis museum at Naxos in Greece. This *in situ* museum, located in the capital of the island of Naxos, emerged when a significant archaeological site was discovered during the modification of the central square of 'Mitropolis' undertaken by the Municipality of Naxos and the Hellenic Organisation of Tourism in the 1980s (Couvelas-Panagiotatou 1999; 2000a; 2000b; Mikelakis 2002, 20). The museum exhibits not only immovable architectural remains covering a period from prehistoric until Roman times but also replicas of movable objects presented exactly as they were found. This example reveals the attempts by archaeologists to contextualise the discovered movable finds in their original setting by displaying them in association with the immovable architectural remains. The underlying principle seems to have been the contextualisation of the objects even if they are replicas. This example shows that contextualisation in the museums of the twenty-first century does not necessarily presuppose the authenticity of the displayed objects which aims at exciting visitors' admiration of the aesthetics of the genuine. In the case of the museum in Naxos, the aim was to make visitors understand the use and meaning of the objects and the displays in their real context.

In addition to the educational museum methods that apply at *in situ* museums for facilitating communication and interpretation of the immovable archaeological remains, there are some examples of *in situ* museums where the immovable archaeological remains are museumified and presented as if they are parts of a work of art. While artefacts are often displayed in showcases in a predominantly aesthetically pleasing way, immovable archaeological remains are usually enhanced with a simple informative panel or text label. However, in art galleries immovable architectural remains may constitute part of the general art setting as in the case of the Macedonian Museum of Contemporary Art in

Thessaloniki, Greece. In this example, part of the ancient road that was discovered in 1996 during extension works is preserved *in situ* and displayed along with the collections of modern art. The remains of the ancient road were considered of particular historical and topographical significance since they constitute a unique find of Thessaloniki's ancient road system (AD 1996, 427). Decorative metal spirals have been placed along the ancient remains functioning as a link to the modern art exhibition.

It could be argued that the examples of the Guildhall Roman Amphitheatre in London (inaugurated in 2001) and the Aboa Vetus in Turku, Finland, (inaugurated in 1995) also prove that archaeological remains can be successfully presented within the broader context of an art gallery. The Guildhall Roman Amphitheatre incorporates remains of a Roman amphitheatre that were discovered during the extension of the Guildhall Art Gallery in 1992 (Bateman 2000; Crooks 1995). Three-dimensional virtual reconstructions of human figures occupy the surrounding walls of the building.

The innovating trends applied on *in situ* museums have also affected the nature of the structures that enclose the *in situ* archaeological remains. The archaeological crypt of Vergina, in the homonymous archaeological site in Northern Greece that was designed by the architect Iordanis Dimakopoulos in 1993 is a subterranean structure that has externally the appearance of a tumulus (Figure 6). It actually replaced the initial shelter that was designed to offer basic protection to the movable and immovable finds discovered by professor Manolis Andronikos rather than to render the site accessible to the public. In this case, the construction of an *in situ* museum that could cater for both visitor access and conservation was deemed essential following principles advocated by contemporary heritage management. The structure protects the ancient monuments effectively by controlling the levels of temperature and humidity required for the conservation of the remains (Dimakopoulos 1997). At the same time, the structure itself functions as a museum exhibiting finds from the Royal tombs. This museum fulfils the basic principles regarding the *in situ* conservation of archaeological remains in a contemporary context. Not only the architecture of the museum building is distinctive and close to the original setting of the Royal tombs but also it successfully provides the balance between conservation and visitor access. The underlying principle of respecting the aesthetics of the surroundings and contextualising the archaeological remains is apparent. This issue, as will be shown in the following chapters, is also a common cause of dispute among architects and archaeologists. Furthermore, the aesthetic integration of a modern building into its surroundings is occasionally used by other parties as a means to oppose a decision to conserve archaeological remains *in situ*.

Figure 6 - Museum of Royal Tombs, Vergina, Greece. (Photograph: Kalliopi Fouseki, 29/07/2005).

Aesthetics can be either enhanced or threatened in the case of *in situ* museums. Aesthetics in conjunction with innovation can indeed play a significant role in dispute genesis, escalation and resolution. In order to analyse the distinctive, innovative features of *in situ* museums, it is essential to explore them from two different perspectives, first as an architectural and secondly as an archaeological ensemble. Examining *in situ* museums as architectural ensembles the main characteristics that can be identified are as follows:

- integration of the modern structures-museum buildings into the urban or natural landscape (exterior space)
- the integration of the archaeological remains into a building have often dictated alterations to the design (interior space)
- the role of an *in situ* museum as a link between the exterior space/landscape and its interior space.

The construction of modern buildings that host cultural activities such as museums raises similar concerns that are similar to the aesthetic integration of a modern structure into its historic surroundings. However, the specific characteristic that differentiates *in situ* museums from other architectural structures is the coexistence of the ancient element with the modern/present in the case of *in situ* museums. While the co-existence of the ancient element with the present may be a major issue in the construction of shelters for archaeological sites, in the case of *in situ* museum there is a further distinctive characteristic. This relates to the fact that the initial plan for the construction of a building with a different function from that of a museum may eventually need to change after the discovery of archaeological remains. Overall the original plan to construct a museum building, its construction may have to be redesigned in order to enclose the accidentally discovered archaeological remains. The accidental and unplanned discovery of the archaeological remains usually cultivates a series of disputes and debates among developers, archaeologists

and private owners, which, the solution of an *in situ* museum aims to resolve.

Furthermore, the integration of *in situ* museums as a whole into an exterior setting and the integration of archaeological remains into an interior modern setting are also a matter of aesthetics, which is often an area of dispute between architects and archaeologists. Disputes arise mainly due to the fact that the notion of aesthetics is subjective and complex and because individuals and groups of people perceive it in different ways.

This analysis relates the notion of aesthetics to the notion of curiosity, exploration, attraction and motivation which raises a specific interest in discovering the site itself, when it is aesthetically presented. In the case of *in situ* museums the perception of aesthetics is formed through an amalgam which includes perceptions of: the landscape/setting, archaeological remains and objects, museum building and the cultural and social context/prerogatives of each visitor or member of the public. The issue of how archaeological remains and objects are to fit aesthetically into the surrounding modern building again may raise disputes between archaeologists, museum professionals or architects. Above all, how the public will perceive the building in both its surroundings and in association with the displayed finds as well as the presentation of the archaeological remains is a matter of individual taste. The question which consequently arises is how a museum display can function as a compromise among the diverse perceptions regarding the aesthetics.

In situ museums as archaeological ensembles can be distinguished from open-air or sheltered archaeological sites and other types of museums for various reasons. Firstly, the notion of authenticity/originality is dominant in the case of *in situ* museums. This element is reinforced by the *in situ* conservation of the archaeological remains in their original context which provides, especially when combined with displayed movable objects, a lively experience for the visitor. The original context is two-dimensional. On the one hand, it is connected with the original location where the remains and finds were discovered.

Secondly, the potential for displaying and presenting immovable archaeological remains with movable objects is a significant element that provides a variety of innovative opportunities in terms of presentation, interpretation and communication.

It can be argued that the context of an *in situ* museum is both spatial and temporal. The interior spatial context is determined by the presence of the archaeological remains and the interior of the building while the exterior spatial context is determined by the museum structure and its surroundings. The temporal context of the past is also determined by the archaeological remains conserved *in situ* and coexists with the temporal context of the present, determined by the presence of the modern building and the modern exterior setting.

The interplay of the spatial and temporal context is also an innovative element that has been perceived by visitors as quite interesting and attractive as was revealed by the analysis of 388 visitor comments included in the visitor book of the Mitropolis Museum at Naxos in Greece. This survey was undertaken in summer 2005 and showed that visitors, despite the fact that the site is enclosed by a contemporary structure, still perceive a specific sense of the place. Their perception was not proved to be affected by the authenticity of the displayed objects and the remains – bearing in mind that some of the latter are actually replicas. The majority of the comments (65%) were quite general and provided little information about the visitor experience *per se*. However, from the remaining comments an estimated 35% did offer an insight into the general perceptions of visitors regarding the *in situ* museum. Particularly 5% of these comments referred specifically to the effectiveness of the museum in enriching their visitor experience by providing them with a sense of place – in this case sense of place is connected with the ability of the museum to tell a story. These results support the idea that an *in situ* museum functions as a medium that enhances the sense of place and justify the views of the architect who designed the museum building. The latter had stated before the completion of the project: 'the museum aims to convey the visitor the sense of the ancient market, the ceramic workshop and the cemetery' [author's translation] (Couvelas-Panagiotatou 2002, 193).

The role of contextualisation in the learning, meaning-making and understanding process cannot be assumed with certainty unless a thorough visitor survey takes place. However, there are some indications provided by the visitor book at the Mitropolis museum at Naxos showing that at least meaning-making and understanding are facilitated. Learning is mainly facilitated by the specific, innovative physical context which motivates visitors to explore more about the site. Learning also facilitates memory, which is an active process involving the connection of past experiences to recent ones, and memory, consequently, facilitates learning since visitors have the feeling that they participate in storytelling. Visitors commented on those parts of the museum that exhibits movable objects *in situ*. Of those who mentioned specific aspects of the museum that they remembered the most 2% referred to the offering tables; 6% to the graves; 1% to the ship and death section; 2% to the remains of the ceramic workshop; and 1% different moveable artefacts.

To sum up, the distinctive characteristics of the *in situ* museums include the material coexistence of the ancient (the remains) with the modern (the overall surrounding structure), the co-existence of multiple functions of the same space (for example as an accessible museum and a bank or parking lot etc), the preservation of authenticity (original/*in situ* location of remains), the possibility to co-display movable and immovable elements and the facilitation of learning and meaning-making.

All of these features are responsible for rendering a relevant underground museum display located in the basement of a modern building as a place 'that fits perfectly to what archaeology is, the revelation of old and miraculous things that lie hidden beneath the visible daily world' (Chippindale 1989, 413). The *in situ* conserved remains can potentially motivate people to go underground and find their past (Chippindale 1989, 413). In this case a main motivation for the visitor could be curiosity and the willingness to explore the 'unknown' past. This particular motivation can make *in situ* museums occasionally quite popular. As Chippindale argues, the 'setting of the Jorvik Viking Centre in York under the boutiques and the chain stores, squeezed into a very cramped cellar on the exact spot where those Vikings lived is more responsible for its popularity than we realize' (Chippindale 1989, 413). The innovative way of presentation in the case of the Jorvik Viking Centre should not be underestimated (Chippindale 1989, 413).

4.5. Summary

The innovative characteristics of *in situ* museums that were presented in this chapter have inherent disputing trends. These could be discussed as pairs of juxtaposed interrelationships including:

1. authenticity of the real - authenticity of the virtual
2. visitor access - conservation
3. the different uses of a building
4. aesthetics of the interior space – aesthetics of the exterior space
5. reconstruction as a means of learning - authenticity

These juxtaposed interrelationships will be thoroughly analysed in the case studies of this book. Their identification by the heritage manager is an essential step in dispute management resolution.

This chapter has demonstrated how *in situ* museums have evolved from inaccessible spaces to spaces that cater for the presentation and enhancement of their *in situ* remains using innovative interpretative means. Innovation in management science is mainly associated with the use of multimedia technology which has gradually become an important element in *in situ* museums in the last decades. Such technological means seem to gain popularity despite the dominance of 'traditional' methods such as informative panels and text labels. Innovation has been adopted by both private and public museums mainly in order to render displays more understandable and also in order to raise visitor numbers, and consequently, revenues.

This chapter has also shown how innovative examples have been diffused from country to country. For example, the display of movable objects in showcases and *in situ*, first encountered at Nyon in the 1960s, has been later adopted in several cases such as the Naxos Mitropolis Museum. The example of the Jorvik Viking Centre and the Medieval Museum in Stockholm which employed extensive reconstructions has also been followed in the case of the Aboa Vetus museum in Turku. The *in situ* preservation and display of the Eastern Gate remains of Sofia in a subway (1980s) occurred in Athens and Naples in the late 1990s. The use of transparent material in the case of Sargans (1960s) for enhancing the visibility of the archaeological remains has been applied in Bruxella (1990s), in the Acharnikae Gate of Athens (National Bank of Greece) as well as in Chania in Greece.

Two main questions are raised by the above remarks. The first relates to the specific ways in which innovation at *in situ* museums is diffused among countries whereas the second concerns the potential role of innovation in dispute management and resolution. Regarding the first question, innovation theorists have developed models and strategies to explain how innovations become diffused among countries. They have also stressed the importance of organising conferences and funding research for developing innovative programmes (Brown 1981; Rogers 1995). The second question will further be examined in the case study analysis that follows.

The examples of *in situ* museums mentioned in this chapter reveal that innovation can be diffused even without the existence of specific strategies and techniques developed by organisations. It is obvious that in the current 'age of information' and globalisation with the wide use of mass communication, innovation can easily be diffused in the museum/heritage sector through the development of networks among several countries and through international organisations such as ICOM (International Council of Museums) (see about innovation networks Graf 2006). The formation of networks is also facilitated nowadays through presentations of innovative projects in conferences and by the comfort of easy travel around the world.

Although *in situ* conservation and integration into a modern building provides a solid basis for developing innovative ways of presentation and innovative activities, what is further needed is the constant development of innovative activities. Innovative examples of *in situ* museums, as the case of Jorvik Viking Centre, have revealed that divergent opinions and perspectives can be accommodated in innovative projects. In addition, well conceptualised and planned innovations may lead to increase of income and general economic revitalisation of an area.

CHAPTER FIVE: DISPUTE MANAGEMENT AT ARCHAEOLOGICAL SITES DISCOVERED DURING PRIVATE DEVELOPMENT PROJECTS

5.1. Introduction

Having conceptualised *in situ* museums and their distinctive and potentially conflicting characteristics, the next three chapters analyse dispute situations that occurred after the discovery of archaeological remains during the development of private, public and museum projects respectively. Examples of private projects include the construction of buildings, such as a shopping centre, an office complex, or a private property. The main aim of private projects is the fulfilment of economic benefits for a private owner or a corporation. On the contrary, public projects aim at offering economic and social benefits to a broader community or a nation. As for the public projects, they may include the rehabilitation of an open public space such as the construction of a square, the construction of subways, car parks and motorways for facilitating the traffic, and the creation of public buildings such as hospitals, schools and churches. Socio-economic benefits are also achieved by the construction of a museum building. In view of this, a museum building is a public project. However, what differentiates a museum project from other public projects is the fact that a museum provides the public also with cultural benefits (e.g. education, leisure, engagement). The question that arises is whether disputes differentiate according to the nature of the project.

In relation to the above question, the analysis of the case studies reveals that the nature of the project plays a much more significant role in dispute genesis, escalation and resolution than the geographical area, chronological period or the administrative and legislative framework of each country. The case studies were purposefully chosen to cover a wide geographical and chronological range deriving from several countries with different planning laws and regulations. However, despite these differences, common and repeated phenomena and patterns can be identified. The identification of commonalities (constants) constitutes the basis for the formation of the operational dispute management model in chapter 8. The variables that may affect the constants are not related to the geographical area or time period, as will be shown, but to the nature of the project as well as to other key dispute elements that will be identified gradually throughout the book.

The analysis of the disputes presented in the case studies is divided into three main sections namely the stages of dispute genesis, dispute escalation and dispute resolution. Despite this linear sequence, the stage of dispute escalation is characterised by several de-escalation phases. One could argue that there can be no specific sequence of dispute stages since the human element, which is often unpredictable, is dominant and each case is unique. Nevertheless, at least in these particular case studies, the above general sequence of dispute stages was proved to function well.

This particular chapter analyses dispute situations that occurred after the discovery of archaeological remains during the development of private projects and will be followed by chapters concerning public and museum projects respectively.

In this chapter examples of archaeological remains that were discovered during the construction of modern, private structures are illustrated. The main case studies include the Wood Quay in Dublin (Ireland) and the Rose Theatre in London (UK). The cases of Jorvik Viking Centre in York (UK), Aboa Vetus in Turku (Finland) and the Billingsgate Bathhouse in London (UK) will also be briefly presented in order to further illuminate the dispute situations related to the *in situ* conservation and presentation of archaeological remains within a modern, private building.

The case studies of this chapter have similarities as well as differences and reveal different types of disputes and different strategies and tactics that the involved parties used in order to avoid or resolve dispute. What links the selected case studies is mainly the great impact that the discovery of archaeological remains had on the public. Yet, what differentiates them is the final outcome regarding the conservation and presentation of the archaeological remains. The Wood Quay example did not lead to the creation of an *in situ* museum although the public demand was for the *in situ* conservation of the remains and the use of the site for educational tours. Despite the fact that this example did not end up in the formation of an *in situ* museum, this case study provides significant information regarding the role of the public in the *in situ* conservation and presentation policy and in the decision-making process. This case study will also be compared with the rest of the case studies, allowing the extraction of conclusions and the enrichment of the suggested dispute management model with further guidelines. The example of the Wood Quay is followed by the analysis of the Rose Theatre, which led to similar problems caused by modern development that threatened an important archaeological site. However, this controversy led to the *in situ* conservation but not to the presentation of the site, although there were, and still are, attempts to render the site accessible to the public. The Jorvik Viking Centre shows how private funding and innovative presentation can lead to the genesis, escalation and resolution of disputes related to financial obstacles. The role of private funding as a driving force in dispute will be further illuminated in the cases of the Aboa Vetus museum and the Billingsgate Bathhouse.

5.2. The case of Wood Quay in Dublin, Ireland

This chapter begins with a timeline of the history of the case study in order to present synoptically the history of disputes in this example (Table 4). This timeline facilitates the analysis of the disputes in the sections that follow.

Table 4 - Timeline of the Wood Quay case study indicating phases of dispute genesis, escalation, de-escalation and temporary resolution

TIMELINE OF DISPUTES IN WOOD QUAY, DUBLIN, IRELAND

1951 Dispute Genesis	City Council of Dublin decided to construct an office-block in Wood Quay.
1955 Dispute Genesis	Dean of Christ Church Cathedral opposed the project due to the disruption of the view towards the cathedral caused by the modern building
1956 Escalation	The University College Dublin (UCD.) Architectural society opposed the construction of a modern building in the historic complex.
1956-68 Resolution	The compromise solution was the use of different material and different façade.
1968 Genesis	Dublin Finance & General Purposes Committee purchased the site of Wood Quay.
End of 1968 Genesis	The media (newspapers) pressed the Dublin Corporation to conduct preliminary excavations on the site. Meanwhile the Corporation had invited development proposals.
01/1969 De-escalation	The National Museum of Ireland started excavations on the site.
10/1969 Escalation	The excavation finds were published in newspapers which raised general concern.
12/1969 De-escalation	The Dublin Corporation granted a planning permission to the Green Property Co. Ltd. for construction on the site.
1971 (Summer) De-escalation	The National Museum of Ireland declared that had completed the archaeological excavation of the site. **[1st announcement of excavation completion]**
01/1972 Escalation	The Director of the National Museum of Denmark expressed his anxiety regarding the future of the site to the Director of the National Museum of Ireland.
07/1972 De-escalation	The Minister for Local Government granted planning permission to the Green Property on the condition that the area closer to the river would be fully excavated by February 1973 **[1st announcement of excavation continuation]**
09/1972 De-escalation	The Green Property withdrew from the scheme.
04/1973 De-escalation	The Dublin Corporation borrowed the money themselves to go ahead with the project.
05/1973 De-escalation	The Dublin Corporation sent the National Museum of Ireland a notice to quit the excavation by mid-June.
05/1973 De-escalation	The National Museum of Ireland agreed and left the excavation **[2nd announcement of excavation completion]**
08/1973 Escalation	The public became aware for the first time of the archaeological destruction.
11/1973 Escalation	The National Monuments Advisory Council sent a letter to the National Museum of Ireland regarding the damage to the Viking Wall of the site.
11/1973 Escalation	The Director of the National Museum of Ireland transferred the responsibility for further archaeological excavation to the Office of Public Works.
11/1973 Escalation	Public controversy led the Government to halt the development on the site and to request that the Corporation examine alternative locations.
12/1973 De-escalation	The City Manager presented a report on five alternative sites which had been examined among which the site at Waterford St. was considered suitable. However, a new design was deemed to cause huge delays and increased cost.
01/1974 De-escalation	The Minister for Local Government told the Corporation that the Wood Quay site should remain a free space due to its archaeological significance.
02/1974 Escalation	The Minister for Local Government changed his mind writing to the City Manager that the Civic Offices should be built at Wood Quay.
03/1974 Escalation	At a meeting at Mansion House open to the public the full excavation of the site was requested by the public.
03/1974 De-escalation	The Corporation, the Museum and the Architects divided the development area into four zones with a phased programme of excavation over three years **[2nd excavation continuation]**
05/1974	Excavations restarted.
09/1974 De-escalation	The Corporation accepted a tender of £250,000 for preliminary site-work including the construction of a retaining wall around the perimeter of the site.
10/1974 De-escalation	The City Council debated the preliminary works on the site conducted by the Corporation. However, the majority of the City Council decided the continuation of the project.
10/1974 De-escalation	The Corporation decided, for the first time, to finance the excavation works in order to accelerate their completion.

01/1975
Escalation
A 60-metre length stretch of the wooden quay walls was found. Despite this discovery the National Museum declared that the excavations would be completed in a month. This caused public agitation. [3rd **announcement of excavation completion**].

04/1975
De-escalation
Public agitation led to the announcement of a six-week extension for the excavation which revealed remains of many wooden boats dating to the twelfth century AD, the most extensive group of this period known in Western Europe [3rd **excavation continuation**].

09/04/1975
Escalation
The Director and Keeper of Irish Antiquities at the Museum informed the Corporation that the area was fully investigated [4th **announcement of excavation completion**].

04/1975
Escalation
This caused further public protest directed towards obtaining proper archaeological excavations on the site.

25/04/1975
De-escalation
A new extension was given [4th **announcement of excavation continuation**].

06/1975
Escalation
The archaeological destruction raised international concern.

07/1975
De-escalation
Excavations on Area 2 were started by the National Museum.

04/1976
Escalation
The Friends of Medieval Dublin (FMD) association was formed.

06/1976
Escalation
The Corporation offered an extension of excavation in Area 2 until November. Later in the court, it was discovered that the Corporation demanded £5,000 for the removal of spoil earlier in the year and threatened the museum with legal proceedings if the bill was not met.

06/1976
Escalation
The Museum refused the offer and declared that the excavation had been completed [5th **announcement of excavation completion**].

1977
De-escalation
The Corporation was ready to sign the contract for the construction of the building.

1977
De-escalation
The 'FMD' proposed to the Dublin Corporation the organisation of guided tours during the summer period.

07/1977
Escalation
The 'Friends' noticed that one part of the site, which had not been archaeologically excavated, was due to be removed mechanically in the autumn.

08/1977
Escalation
Representatives of the Friends and the Dublin Civic Group met Corporation officials and the architects of the proposed scheme with the aim of postponing the building construction.

Negotiations failed.

10/1977
Escalation
A public meeting was organised by Friends at the Mansion House resulting in an appeal to the Minister of Education.

10/1977
Escalation
The Minister of Education announced the initiation of excavations [5th **excavation continuation**]. However, despite the Minister's declaration workmen on the site informed the Friends that bulldozers had been ordered to move in on the unexcavated part of the site.

11/1977
Escalation
Appeals were made to the Corporation and the Commissioners of Public Works to state whether the area was a national monument. The decision declared Wood Quay a national monument.

11/1977
Escalation
The Dublin Corporation took advantage of a loophole in legislation and asked the Commissioners of Public Works to join with them in giving consent to demolish the site.

Public protest led the Minister of State at the department of Finance to announce the continuation of the excavations for no more than six weeks [6th **announcement of excavation continuation**].

09/1978
Escalation
Massive protest at the Mansion House known as the Viking March.

1978
Escalation
The Labour party and the City Council suggested alternative solutions such as the relocation of the building. But the latter never happened.

01/1979
Escalation
Bulldozers destroyed significant archaeological remains. Archaeologists working on the site stood in front of them and asked for intervention of the High Court which decided that development should be interrupted until the final appeal was decided.

01/1979
Escalation
The Corporation appealed against the High Court in the Supreme Court. The Corporation was given permission to build.

05/1979
Genesis
Internal disputing discourses on the future of the site within the City Council. The Wood Quay Action Group immediately associated the Wood Quay claim with the political elections. The councillors who supported the preservation of Wood Quay won the elections but still did not manage to protect the site.

1980
Resolution
The dispute was not actually resolved but stopped eventually since the decision to construct the building had already been made.

The story of Wood Quay started in 1951 when the City Council of Dublin recommended that the Finance and General Purposes Committee borrow the sum of £60,000 to erect a civic office-block at Winetavern Street in Dublin (Haworth 1984, 20). Four years later, and before any construction works had started, the Dean of Christ Church Cathedral argued that the high modern building would disrupt the view towards the cathedral (Haworth 1984, 20). In light of this, the Finance and General Purposes Committee suggested in November 1955 that the principal block be lowered by one storey (Haworth 1984, 20). Similar concerns regarding the aesthetic integration of a modern building into the historic complex of Dublin were expressed by the Architectural Society of the University College Dublin (UCD) (Haworth 1984, 20). As a result, in 1960 the City Council asked from the Finance and General Purposes Committee to provide a building in cut stone (Haworth 1984, 20; see also Rosney 1984).

In 1961, the site, previously owned partly by the Dublin Corporation and partly by private businesses and inhabitants, was purchased by the Finance and General Purposes Committee in 1961 through the Winetavern Street/Wood Quay Area Compulsory Purchase (Provision of Civic Offices) Order 1961. The Purchase Order was confirmed only in 1964 after public enquiry and was legally acquired in 1968 (Haworth 1984, 20). Towards the end of 1968, public pressure was placed on the Dublin City Corporation through newspapers for the conduction of preliminary excavations on the site probably after intervention from academics and archaeologists who were aware of the archaeological importance of the area (Haworth 1984, 22) . As a result, in January 1969 the National Museum of Ireland started excavating the site. Meanwhile, the Corporation had already invited a number of developers to submit plans for the civic offices and their various schemes were put on display (Haworth 1984, 22). During the excavations part of the Viking wall of the Wood Quay was revealed which was perceived by the archaeological community as a very significant find.

In October 1969, news about the archaeological finds were published in newspapers and raised a broader interest in the archaeological significance of the site, especially among the academics including the Director of Winchester excavations, Martin Biddle, who realised the national and international importance of the site (Haworth 1984, 24). Despite the importance of the archaeological finds and the fact that the excavations were still in progress, the Corporation invited the Green Property Company to apply for planning permission to build on the site which was finally granted in 1970 on Christmas Eve (Haworth 1984, 24). In summer 1971 the National Museum announced the completion of the archaeological investigation on Winetavern street (Haworth 1984, 24). It was later revealed that the museum had excavated only a small part of the site (Haworth 1984, 24). In January 1972, the Director of the National Museum of

Denmark wrote to the Dublin city manager that the discovery of the Viking town had attracted attention all over Scandinavia (Haworth 1984, 24). This letter was passed to the writer's Irish counterpart, Dr Lucas, Director of the National Museum of Ireland who was insisting that only the city wall was worth conserving (Haworth 1984, 24). In July 1972, the Minister for Local Government granted planning permission for the construction of the offices on the condition that the unexcavated site closer to the river would further be investigated by the Museum of Ireland by February 1973 (Haworth 1984, 25). This decision increased the cost of the designed scheme still further and led the Green Property to withdraw in September 1972. The withdrawal of the Green Property in turn led, the City Manager to go ahead with the scheme in March 1973, borrowing the money on behalf of the City Council (Haworth 1984, 25). In May 1973, the decision by the Corporation to interrupt the excavations caused to huge public outrage since the latter became aware of the destruction of valuable archaeological remains through the media (Haworth 1984, 24). In November 1973, a letter about the damage at the Viking wall of the site was sent by the National Monuments Advisory Council to the Director of the National Museum. The Director's reply was that 'The museum has completed its investigation of the site and has now no official connection with it…The museum most emphatically does not wish to be associated with any …adverse comments on the Corporation or its officers' (in Haworth 1984, 27). He also mentioned that architects had been warned by the museum of the possible discovery of further sections of the wall during the clearance work of the site and he suggested that the architects should discuss this matter with the Office of Public Works (Haworth 1984, 27). It is important here to mention that at that time only five percent of the site had been excavated (Haworth 1984, 27).

It has been claimed that the main reason for which the National Museum had agreed on the continuation of the construction works by declaring that the excavations had been completed was that it was principally interested in the recovery and conservation of the movable artefacts rather than the remains (Haworth 1984, 27). This was partly revealed in the minutes of a meeting held with the Corporation a week after the discovery of the Viking wall where the director was recorded saying that: 'the museum is principally interested in the recovery and conservation of artefacts' (Haworth 1984, 27).

In November 1973, the public concern for the future of the archaeological remains, led the Government to order a halt to the development on the site and to request that the corporation examine possible alternative locations for the offices. A month later the City Manager presented a report on five alternative sites of which only the site at Waterford Street was considered suitable in all respects. However, this decision required a new design scheme which would have caused further delays and costs. Therefore this decision was abandoned (Haworth 1984, 27). In January 1974, the Minister for Local Government also suggested to the Corporation that the Wood Quay should stay an open-space, free of structures, because of its significant location in relation to Christ Church Cathedral and its archaeological importance (Haworth 1984, 27-29). One month later, the Minister for Local Government changed his initial proposal by stating that the office building could be built on the eastern half of the site. The reasons for the reconsideration were not explained (Haworth 1984, 27). This action provoked further public protests including an open meeting at the Mansion House on 12 March 1974 addressed by well known archaeologists who requested the full excavation of the site before the construction of the building. As mentioned above, the National Museum of Ireland had excavated only part of the Wood Quay site considering that there was no necessity to excavate other parts due to the small archaeological significance of the site. On the following day a joint open meeting between the Corporation, the Museum representatives and Architects from the University of Dublin was held at the Mansion House. During this meeting, the parties agreed on dividing the development area into four zones with a phased programme of excavation over three years (Haworth 1984, 28). Despite this agreement, the Corporation accepted simultaneously a tender of £250,000 for preliminary site-work including the construction of a retaining wall around the perimeter of the site (Haworth 1984, 30). The City Council debated the above actions although the majority supported the continuation of the development works. As a result, the excavations took place along with the construction works. During the excavations a 60-metre length part of the Viking wooden quay walls was discovered. Despite this important discovery the Museum announced the completion of the excavations a month later, a fact that raised public agitation which led to the announcement of a six-week extension of the archaeological excavations (Haworth 1984, 31). During this excavation period remains of many wooden boats dating to the twelfth century AD were discovered. Although they constituted a unique find discovery for Western Europe the Keeper of Irish Antiquities again announced the completion of excavations in April 1975 which again caused public protest and again led to extension of the archaeological works (Haworth 1984, 32). Excavations at Area 2 started in April 1975. A year later a number of people in Dublin including archaeologists, medieval historians, historical geographers, architects, town planners, local historians as well as city aldermen, formed the association of Friends of Medieval Dublin (FMD) with the objective of fostering an appreciation of medieval heritage of Dublin (Martin 1984, 38; see also their website http://fmd.ie/). They also published maps of medieval Dublin for city planners and developers. In June 1976 the Corporation offered a further extension for archaeological excavations to the Museum but the latter refused. The reason for this refusal, as was revealed later in court, was the fact that the Corporation had demanded from the Museum the sum of £5,000 for

the removal of spoil a year earlier and had threatened with legal proceedings if the bill was not settled (Martin 1984, 32).

In Christmas 1977, the discovery of the Norman wall (11th century AD) reignited the controversy and motivated archaeologists to carry out further excavations in order to uncover the ruins of a legendary church, the St Olaf's Church (Lansaw 1984). In summer 1977, when the Corporation was about to sign the contract for the construction of the building, the FMD proposed to the Dublin Corporation that guided tours of the site at Wood Quay be organised during the summer (Martin 1984, 38). Permission was granted by the Corporation but some months later, in July 1977, the intention of the corporation to remove a part of the unexcavated site mechanically again caused strong public reaction (Martin 1984, 38). In August 1977, representatives from the FMD and the Dublin Civic Group - a group established in 1961 with the aim of investigating the threats to Dublin's cultural heritage (see Hefferman 1988, 27) - met Corporation officials and the architects with the aim of postponing the signing of the building contract. In October 1977, the FMD organised a public meeting in the Mansion House in order to alert the public of the threat to the site (Martin 1984, 38).

An overflowing audience expressed its opposition to the building of the civic offices until the site had been scientifically excavated. They made an appeal to the Minister of Education, John Wilson (Martin 1984, 38). The Minister in turn announced that there would be a stay of execution at Wood Quay for six months and that money would be made available for an archaeological team to work there (Martin 1984, 39). As a result archaeologists started working on the site. Despite the continuation of the excavations workmen on the site informed the FMD that the bulldozers had orders to move in on the unexcavated part of the site and destroy the Viking earthen defence banks on 28 November 1977 (Martin 1984, 40). The case opened immediately and a lengthy legal process ensued with unavailing appeals to the Corporation and to the Commissioners of Public Works to decide whether the area in question was a National Monument (Martin 1984, 40). The legal decision resulted in the declaration that Wood Quay was a National Monument (Martin 1984, 41). The Dublin Corporation asked the Commissioners of Public Works to join with them in giving consent to demolish and totally remove the National Monument, taking advantage of a loophole from sub-section 3 of section 14 of the National Monuments Act of 1930 (Martin 1984, 41). According to this loophole 'the commissioners and every local authority were authorised to give a consent for demolishing whenever they think it expedient in the interests of archaeology or for any other reason so to do' (Martin 1984, 41). This raised further public protests forcing the Government to intervene with a temporary compromise to meet the popular outcry. In August 1978, the Minister of State at the Department of Finance announced that excavations at Wood Quay should continue for a period of not more than six weeks. 'When the excavations were completed and unless some new archaeological finds of great importance had been made, the Corporation would be granted permission to proceed with the building of the civic offices' (Martin 1984, 42). However, in the same month, a joint consent to go ahead with the destruction of the site between the Commissioners of Public Works and Dublin Corporation had been secretly signed (Martin 1984, 42). In September 1978, public indignation rose rapidly and was channelled into a march by the FMD at the Mansion House (known as the 'Save the Wood Quay' campaign (Simpson 2014). The Viking March was supported by rural Ireland (National Council of Muintir naTire), the trade union workers, Irish hotels and tourism representatives, historians, academics and school children with their teachers (Martin 1984, 47).

The Government issued a formal statement on the problem declaring that it 'had directed that the Commissioners of Public Works should consent to an extension of time to complete further investigation of the site' (Martin 1984, 48). Proposals for relocating the building to another plot were expressed by the Labour party and the City Council, but, despite the national campaign of the FMD, the recommendations of the National Monuments Advisory Council and the Committee of Culture and Education of the Council of Europe, the development works continued (Martin 1984, 51). The Labour party suggested the relocation and redesign of the offices on a part of the Wood Quay that had been bulldozed leaving the rest of the site free of any structural intervention. Thus, the National Monument would have been conserved and the view towards the cathedral would not have been obscured (Martin 1984, 51).

In January 1979, bulldozers moved into an area of prime archaeological interest at the base of the supporting steel sheeting at Wood Quay and began to remove material provoking reactions by archaeologists working there who stood in front of the bulldozers. They requested that the historian F.X. Martin and retired professor of Medieval Archaeology at the University College Dublin, who was also chairman of the FMD society, secure a High Court injunction restraining the Corporation from proceeding with the bulldozer work (Martin 1984, 54). The Corporation argued in court that a joint consent for demolition had been agreed on 29 August 1978 and that the bulldozing of that area was necessary for strengthening the sheeting wall with supporting concrete (Martin 1984, 55). Mr Justice Gannon interrupted the bulldozing until the full trial (Martin 1984, 55). Within an hour of the High Court decision, the Corporation appealed against it in the Supreme Court. The Supreme Court in turn upheld the appeal for the Corporation and the Commissioners of Public Works against the High Court decision. The Corporation was given the permission to continue with the demolition and the

High Court and Supreme Court costs were awarded against Prof. Martin (Martin 1984, 55). The Committee of Culture and Education of the Council of Europe pleaded with the Irish Government to preserve Wood Quay (Martin 1984, 56). The Council's Assembly requested the Irish government to delay construction work but the government did not respond (Martin 1984, 55). In May 1979, a special meeting at the City Council resulted in a sharp reversal of policy with the councillors voting by 22-15 to request a renegotiation of the contract for the civic offices that would leave the National Monument area free from buildings (Martin 1984, 56). Citizens mounted a campaign to occupy the site in order to try to give effect to the common wishes of the City Council and Council of Europe.

The Wood Quay Action Group with the support of the FMD decided to produce 'Vote for, Canvass Against' election leaflets for each of the eleven constituencies of the City Council. This action reveals the political dimension that the issue had acquired, a common characteristic also in other case studies, as will be shown in the following section. Many councillors who opposed the protection of the Wood Quay site were defeated in the elections while the new City Council was ready to save the site (Martin 1984, 60). The Lord Mayor of the City Council, Mr Cumiskey, who was elected that day, asked the building contractor, John Paul, to halt the construction works. John Paul forced the occupiers to abandon the site through a decision from the Supreme Court (Martin 1984, 55). The City Council managed to extend the excavations until March 1981 but the office block was finally constructed due to legal advice, threats of surcharge and suggestions of withdrawals of services to councillors (Martin 1984, 61). As a result, the remains were finally destroyed despite the time-consuming excavations and the building was constructed over the archaeological site. The only remains that were preserved *in situ* in the basement of the office block were the remains from the Viking city wall (Archiseek 2007) with the aim to create an *in situ* museum which finally was never realised (Clarke 2004; Lansaw 1984).

5.3. Analysing the disputes in the case of Wood Quay

The example of Wood Quay illustrates a complex network of involved parties which consists of various heterogeneous parties who got involved in different stages of the dispute and it can be divided into ten sub-networks following the different chronological stages. The first two networks are not related to the archaeological significance of the site but to the aesthetic and historic-symbolic significance of the historic complex within which the modern building was constructed. The next eight sub-networks are related to the archaeological significance of the site and are more complicated than the first two. The dominant parties in each network are the Corporation on the one hand and the media/public on the other. These involved parties can be divided into three main groups on the basis of their objectives. The first group consists of those who desire the protection of the site, the second group of those who desire the construction of the office block, and the third group of those who support or oppose the construction of the office block according to the changing political circumstances. The main intermediaries that link or divide the involved parties are the site of Wood Quay, the different values attached to it (archaeological, economic, symbolic, political, educational) as well as the administrative and financial framework.

In detail, in the 1950s in the case of Wood Quay, opposing reactions by the Dean of the Christ Cathedral and the University of Architecture to the construction of a modern building in the historic centre of Dublin cultivated a pre-dispute situation providing a fruitful ground for the genesis of disputes in the 1960s and 1970s. This actually constitutes a guideline for the development of a dispute management model. As will be shown in the following case studies, minor reactions at a pre-conflict stage can constitute the basis for further major conflicts and disputes. Therefore, it is imperative that a heritage/dispute manager examines the history of disputing debates of a site.

Despite temporary negotiations in 1977, the Wood Quay dispute soon escalated to a confrontation and a state of crisis. This outcome has further implications for heritage/dispute management. Temporary negotiation outcomes which give the impression of a dispute resolution should not be perceived as permanent solutions. On the contrary, a heritage manager should keep in mind that the dispute could potentially evolve into a crisis if the outcome is temporary and does not fulfil the needs of the involved parties.

Along with the extra-organisational disputes, there was an inter-organisational dispute between two heritage organisations: the National Museum of Ireland and the National Monuments Advisory Council. The main issue in dispute was the different approach to the preservation of the archaeological remains and the selection of the heritage elements that were deemed important enough to preserve. The National Monuments Advisory Council valued the archaeological site as an ensemble while the National Museum of Ireland focused on the preservation of the movable objects discovered on the site. The extra-organisational disputes occurred between those who desired the completion of the excavations and the preservation of the archaeological site and those who were supporting the construction of the office block in the Wood Quay area. The first group includes the general public and the media, while the second group includes the Corporation, the local government and the National Museum of Ireland. Initially the public group included intellectuals and academics. At a later stage, the extra-organisational disputes led to intra-organisational disagreements such as the dispute

between the employees and the employer/Corporation and the dispute among the Councillors of the City Council. The role of media was instrumental in fostering disputes regarding the protection of the archaeological site as they generated public awareness and facilitated the formation of local societies and national groups aiming to protect medieval history and archaeology.

One of the main reasons for the escalation of the dispute was the contending style of the main parties in dispute. In the case of Wood Quay the main party opposed by the public was the Corporation that adopted and retained a contending style against those who supported the preservation of the archaeological site. Therefore, despite the initiation of the excavations in 1968 by the National Museum of Ireland after pressure generated by the media, the Corporation invited the Green Property Company to build the office block. This shows that while the Corporation adopted a yielding style by accepting excavation of this site, it never yielded its main objective, which was the construction of the office block. What is unknown is the extent to which the Corporation expected the presence of archaeological remains in this area. The expectations and predictions would have strongly depended on information provided by the National Museum of Ireland. Interestingly, the director of the National Museum of Ireland, whose role in the Wood Quay was critical, Pat Wallace, has admitted at an interview conducted in 2005 that 'my biggest problem was not the Dublin Corporation, which did not value the site, but my employer, the National Museum, because it did not back me up. It was outsiders, mainly historians such Fr F.X. Martin, who salvaged time for me to finish the job' (Wallace and Canavan 2005, 49).

The media continued to play a powerful role since promoting the excavation results raised a broader interest among academics and the general public. As a result, the announcement of the National Museum of Ireland that excavations had stopped raised strong public reaction not only at national but also at international level, for example due to the significance of Viking archaeology for Scandinavian countries. Despite the public reaction, permission for construction was given by the Minister for Local Government who probably had not predicted that public reaction would continue unremittingly. After the bankruptcy of the Green Property Company and the interruption of the excavations, the public again reacted leading the government to order a halt to the construction of the office block and to suggest its relocation to another plot. This fact shows that the contending style of the public in response to the contending style of the Corporation persuaded politicians to intervene as mediators adopting a compromise strategy probably because of fear of political losses. This changed the initial attitude of the Minister for Local Government who despite having initially granted permission for the construction of the office block, later suggested that the office block be built on the eastern side of the site, the area that had been totally excavated. This reveals the flexibility of dispute management styles that governmental bodies adopt according to the political effects that massive public reactions have. It also shows that the contending style of the public may work in its favour.

Despite the compromise style of the Minister for Local Government the public retained the contending style and gathered at the Mansion House demanding the continuation of the excavations. The formation of the local society also aimed at the fulfilment of this objective. After the completion of the excavations (promoted by the Corporation and the National Museum of Ireland) the FMD proposed the organisation of guided tours during the summer period, a proposal that was accepted by the Corporation. This is actually the first time that a reconciliation took place between the Corporation and the public. The initiative was undertaken by the local society who transformed their initial contending style to a compromise one. Despite the persistent contending style of the Corporation and the mistrust this caused towards the Corporation and the National Museum of Ireland (low probability of performance) the FMD adopted a yielding and compromise style that was temporarily effective. Despite this positive climate the intention of the Corporation to remove an unexcavated part of this site caused further reactions among the employees (intra-organisational dispute) who informed the FMD about the planned destruction. The latter again adopted a problem-solving style trying to negotiate with the Corporation who nevertheless insisted on their initial objective. Therefore, the FMD did not limit their efforts to negotiating but also organised a public meeting, made an appeal to the Minister of Education and took legal action to achieve the declaration of the site as a National Monument. In this way, the FMD adopted a mixture of strategies including both negotiation and litigation. These initiatives again brought temporary positive results (continuation of the excavations and the declaration of the site as a National Monument). The Corporation retained its contending style and collaborated with the Commissioners of Public Works taking advantage of loopholes in the legislation, a fact that shows the potential ineffectiveness of legal measures or the uses and abuses of the latter by the financially powerful parties. This led to public reaction and the Viking March that necessitated the intervention of the Government and the political parties who adopted a compromise style. The local societies took advantage of the fact that the issue was a political one causing intra-disputes among the city councillors and therefore local people voted only for the supporters of the Wood Quay site.

The escalation phase included some de-escalation phases during which temporary compromises were achieved after mainly the intervention of third parties including mainly administrative and political bodies. The FMD also prepared maps of Medieval settlements in the city which developers could potentially use in the future as a basis for avoiding to build on sites of archaeological significance. The FMD also suggested, during negotiation transactions with the Corporation, the organisation of guided tours in the site which could have potentially provided a common ground for achieving a solution based on the economic interests derived from both rendering the site accessible to the public and from the construction of the building. The alternative offers were proposed by mediators rather than directly by the parties in dispute. The main alternative offers included the relocation of the building and the completion of the excavations before the construction of the building. None of these were accepted by the disputing parties.

Usually after a crisis there is the post-dispute stage, as in the case of Wood Quay, which either provides the final outcome of a dispute situation or leads to further disputes depending on the solutions and the situation. In this case, the dispute was never resolved, the demand of the public to preserve the site was never achieved and the most powerful party (the Corporation) won. However, the losses for the Corporation, in terms of time and costs, were huge. The main reason for which a negotiation was never achieved was the contending style of the parties that prevented them from recognising potential common interests. Some of those interests included the economic exploitation of the site for tourism development. The suggestion of the FMD to organise tours for the public was revealing of their desire to exploit the site economically. This actually was used by the FMD as a means of negotiation but proved to be unsuccessful since the core aim of the Corporation to build the office block on top of the remains did not change. A common ground was never achieved since there was lack of constant communication and negotiation and because the Corporation proved to be an unreliable negotiating party.

5.4. The case of Rose Theatre in London, UK

The example of the Rose Theatre is typical of a nationally valued monument endangered by the construction of a modern building. In contrast to the Wood Quay where the archaeological site was revealed accidentally and was characterised as a National Monument only after public demand, in the case of the Rose Theatre, the discovery of the particular remains had been predicted by the specialists (Miles and Brindle 2005) and the site was immediately associated with a nationally and internationally famous monument. It was agreed that the remains would be conserved *in situ*, although without the possibility to visually present them and without access to the public. This was the result of a public reaction and a compromise between the developers/private owners and the public/archaeologists. However, the presentation and interpretation of the archaeological remains to the public remained one of the major concerns (Table 5).

The Rose Theatre was built in 1587 by the impresario Philip Henslow in the proximity of Southwark Bridge Road. It was followed by the Swan (1595), the Globe (1599) and the Hope (1613). Two of William Shakespeare's plays were first presented at this theatre (Orton 1989, 62).

In 1957, Southbridge House, an office block, was built on the site. At that time the piles of the new building were driven through the known site of the Rose but with no provision for archaeological recording (Miles and Brindle 2005). In 1987 the building became redundant and the Heron Property Group applied for planning permission to construct a new building on the site (Orton 1989, 62). This gave the opportunity for the excavation of the site and the exposure of the Rose Theatre. The excavations conducted by the Museum of London's Department of Greater London Archaeology revealed the foundations of the 'Rose Theatre', the first of the four Tudor/Jacobean playhouses on London's South Bank (Wainwright 1989, 430). In the same year, the Museum of London (MoL) advised the London Borough of Southwark to attach an archaeological condition to any consent that might be given relating to the construction of an office block on the site (Sheldon 1990, 286).

During the construction works the archaeological remains of the theatre were discovered. The Heron Property agreed to a two-month evaluation followed by a period for further work. In October 1988, after the discovery of the remains by Heron Property, the Imry Merchant Developers PLC undertook the development of the site and agreed to finance the excavations (Wainwright 1989, 430). In the light of the archaeological discoveries and the view of the Museum of London that the remains were those of the Rose Theatre, the developers subsequently agreed to extend the excavation period until 15 May 1989. On this day a big protest prevented piling for the new building that would ultimately destroy the remains, a debate which had already started on 10 May 1989 in the House of Commons.

Virginia Bottomley, Under Secretary of State for the Environment, claimed that the remains of the Rose would be 'substantially conserved' and Margaret Thatcher, the then Prime Minister added that damage would be kept to a 'minimum' (Biddle 1989, 753). This would be achieved by constructing the building on stilts which would raise it over twenty feet above the remains (Goyder 1992, 354). However, the actors' community was not convinced by these claims and therefore protested against any development work on the site by blocking its entrance. The protest had been initiated by Ian McKellen and other distinguished actors with slogans like 'Don't let them doze the Rose' (Chippindale 1989, 411). After the sudden blocking of the entrance to the site by the campaigners, it was agreed that staff from the Museum of London (MoL)

would serve as on-site agents of English Heritage. The main responsibility of the MoL was to keep the remains damp to prevent their physical deterioration (Sheldon 1990, 287). English Heritage was to examine the long-term problems of conserving the site and the MoL was to submit schemes for further excavation which might be necessary (Sheldon 1990, 287).

On 15 May, English Heritage tried to persuade the developers to redesign their foundations in a non-damaging fashion, to ensure full protection of the remains while the office building was going up and to redesign the building in a way that would eventually allow the uncovering and display of the remains. Despite the increased cost, a redesigned scheme was released in 1989. The redesigned scheme involved protection of the site during construction, removal of all piling from the area likely to contain remains of the theatre foundations, and provision of sufficient headroom over the remains to allow for their future display. In addition, the developers agreed that prior archaeological investigation of any area affected by the adjacent piling should take place. The total cost of these changes had been estimated by developers to around £10 million (Wainwright 1989, 432). While the developer was preparing the redesign-plan, the 'Theatres Trust' set up by an Act of Parliament to promote the better protection of theatres for the benefit of the nation, commissioned an independent study from Ove Arup and Partners (Biddle 1989, 758). The height of the Arup hall deprived the developer of 75.000 sq.ft. that could have been both compensated for and replaced by an extra floor in the new office block. However, this solution could have been risky since, as has been demonstrated in other case studies, extremely high buildings in historic areas can cause further negative reactions by architects.

The revised plans of the developers were submitted to Southwark Borough Council for planning permission that would allow the construction of the building to proceed (Wainwright 1989, 432). The Secretary of State announced that the developers had agreed voluntarily to delay the development by up to one month, to allow time for further discussion on the best way of preserving the remains and for consideration to be given to the possibility of public display

.

English Heritage began undertaking further archaeological work on 5 June. According to Wainwright, the MoL refused to authorise staff to undertake further archaeological work, an action that led to English Heritage's on 7 June to assume responsibility for the conservation and essential recording of the site from 12 June onwards (Wainwright 1989, 432). The MoL was reportedly reluctant to carry out that work then because it involved digging holes immediately adjacent to the known remains of the theatre in accordance with a redesigned scheme which was not due to go before Southwark Council for consideration until 3 July (Sheldon 1990, 287). This however did not mean that the MoL refused to excavate (Sheldon 1990, 287). The MoL sought a preliminary assurance from English Heritage that they could withdraw from the excavations should circumstances, such as a legal challenge, make this advisable (Sheldon 1990, 287). However, this request was not accepted by English Heritage. Its Chief Executive stated in a letter to the Director of the Museum of London that the latter was informed that its concerns were now in dispute with the duty, held by English Heritage, for the safety of the remains and that the MoL would be replaced on the site by English Heritage's own central Excavation Unit (Haynes et al. 2000, 265).

The public was not satisfied with this solution since their main demand was for the monument to be scheduled. However, scheduling at this stage and subsequent frustration of the extant planning consent would have involved payment of compensation that was estimated at £60 million and was consequently rejected by the State as an option (Wainwright 1989, 432). The Rose Theatre Trust applied for a judicial review of this decision (Wainwright 1989, 434). On 30 June, the Rose Theatre Trust successfully applied for an injunction against Imry Merchant Developers to prevent preparatory work being undertaken in advance of the outcome of the Judicial Review. This injunction was lifted on appeal on 3 July. That same day Southwark Borough Council deferred considering the planning application until 25 July pending a decision by the Secretary of State on whether to call in the application and also to await the outcome of the Judicial Review. The Secretary of State refused to call in the application and the application for judicial review of the decision not to schedule the remains of the Rose Theatre was rejected mainly for financial reasons (Wainwright 1989, 435). On 25 July 1989, planning permission was finally granted in refusal to schedule the site while developers and Southwark Council agreed on a legal basis that provision for displaying the finds to the public would be taken (Sheldon 1990, 287).

Finally, Rose Court was completed in 1991 and handed over to new owners (Miles and Brindle 2005). Originally it was expected that the protective covering over the remains of the Rose would only need to remain in place during construction work of the Rose Court building, a period of approximately two years. The developer, Imry Merchant, contributed £230,000 towards the redisplay of the theatre's remains, and placed this in the keeping of Southwark Council (The Rose Theatre Trust, 2006). Meanwhile, on Friday 28 February 1992, after almost three years of concerted lobbying by the Rose Theatre Trust, the Government announced that it had decided to include the remains on its Schedule of Ancient Monuments. The trust – a registered charity and limited company- was given licence by the new owners to occupy and use the basement containing the archaeological remains (Miles and Brindle 2005). In 1993 the Trust appointed Jon Greenfield, the architect of the new Globe, to produce

plans for the site (Miles and Brindle 2005). English Heritage became responsible for inspecting the site on a regular basis and ensuring that the covered remains were being kept in a stable environment to prevent their deterioration. Southwark Council made some of the money originally contributed by Imry Merchant available to the Trust in order to create a temporary exhibition in 1999. The aim of this exhibition was to reawaken public interest in the site and to help raise the money needed for full excavation and a permanent display. The Rose Trust proposed the excavation of the whole theatre site to natural gravel, the removal and conservation of the hard features, the lining of the site with a waterproof structure, the refilling of the site with an inert matrix to the level of the theatre remains, the reinstatement of the hard materials and simulated soft surfaces, the construction of viewing galleries and the installation of exhibitions in the basement area and the bridge arches. English Heritage undertook the long-term conservation of the remains as well as to attract a sufficient number of visitors in order to generate sufficient revenue (for a detailed account see also Eccles 1990).

Table 5 - *Timeline of dispute at Rose Theatre indicating phases of dispute genesis, escalation, de-escalation and temporary resolution.*

Date	Event/action
1987	The Heron Property applied for building permission on the site
1987	MoL advised Southwark borough to attach an archaeological condition which led to the initiation of archaeological excavations [**1st phase of archaeological excavations**].
1987	The remains of the theatre were immediately discovered.
1987	Heron Property agreed to accept a two-month archaeological evaluation [**2nd phase of archaeological excavations**].
10/1988	The Imry Merchant Developers PLC undertook the development.
1988	In the meantime further archaeological finds were associated with the Rose Theatre.
1988	The Imry Merchant Developers decided to postpone the excavations until the 15 May 1989.
10/05/1989 Genesis	A debate started in the House of Commons regarding the construction of the office block.
15/05/1989 Escalation	Public reactions against the building construction started by blocking the entrance to the site.
05/1989 De-escalation	After the sudden blocking of the entrance to the site by the campaigners, it was agreed that staff from the Museum of London would be responsible for keeping the remains damp.

15/05/1989
De-escalation — English Heritage (EH) undertook the examination of the long-term problems of conserving the site and the MoL was to submit schemes for further excavation which might be necessary.

15/05/1989
De-escalation — EH tried to persuade the developers to redesign their foundations in a non-damaging fashion, to ensure full protection of the remains while the office building was going up and to redesign the building in a way that would eventually allow the uncovering and display of the remains.

06/1989
De-escalation — A redesigned scheme was released and excavations continued by EH while the Rose Theatre Trust applied for a judicial review [3rd phase of excavations].

Summer 1989
De-escalation — The revised plans of the developers were submitted to Southwark Borough Council for planning permission that would allow the construction of the building to proceed.

Summer 1989
De-escalation — The Secretary of State announced that the developers had agreed voluntarily to delay the development by up to one month, to allow time for further discussion on the best way of preserving the remains and for consideration to be given to the possibility of public display.

05/06/1989
De-escalation — English Heritage began undertaking further archaeological work [4th phase of excavations].

07/06/1989
Escalation — The MoL was reportedly reluctant to carry out that work then because it involved digging holes immediately adjacent to the known remains of the theatre in accordance with a redesigned scheme which was not due to go before Southwark Council for determination until 3 July.

07/06/1989
Escalation — English Heritage undertook the responsibility for the conservation and essential recording of the site from 12 June onwards.

Summer 1989
Escalation — The public was not satisfied with this solution since their main demand was for the monument to be scheduled.

Summer 1989
Escalation — The State refused scheduling of the site.

Summer 1989
Escalation — The Rose Theatre Trust applied for a judicial review of this decision.

30/06/1989
Escalation — The Rose Theatre Trust successfully applied for an injunction against Imry Merchant Developers to prevent preparatory work being undertaken in advance of the outcome of the Judicial Review.

03/07/1989
Escalation — This injunction was lifted on appeal. The Southwark Borough Council deferred considering the planning application until 25 July pending a decision by the Secretary of State on whether to call in the application and also to await the outcome of the Judicial Review.

25/07/1989
Escalation — The Secretary of State refused to call in the application and the application for judicial review of the decision not to schedule the remains of the Rose Theatre was rejected mainly for financial reasons.

25/07/1989
De-escalation — Planning permission was finally granted in refusal to schedule the site while developers and Southwark Council agreed on a legal basis that provision for displaying the finds to the public would be taken.

1991
Resolution — Completion of the Rose Court.

1992
Resolution — Scheduling of the site.

5.5. Analysis of disputes

The case of the Rose Theatre reveals that a latent, invisible dispute existed, as in the case of Wood Quay, which caused further disputes immediately after the discovery of the remains despite the compromise solutions and attitudes of the developer. This implies also that when nationally significant remains are discovered during the construction of a modern building disputes may occur suddenly and rapidly. Mild confrontation quickly succeeded the crisis which led to the particular end-result and then further disputes. This also implies that sudden and rapid dispute situations may lead to sudden and rapid outcomes.

The main parties that got involved in the case of the Rose Theatre included developers, heritage organisations, governmental bodies and the public. The involved parties can be divided into two main groups. The first group included mainly the developers who wanted the construction of the office block and the second group those who wanted the preservation of the site. The second group was slightly more heterogeneous. It consisted of English Heritage, the governmental bodies and the local societies that all wished to see the site presented to the public and scheduled as a National Monument.

The intermediaries that linked the parties into a network were the archaeological remains of the Rose Theatre and the national/symbolic significance that the site had for the public, the existing legislative framework regarding excavations during development projects, the governmental bodies that had to ratify a decision (administrative context), the available funding resources and the media. The available funding resources determined, to a great extent, the participation or non-participation of some of the actors. Regarding the administrative context, Southwark Council was the main body responsible for the ratification of a final decision regarding planning permission. This decision was also influenced by advice provided by the Museum of London and the Secretary of State. The media again played a significant role in publicising the case. Available funding or willingness to pay determined the decision by the Secretary of State not to schedule the site and by the Heron Corporation to abandon the project.

The obligatory passage points through which the involved parties had to go were initially the completion of the excavations and then the conservation of the site. On the basis of this, the solution that was proposed was the construction of an underground *in situ* museum. However, this solution was not perceived by the public to be adequate both because they did not trust the initial promises of the government and because they were opposed to the suggested architecture of the new scheme.

As in the case of Wood Quay, politicians supported the idea of preserving the site on the basis of fulfilling their need for recognition and political development. The public clearly expressed their preference for the preservation of the site as a means to protect their cultural, national identity. The developers in the case of the Rose Theatre, in contrast to Wood Quay, adopted a more integrative/compromise style when negotiating with the main heritage organisations –especially with English Heritage. Perhaps examples such as Wood Quay were considered as situations to be avoided since they proved that when corporations oppose public demand, the project is delayed and the cost is increased. However, despite the compromise attitude of the developers, public reactions continued since the demand was not only for complete excavation but also for presentation and scheduling of the site. This proves that the integrative style does not always produce an equivalent response, as Transactional Analysis has implied. There are specific conditions which need to be fulfilled such as the assessment of the total number of goals and wishes of the other party and the assessment of the prioritisation of their goals.

The public undertook two main alternative actions which were actually used simultaneously as in the case of Wood Quay. The first included blocking dynamically the entrance to the site and the second pursuing judicial appeals for scheduling the site.

The compromise attitude adopted by the developers and the government from the initial stages revealed that a common interest and concern was the avoidance of dispute and time-consuming judicial procedures that would delay the completion of the development project as had happened in the case of Wood Quay. Regarding the tension between English Heritage and the Museum of London, a common interest was the preservation of

the site on a long term basis. Avoidance of dispute and preservation of the site were the main elements on which a common ground was finally established for finding a balanced solution that allowed the co-existence of the modern building with the archaeological remains.

The Heron Property Group adopted a compromise style from the beginning of the project since they accepted the need to conduct excavations at the site. This shows that there was a positive climate between the responsible heritage organisation and the developers, which formed a positive ground for avoiding potential disputes. However, although this positive climate ensured the avoidance of disputes between archaeologists and developers it did not secure the prevention of disputes between the public and the developers. The public mistrusted any promises provided by politicians and developers that the remains would not be damaged. The public demand was for the scheduling of the monument. This demonstrates what Goldman and Rojot have stated in their cost-benefit bargaining model theory (see chapter 3) regarding the interrelationship between the willingness of a negotiator to offer to meet the needs of the public, as in the case of the Rose Theatre, with the perception of probability of performance (POP). If the general public perception of developers is negative, then their willingness to fulfil the demands of the public are either regarded as suspect or ignored by the latter. The final compromise offer was the *in situ* conservation and integration of the site into the modern building. This however did not resolve the problem since it raised further difficulties regarding the conservation of the site and the claim to enhance its presentation and interpretation.

5.6. Other examples of disputes in European *in situ* museums

The dilemma of integrating archaeological sites into modern buildings can be demonstrated by several other examples. This section presents briefly the cases of the Jorvik Viking Centre in York, UK, the Aboa Vetus Museum in Turku, Finland and the Billingsgate Bathhouse in London, UK.

The Jorvik Viking Centre

The case of the Jorvik Viking Centre was selected as a good example to demonstrate how private funding and the economic exploitation of an archaeological site can actually be effective in terms of the latter's conservation, at least for the short-term. As James notes, the 'heritage centre' concept adopted in the case of the Jorvik Viking Centre, proved to work for the first fifteen years since the Jorvik Viking Centre closed in 2000 as a result of the declined visitor numbers (James 2000). He also argues that an *in situ* museum imposes inflexibility in terms of how it can adapt to change (James 2000). However, this does not seem to be the case as the current situation reveals (www.jorvik-viking-centre.co.uk) Furthermore, it reveals how private funding can affect presentation in a way that may not be easily acceptable to academics or other specialists, thereby leading to internal disputes and debates. This example also raises the issue of ethics in presentation and interpretation, an issue which is very relevant for archaeologists, museologists and heritage professionals in general. In addition, the Jorvik Viking Centre illuminates further issues in dispute which may occur during the discovery of significant archaeological remains on development projects.

Before examining the tactics that the York Archaeological Trust (YAT), the main organisation involved in excavating Jorvik, followed in order to prevent the dispute, it is essential to review its history briefly. The YAT, a charitable foundation which is responsible mainly for the conduction of rescue excavations in the city of York and the education of the public in archaeology, conducted excavations between 1976 and 1981 at the Coppergate area on the occasion of the construction of a shopping centre (Addyman 1990, 257). The majority of the discovered remains belonged to the Anglo-Scandinavian period (AD 850 – 1050). The excavations revealed part of the commercial area of Jorvik, with street-front shops, workshops and yards (Addyman 1990, 257). The archaeological remains were very well preserved and offered the chance for specialists and the public to glimpse at vernacular buildings of the Pre-Conquest period (Addyman and Gaynor 1984, 9). The YAT suggested a series of alternative solutions regarding the conservation of the site (Addyman and Gaynor 1984, 9).This was also the result of market research focusing on the use of visitor comment cards that demonstrated that the large majority of visitors at Coppergate felt sad and angry at the possibility that remains would have to be destroyed by the new development (Addyman and Gaynor 1984, 9).

In the case of the remains found at Coppergate, reburial was considered as an option but entailed the risk of adverse public reactions. A second potential option was the removal of the remains and their display in the Yorkshire Museum. However, this particular museum was deemed totally inadequate for hosting the material because it was too small and too old (Addyman and Gaynor 1984, 9). A third option was the creation of a special display area away from the site (Addyman and Gaynor 1984, 9). In the end, the possibility of conserving the remains *in situ* underneath the designed shopping centre was considered to be the most appropriate option and the most acceptable to the public (Addyman and Gaynor 1984, 9).

The scheme was rejected by York City Council, which indicated that an alternative scheme for a ground level museum, adjacent to the existing Castle Museum, might be a better option and could be more favourable to the public. In effect, the York Archaeological Trust prepared a new scheme, which aimed to combine a new generally themed archaeological museum with the proposed archaeological exposition of a neighbourhood of Viking-Age York (Addyman and Gaynor 1984, 9). This was also rejected by York City Council, which provided YAT with the option of returning to its first scheme that proposed an underground archaeological basement below the shopping arcade (Addyman and Gaynor 1984, 9). Nevertheless, the implementation of this project was not considered an easy task because the cost was estimated to be high and conservation issues would have restricted accessibility and display.

In order to solve the funding problem a scheme with potential commercial viability was devised. This scheme, which received the essential prerequisite of a £250,000 grant from the English Tourist Board, proved to be attractive and sound enough to gain a loan of £14 million from a consortium of seven banks syndicated by N.M. Rothschild and Son for the YAT. The balance of the £2.6 million, equivalent to the cost for the construction and fitting out, was provided by a loan from Wimpey Property Holdings PLC, the developer. This scheme was based upon projected visitor figures of 500,000 per year, with an entrance charge at about the level of a cinema ticket together with a profitable shop (Addyman and Gaynor 1984, 10-11). Although such a visitor figure would have placed the Jorvik Viking Centre amongst the most successful attractions in the country, it was nevertheless felt to be achievable only together with an imaginative display and systematic marketing. These estimates were also based on the fact that the Jorvik Viking Centre would be located near three famous attractions of York (the Minster, the National Railway Museum and the Castle Museum), and therefore it was reasonable to expect a great number of visitors as well. Moreover, it was felt that the majority of visitors to York came to enjoy the city's historic ambience and would thus already be, at least potential, customers for an archaeological centre designed to present the story of a formative period in the growth of the city (Addyman and Gaynor 1984, 10-11).

However, this innovative and imaginative way of displaying archaeological remains was criticised, mainly by academic archaeologists, as inauthentic and fake. These criticisms derive from the question of how to balance presentation on an ethical way in relation to the authenticity of the site. The Jorvik Viking Centre is imaginative, creating the illusion of authenticity by recreating smells and sounds but this aspect has attracted contradictory opinions. It has been claimed that even the *in situ* remains, a very small part of the whole exhibition, have been shifted slightly and are not strictly *in situ* (Schadla-Hall 1989, 62). Despite such criticisms, the Jorvik Viking Centre remains one of the most popular tourist destinations in the UK, a fact that demonstrates that what really matters, at least from a visitor's point of view, is not the *in situ* conservation but the *in situ* presentation of the site. What seems to matter is that the display of the Jorvik Viking Centre is located exactly where the Viking settlement was discovered. Similar issues, although to a lesser degree, seem to emerge in the case of the *in situ* archaeological remains preserved in various stations of the Metropolitan Railway of Athens (Greece). In some of these stations replicas of immovable and movable objects have been displayed in showcases, at the underground level where they were discovered, creating a sense of place and of authenticity (Figure 7).

Figure 7 - Syntagma Station, Athens, replica of a water pipe discovered during the construction of the Metropolitan Railway. (Photograph: Kalliopi Fouseki, 12/07/2005).

The network in the case of the Jorvik Viking Centre includes the main heritage organisation responsible for the site (York Archaeological Trust), the visitors/ the public, the governmental bodies responsible for tourism and development, the developers and the archaeologists/academics. The network is quite homogeneous in contrast to the networks of the previous case studies, since the main parties had a common goal which was the co-existence of the archaeological site with the development of the shopping complex. This shows that the more homogeneous a network is the fewer the disputes that occur while complex networks tend to involve more disputes.

Overall, the co-existence of the remains with the shopping centre seemed to be a successful solution and did not cause external disputes raised by the media or the public. The only disputing discourse was generated among the academics some of whom opposed the transformation of the site into a tourist theme park.

The main issue in dispute among academic archaeologists and archaeologists-practitioners was the economic exploitation of the site which resulted, in the eyes of the former, in the presentation and conservation of the remains in a manner that was not authentic. Therefore, both the examples of Jorvik and of the Rose Theatre, reveal that even if there are common goals (in this case, the conservation of the site) there can still be differences regarding the different approaches and ways of preserving the remains. In view of this, innovation can be successful as far as it ensures a collaborative multidisciplinary approach.

At the Jorvik Viking Centre, as mentioned above, the common goal from the beginning was the preservation of the site along with the construction of the shopping complex. This required extra funding. The necessity to raise more funds required the presentation of the site in the manner of a theme-park.

The element that differentiates the case study of the Jorvik Viking Centre from the examples mentioned before is the fact that a series of alternative options had been suggested by the York Archaeological Trust from the very beginning of the project. These suggestions prevented any disputes and disagreements with the involved parties, such as the York City Council and the developers. If the YAT had suggested only one scheme regarding the preservation of the remains which would have then been rejected by York City Council, tensions and disputes would have possibly raised. However, because the YAT had five alternative ideas/options, the initial rejection for the creation of an *in situ* museum by York City Council did not cause any delays in the project. Preparing a series of alternative solutions is a key element of the garbage can model as has been analysed in chapter 3. As demonstrated by this example, it is also a key element in the dispute management strategy for heritage places since it can effectively prevent the emergence of disputes and tensions.

While external disputes were successfully prevented in the case of the Jorvik Viking Centre internal tensions emerged related to the ethics of conservation and preservation of the remains. Similarly, in the case of the Aboa Vetus Museum in Finland a dispute arose between the museum owner/sponsor and the archaeologists working on the excavations.

The Aboa Vetus

The Aboa Vetus Museum, which opened to the public in 1995, is located in Turku, Finland, and is part of a building complex which also includes the Ars Nova modern art museum. Aboa Vetus (which means Old/Ancient Turku in Latin) houses archaeological remains dating to the medieval period of the city of Turku, the old capital of Finland. The contemporary museum that displays the archaeological remains was constructed after the discovery of the latter in 1993 during renovation works at the so-called Rettig Palace. The building itself, built in 1928 and named after its former owner Hans von Rettig, a wealthy businessman and vice-consul for Sweden, was purchased in 1991 by the private foundation of Matti Koivurinta in order to house his significant collection of modern art paintings (Alexopoulos 2000).

Following the discovery of the archaeological remains in 1993, negotiations took place between the Ministry of Education and the National Board of Antiquities of Finland for the conduction of large-scale excavations and for the subsequent creation of an *in situ* museum that would integrate the excavated buildings to the modern art gallery (Uotila and Sartes 2000, 375). The Turku Provincial Museum carried out excavations which revealed buildings dating from the fourteenth to the nineteenth century AD and, among other things, medieval streets flanked by rows of masonry and cellars of buildings with vaulted ceilings (Sartes 2002, 375). This discovery led to the continuation of the excavations in 1994 by the National Board of Antiquities, which revealed storerooms and foundations of houses belonging to merchants and craftsmen of the medieval period (AD 1300-1500). The remains were very well preserved because the foundation of the Rettig palace had been excavated with spades and shovels rather than bulldozers. The old layers and structures were left in place, protected under the grounds of the large walled-in garden that was laid at the site (Uotila and Sartes 2000, 375).

In order to enter the Aboa Vetus museum the visitor passes through the main entrance of the building where segments of the archaeological remains have been left *in situ* next to a bookshop, a café and a corridor leading to the Ars Nova galleries. Other segments of the excavated site are also situated outdoors by a small garden as well as indoors underneath the floor, the latter being visible through transparent material. The Aboa Vetus museum itself is on underground level and accessed through a staircase. The visitors can walk through the remains of various medieval stone and/or brick structures. The museum space includes showcases for the display of movable finds such as tools, jewellery, pottery, glass etc. The interpretation and presentation is enhanced by various media such as informative panels, illustrations, maps, interactive exhibits for both children and adults, multimedia presentations (Alexopoulos 2000).

Throughout the excavation of the medieval remains constant consultation and discussions were taking place between the various parties involved in the project. Although M. Koivurinta, the owner of the Rettig Palace and the Ars Nova museum, was interested in the creation of an archaeological museum with *in situ* remains, he was finally engaged in debates with the archaeologists working on the site regarding the interpretation of the site (pers.comm. 12 December 2006). The actual use and nature of some of the architectural remains was uncertain and under investigation and therefore archaeologists were reluctant to include these 'uncertain' theories in the interpretation of the site and present them as facts to the wider public. On the other hand, there were pressures, mainly by the owner of the museum, to present 'stories' that could be appealing to the visitors and would enhance the understanding of the medieval ruins (pers.comm. 12 December 2006). One of the sections of the *in situ* museum with 'contested' interpretation is a room associated with the so-called church of Saint Henry (Henrik). The presentation of the space implies its use as a place of worship enhanced by church music, the use of candles (which visitors can

light), an icon of the Virgin Mary as well as a relevant short informative audio recording.

Generally the owner of the Aboa Vetus and Ars Nova museums has been described as strong minded and a difficult person to negotiate with (pers. comm. 2004). Nevertheless, archaeologists were allowed to express their views and influence the process of selecting the excavated remains that would finally be preserved *in situ*. Furthermore, the willingness of M. Koivurinta to pay for the excavations and the interpretation of the site as well as to employ a permanent curator for the museum have been acknowledged by my informant (pers.comm, 12 December 2006). In conclusion, the example of the Aboa Vetus has revealed how private ownership and funding are factors that can potentially exercise pressures in favour or specific intepretations not necessarily accepted by the scientific community, in this case the archaeologists. The extent to which any party influences what is chosen to be appropriate or appealing to the wider public can challenge the ethics of heritage interpretation. Therefore interpretation can also constitute a source of disputes and tensions.

Billingsgate Roman Bath House

The last example of this section examines the difficulties that arise when *in situ* presentation and accessibility of archaeological remains dispute with the desires of private benefactors.

The archaeological remains of the Billingsgate Roman Bath House were discovered in 1848 during the construction of a Coal Exchange at Billingsgate in Lower Thames Street (Marsden 1968, 3). One of the rooms, of the originally extensive bathouse, the *tepidarium*, was preserved by the Corporation of London through the city architect Mr. J.B. Bunning (Marsden 1968, 3).

In 1859, the erection of a block of warehouses next to the Coal Exchange led to the discovery of the *caldarium* and *frigidarium*. These were preserved beneath the Victorian basement floors but were not visible to the public (Marsden 1968, 3). This site was among the first to be legally protected by scheduling under the 1882 Ancient Monuments Act (Baillie 2002). The demolition of the Coal Exchange and the widening of Lower Thames Street in 1967-8 led to new excavations undertaken by Peter Marsden, with volunteers from the recently formed City of London Archaeological Society (COLAS). Further excavations took place in 1969-70 and 1974, culminating in the consolidation and capping of the surviving walls with cement mortar by the Ministry of Public Buildings and Works, and their preservation in the basement beneath the new building that was constructed on the site.

By 1987 it became clear that the 1970s consolidation was causing damage to the surviving Roman walls and floors, because of the chemical nature of the concrete capping and the cement and the interference of the latter with ground water evaporation (pers.comm. 22 January 2007). The Corporation of London paid for desalination of the remains (Baillie 2002) and according to Rowsome (1996, 415) has integrated archaeological recording and conservation work as an important part of its strategy. As a result the Museum of London's Department of Urban Archaeology (currently the Museum of London Archaeological Service) was asked to carry out a detailed archaeological assessment of the site as part of the conservation project. The Corporation of London also considered the feasibility of displaying the archaeological remains (Baillie 2002, 416).

Among the problems that the Corporation of London had to weigh up, apart from the cost of the display, was also the fact that the 1970s office block above the Roman building faced an uncertain future (Rowsome 1996, 422). Although the Billingsgate Bath House is strategically placed between the Monument and the Tower of London and had been re-consolidated because of its scheduled status, it remained closed to the public, until recently, when the Corporation office was redeveloped again.

A model of the bathhouse was brought from the museum to aid interpretation, while boxes of Roman building material from the excavations of 1987 were installed to give an atmosphere suit of 'work in progress'. Tours are organised occasionally by the Museum of London and the site can be currently visited on arranged times and days but only in small groups. Nevertheless, the MoL is willing to broaden access and is currently in negotiation with the Corporation about this issue (pers.comm. 22 January 2007).

An interesting question that this case study raises is what are the aspirations of the Museum of London for insisting to make the site broadly accessible and whether economic profit/gain underlies this aim. One could assume as well that broader accessibility can be deemed to have potential for educational purposes. Apparently, in the cases of both the Rose Theatre and the Billingsgate Bath House *in situ* conservation per se does not fulfil the aspirations of the involved parties. What is considered as important is *in situ* presentation. For the Rose Trust *in situ* presentation is estimated to be an effective means to gain funding for preservation of the site whereas in the case of the Billingsgate Bathhouse the MoL aims to enhance education and interpretation. In both examples, the significance of *in situ* presentation is highlighted, a fact that reveals the special importance of the *in situ* museum.

5.7. Discussion

The public reaction to the destruction of an archaeological site caused by the construction of a new building can mainly be interpreted as a conscious or unconscious reaction against the homogenisation of the urban landscape which results from the intensive construction of modern buildings. It can also be viewed as a reaction against the threat to the nostalgia for the past imposed by the financially powerful corporations that seem to dominate the present world.

Both the cases of Wood Quay and the Rose Theatre have revealed that disputes occurring during the accidental discovery of nationally significant archaeological remains are mainly provoked by archaeologists who are interested in the scientific information they can get from the remains or by local societies and local communities who oppose the developers companies often with tension and aggression.

In the examples of the Rose Theatre and the Wood Quay, the aggressive public reaction to the destruction of the archaeological remains was often depicted in cartoons published in the media as a reaction against a certain development corporation that threatens any other value in favour of maximising its own profits. Unconsciously, urban development is associated in people's mind with capitalism and consumption, it is represented by the developers and it threatens the feeling of nostalgia that the 'past' conveys (Lowenthal 1985, 39; 49-52).

If public reactions against the destruction of a nostalgic and highly symbolic past are mainly reactions against technocratic development and resistance against the homogenisation of the present, then the question is: to what extent does the integration of a nostalgic and symbolic past into a modern building –a result of a technocratic present- have the potential of bridging the gap between past and present and unifying and reforming the deformed identities caused by the notion of placelessness/feeling of not belonging to a specific place. In other words, the question is whether an *in situ* museum which allows the *in situ* conservation and *in situ* presentation of archaeological remains into a modern structure, has the power to resolve disputes by restoring the feeling of belonging to a specific place and by preserving a local and national identity.

The homogenisation of the urban landscape that has been emerged from the massive construction of modern buildings in the last decades has resulted in a loss of a sense of place and consequently in the deformation of identity and the creation of a feeling of placelessness in towns (Simms 1984, 154). The creation of *in situ* museums can contribute to bridging these different identities. The integration of archaeological remains, as a symbol of a nostalgic past, reshapes and reaffirms the sense of place, creating new identities, such as in the case of Wood Quay where the discovery of the Viking settlement led to the reinforcement of an identity relating to the Viking past. At the same time, in the case of the Rose Theatre, the site was strongly associated with a national identity shaped by the international reputation of William Shakespeare.

Reactions against a homogenised present become more intensive when the past that is threatened has acquired a national or international significance and, therefore, has acquired a symbolic value that is being sacrificed for economic gain. Both the newspaper cartoons in the case of Wood Quay and the panels that people were holding during the Viking March with slogans such as 'We own Dublin' and 'The past is present, the future is tense' reveal the feeling of common ownership of their national heritage and the contradictory interrelationship between the past, that forms present identities, and the future that is marked by tension, caused by rapid development. These controversies are mainly cultivated by the press. Under its influence, the public organised meetings, massive protests, and even judicial appeals in order to achieve the protection of a valued site.

The case studies in this chapter also raised the issue of ethics regarding the excavation, conservation and presentation of the remains. In the case of the Rose Theatre there was internal tension between English Heritage and the Museum of London revolving around discourses over the ethics of excavation and preservation of remains. The case study also revealed the necessity for ethics in presenting the excavated and preserved as well. This tension reveals the different academic views existing within the same scientific field, which reflect different ideals. The issue of ethics refers also to the presentation or the extent to which economic profit should determine the manner of presentation such as in the case of Jorvik Viking or the case of Aboa Vetus. In these cases an imaginative display raises a series of ethical issues regarding the authenticity of the site. The issue of ethics regarding interpretation and *in situ* preservation can be quite controversial. The question that arises is whether it is ethically right to enhance the visitor experience through the use of sounds and smells that can be questioned in terms of their authenticity. Furthermore, an interesting aspect to explore is how visitors ultimately perceive the experience they are offered and, in terms of education and interpretation, whether such presentation enhances their memory and experience. In relation to this issue a research was conducted in 1999 by John Aggleton and Louise Waskett of the University of Wales, in Cardiff, which involved 45 people who were asked to remember features of the Jorvik Viking Centre in York. The researchers concluded that those participants who were exposed again to the museum's smells could recall their visits more accurately than those who relied on memory alone (Aggleton and Waskett 1999, 1-7).

The results of Aggleton's and Waskett's survey could have important implications in terms of learning at museums. Since memory is enriched through smells, then learning in a museum context that uses smells and sounds, can facilitate long-term learning. The question that arises is whether *in situ* museums, where there is the extra notion of *in situ*, and consequently,

authenticity, add to this invaluable experience. In view of this, the question that needs to be achieved is whether reconstruction of objects, remains, sounds and smells, even when deemed inauthentic, is ethical. If innovative reconstructions offer visitors a memorable leisure experience while generating funding for the *in situ* preservation of the remains, then the ethical issue regarding inauthentic interpretation needs to be discussed in different terms. These issues, common in almost any type of museum, acquire a further dimension in the case of *in situ* museums. The notion of *in situ* enhances the perception of authenticity and the 'sense of place' as shown above, rendering decision-making about letting sponsors intervene in the interpretation a sensitive issue, as was shown in the case of the Aboa Vetus Museum, in Finland, where private ownership and funding restricted the role of archaeologists in terms of interpretation and presentation.

CHAPTER SIX: DISPUTE MANAGEMENT AT IN SITU MUSEUMS: EXAMPLES OF ARCHAEOLOGICAL SITES DISCOVERED DURING PUBLIC WORKS

6.1. Introduction

This chapter explores the nature of dispute in cases where archaeological remains were discovered during rehabilitation public projects. The goal is to examine similarities and differences in the sources of disputes related to archaeological discoveries in private and public projects. Thus the sources of dispute in public projects can be confronted with those illuminated in private projects (chapter 5) to identify similarities and differences related to some archaeological discoveries.

The case studies in this chapter are the Administrative Square (*Πλατεία Διοικητηρίου*) at Thessaloniki (Greece), the Mitropolis Museum at Naxos (Greece) and the 'Archéoforum' at Liège (Belgium). The rehabilitation projects involved the construction of a square in all three case studies as well as the creation of a car park in the case of the Administrative Square. These examples were selected from the 118 sites included in the database on the basis of the 'opportunity to learn and accessibility to information' principle. Bibliographic sources, newspaper articles and websites constituted the main sources of information for the compilation of the data. In addition, personal communications with people who had worked in some of the above sites enhanced the quality and breadth of information.

Chapter 6 highlights the significance of a public open-space for the local community and shows how the solution of the creation of an *in situ* museum can either function as a compromise for the disputing parties or raise further issues in dispute. Consequently the significance that an open-space has for the public can, to some extent, shape the perceptions of the latter towards the archaeological remains that are discovered during an open-space project. More specifically, this chapter reveals that when modernisation leads to social benefits for a community, then cultural benefits derived from the *in situ* conservation of an archaeological site are undervalued by local groups of people and political authorities. In contrast, chapter 5 revealed that reactions against the destruction or reburial of archaeological remains discovered during the construction of a private building can partly be explained as reactions against a commodified and modernised present that threatens a nostalgic past (section 5.3).

The sources of dispute in this chapter are explored through the theory of the significance of an open public space in an urban city developed by Jan Gehl, a Danish architect, currently Professor at the School of Architecture in Copenhagen. Professor Gehl has adopted an interdisciplinary approach in the exploration of the multiple uses of a public open space

including sociology, psychology, architecture and planning (Gehl 2001; Gehl and Gemzøe 1996; 2003). The role of an *in situ* museum as a place that encompasses the values of an open-space is examined within the above theoretical framework.

Finally, this chapter is divided into four main sections. The first three sections analyse the case studies and the fourth section discusses the main reasons for which disputes occurred. The analysis of each case study is divided -as in the previous chapter- into three main parts including dispute genesis, dispute escalation/de-escalation and dispute resolution. At each stage the key elements of a dispute and their interrelationship are identified.

6.2. The case of the Administrative Square in Thessaloniki, Greece

Historical review

The Municipality of Thessaloniki decided in 1987 to construct an underground parking lot (of 1.200 parking places) beneath the so-called Administrative Square (Table 6). The aim of this project was to facilitate traffic circulation in the city. As a result, the Municipality requested planning permission from the Sixteenth Ephorate of Prehistoric and Classical Antiquities, which was rejected by archaeologists due to the archaeological significance of the area (Law 1577/1985, FEK 210 A'/ 18-12-1985; *Eleftherotypia*, 29/09/2004). In 1990, and after constant pressure by the Municipality, the first archaeological trials took place in the northern part of the square (Tasia 1993, 330). The valuable finds of the excavations, which included a bronze medal depicting goddess Athena in relief and parts of a chariot, reinforced the initial decision of the Ephorate to reject the Municipality's planning application. The local Municipality appealed against this decision to the Central Archaeological Council (CAC) which eventually gave permission for the construction of the parking lot on the condition that the excavations would be completed. The installation of piles around the square took place in 1991 and 1992. In the beginning of 1993, CAC approved the construction of the roof of the parking lot while the discovered remains were recorded and reburied. In April 1993, rescue excavations were restarted after pressure by the Ninth Ephorate of Byzantine Antiquities and the Sixteenth Ephorate (Tasia 1993, 330).

The remains that were discovered in the Administrative Square span over a long chronological period from the Hellenistic to post-Byzantine times (Figure 8). The walls of the buildings are very well preserved and stand to a height of 2.80 m. The site lies to the east of a Roman road, 6 metres wide, which formed one of the main arteries of the road network of the city (figs. 35, 36) (Hellenic Ministry of Culture, www.culture.gr).

Figure 8 - Closer view of the archaeological site at Administrative Square (Photograph: Kalliopi Fouseki, 29/07/2005).

A dense network of drainage and water supply channels of various types was discovered including the earliest drainage system of Roman times with a stone built vaulted covering. One of the most significant buildings in the plot is a Roman public building dating to the first century BC. The building (41 x 40 m.) has a colonnaded area on the east side and is identified with the seat of the Roman administrator of the Province of Macedonia. The wall paintings of the building have also been preserved, and, therefore, the latter constitutes one of the rare examples to provide information about the art of painting in Macedonia at the transition from the Hellenistic to the Roman period (www.culture.gr).

The discovery of the above remains in 1993 led to the announcement of two architectural competitions aimed at constructing a square that would integrate and protect the remains under a shelter. Both competitions were unsuccessful since they did not fulfil the main requirements which were the protection of the site at a low cost and the avoidance of any damage to the monuments (*Eleftherotypia*, 29/09/2004).

Simultaneously, the CAC recognised the importance of the archaeological remains and decided not to approve the plan for the construction of the car park (Tiverios 1997). Two years later, in December 1995, the archaeological site was designated as a protected archaeological area (Tiverios 1997).

In 1996, archaeologists started negotiations with the Municipality of Thessaloniki and the inhabitants regarding the claims of the latter that 'the remains are not convincing, they are not significant, they are not ancient' (*Statement in Greek: τα αρχαία δεν μας έχουν πείσει, δεν είναι σημαντικά, δεν είναι αρχαία*) (Tasia et al. 1996, 552). In addition, the president of the 'Committee of the Inhabitants and Professionals of the Administrative Square' stated that none of the archaeologists informed local people about the archaeological significance and uniqueness of the site. The inhabitants and the shopkeepers, whose shops closed as a result of the excavations as their businesses

were isolated from commercial traffic, believed that the remains were just simple walls like those existing all over the city (*Statement in Greek: απλά ντουβάρια, όπως αυτά που υπάρχουν παντού στη Θεσσαλονίκη*) (*Eleftherotypia*, 17/05/2004). Local inhabitants desired the interruption of any further works and the recreation of the square. This claim reveals partly their fear that the presence of the archaeological site would render the place a 'dead site' of no use (*Eleftherotypia*, 29/09/2004). At the same time, this claim is associated with nostalgic memories of childhood spent on the square. The inhabitants referred to the archaeological remains as unimportant walls, a 'hole that attracted mice and snakes instead of tourists' (*Statement in Greek: μια τρύπα που έγινε πόλος έλξης όχι τουριστών, αλλά ποντικιών και φιδιών*). These negative perceptions are expressed fanatically by another citizens' movement for the support of creating more available parking places (Thessaloniki Politon 2006). According to them, the square should provide a multi-storey parking lot in order to solve the traffic problem. They added: 'Why should we want the ancient stuff and all these archaeological finds, when they occupy valuable spaces for cars'. Within this climate of anger, the president of the above movement suggested that the Archaeological Museum of Thessaloniki and the Museum of Byzantine Culture should be replaced by car parks (Thessaloniki Politon 2006).

Despite this negative climate archaeologists of the Sixteenth Ephorate managed to agree upon the creation of an *in situ* museum located beneath the square in April 1996. Although the implementation of this solution resulted in the reduction of the available parking spaces from 1,200 to 100, the suggestion of an *in situ* museum was accepted by the local community and authority. Furthermore, the sixteenth Ephorate, having realised the necessity of informing local people about their archaeological heritage, provided the archaeological site with free informative leaflets.

Although initially the suggestion of creating an *in situ* museum seemed to function as a compromise solution, further debates were caused concerning the location of the museum. Should the museum be located above or beneath the car park? The Municipality desired the construction of the parking lot to be beneath the archaeological site, while the Hellenic Ministry of Culture wanted it to be built above the archaeological remains (*Eleftherotypia*, 15/10/2004). The Deputy-Mayor, Stamatis Karamanlis, claimed that, if the car park was to be located above the archaeological site, then the height of the whole complex would reach the second and third storeys of the surrounding blocks of flats. This raised the issue of integrating aesthetically a modern structure into a densely inhabited area dominated by high blocks of flats and the potential economic losses for the surrounding properties. The General Secretary of the Hellenic Ministry of Culture, Christos Zachopoulos, supported the proposal that the parking lot should be built over the remains, because locating it at a greater depth would have made accessibility of the vehicles impossible (*Eleftherotypia*, 15/10/2004).

The final decision of the Central Archaeological Council was that archaeological remains should be preserved beneath the parking lot and that a square should be created above the car park (*Ta Nea*, 20/04/2005). However, some members of the Council disagreed with this solution, since they were concerned that the available parking places would be very limited and the remains would not be accessible to the public (*Ta Nea*, 20/04/2005). This shows that the construction of an *in situ* museum can function as a general compromise among external parties, especially those who have been in dispute for many years, but, at the same time cause further tensions and disagreements within the decision-making committee, especially when the estimated financial cost is much higher than the cultural benefits. The *in situ* museum has not been built yet, while a new architectural competition was announced recently for the rehabilitation of the square, the creation of the car-park and the construction of the *in situ* museum.

Table 6 - Disputes at the Administrative Square indicating phases of dispute genesis, escalation, de-escalation and resolution.

Date	Event
1987	The Municipality asked for planning permission from the sixteenth Ephorate of Antiquities in order to construct an underground car park.
1987 Genesis	The permission was rejected by the Ephorate.
1987-1990 Genesis	The Municipality insisted on getting the permission.
1990 De-escalation	The first archaeological trials took place.
1990 Escalation	The discovery of important finds reinforced the initial decision of the Ephorate not to grant planning permission.
1990 Escalation	The Municipality appealed against this decision to CAC.
1991/1992 De-escalation	The construction of the car park started.
1993 De-escalation	CAC approved the continuation of the works under the condition that the remains were recorded.
04/1993 Escalation	Rescue excavations were restarted after pressure by the Ninth Ephorate of Byzantine Antiquities.
1993 De-escalation	The discovery of important archaeological remains led to the announcement of two architectural competitions with the aim to construct a square that would integrate and protect the remains under a shelter (the competitions were unsuccessful).
1994 Escalation	The CAC changed position. The car park should not be constructed.
1996 De-escalation	Archaeologists started negotiations with the Municipality in order to find a compromise solution.
1996 Escalation	The local community had already started protesting. They wanted the fulfilment of the rehabilitation square project.
04/1996 De-escalation	An *in situ* museum was suggested by the Local Ephorate of Antiquities. This was accepted.
1997-2007 Genesis	Internal disagreements were caused regarding the exact location of the car park and the *in situ* museum.

Analysis of disputes

The network of the parties that got involved in the case of the Administrative Square can be separated into five main phases. The first phase coincides with the initiation of the dispute in 1987 (dispute genesis) when the Local Municipality asked the sixteenth Ephorate for permission to construct a parking lot. The intermediary that linked these two parties was firstly the administrative and legislative framework that requested the Municipality to ask for planning permission and the site of Administrative Square itself. At the second stage, the network was reshaped after the discovery of important archaeological finds in the area, a fact that involved a third party in the network which is the Central Archaeological Council. Again the administrative framework that provides for the protection of antiquities in Greece was the main intermediary that linked the parties as well as the archaeological remains that were discovered in the square (dispute escalation). The third stage involved further archaeological discoveries which led to the announcement of two unsuccessful architectural competitions for constructing a protective shelter over the archaeological site. This meant that the Municipality had to abandon the plan to build a new car park which generated further tensions and disputes raised not only by the Municipality but also by the local communities. This situation led the archaeologists to act as negotiators and seek for a compromise solution (network phase 4) (dispute de-escalation). The compromise offer was the construction of an *in situ* museum beneath the car park and the square. The offer was generally accepted (dispute resolution) but internal disputes occurred within CAC and external tensions between the Hellenic Ministry of Culture and the Local Municipality regarding the location of the *in situ* museum (network phase 5) (internal dispute genesis and continuing external dispute).

Each section of the analysis identifies the types and levels of disputes (step 2.2. of the descriptive dispute management model), the involved parties and their power (step 2.3), and their perceptions, needs, interests, values, behaviours and goals (steps 2.4.1. and 2.4.2.). A comparative analysis of the changeability of dispute styles and approaches is included at the end of this chapter. This allows the identification of some common behavioural patterns, a summary of which will be included in chapter 8. Common interests that were not initially realised by the involved parties are named enriching the list of commonalities which can constitute a potential common ground for negotiation transactions (step 2.5.). Finally, an exploration on the alternatives that each party used in order to achieve his/her goals (step 3) is essential in order to understand the criteria on which the parties determined their actions and made their decisions.

Dispute Genesis

This section examines the key elements and parameters that led to the genesis of the dispute in the case of the Administrative Square in Thessaloniki. The main sources of dispute are the equality of powers of the involved parties, the perceived incompatibility of goals, needs and values, the different ownership status, the negative probability of performance, and the contradiction between socio/economic and cultural benefits.

In contrast to dispute management theorists who mention that when there is an imbalance of powers disputes are most likely to occur (Pruitt and Rubin 1986), it seems that balance of powers is also a major source of dispute. The Local Municipality's power is a political power reinforced by public voting and the Ephorate's power derives from the existing legislative framework which obliges any developer to ask for planning permission before construction (Law 3028/2002). The equality of power led the parties in dispute to the adoption of a competitive/contending style and therefore at this stage any potential common goals and needs could not be recognised by the parties.

The second key dispute genesis element was the incompatibility of goals and values. The political and economic goals of the Municipality (gain of political power, economic revitalisation of the area and improvement of the quality of life) disputed with the scientific goal of archaeologists which was the completion of the excavations. The incompatibility of goals led them to perceive that they also had incompatible needs. However, both parties intended on gaining public recognition, although this was unexpressed, this can be identified as a common need. This raises two main questions. Firstly, how can a heritage manager/negotiator persuade the involved parties of the existence of common needs? Secondly, in the case of an *in situ* project, how can an *in situ* museum accommodate the perceived incompatible goals on the basis of fulfilling the needs of recognition and development (chapter 8). Persuading and modifying the other party's perceptions requires communication skills and techniques which unfortunately the majority of heritage managers do not have since they are not trained accordingly. The

concluding chapter of this book presents some of these techniques.

The perceived incompatibility of goals and needs is related to the negative perceptions that each party has towards each other (Goldman and Rojot 2002; Pruitt and Rubin 1986). Consequently, one of the main challenges for a heritage manager is to alter the pre-existing negative climate between local political authorities and the archaeological services (negative probability of performance).

A further key dispute genesis element is the contradiction between state ownership of the plot and state ownership of the archaeological site. The power of each type of ownership is interrelated with the power of the parties. The insistence of both of the parties relied partly on the ownership rights they had on the area which legitimised their actions. Again, the question is how an *in situ* museum can bridge the different types of ownership and whether can provide simultaneous access to the parking lot and the archaeological site. Compromises are unavoidably needed as will be shown below.

A further driving force in dispute is a contradiction between socio-economic benefits derived from the car park and cultural benefits derived from the preservation of the site. However, as will be shown below, in this case the cultural benefits have not been recognised by the local community which places a greater emphasis on the socio-economic benefits. The *in situ* museum is challenged to fulfil and promote both the socio-economic and the cultural public benefits.

Dispute escalation and de-escalation

The discovery of historically important archaeological remains rekindled the initial dispute between the Local Ephorate of Antiquities and the Local Municipality. The discovery of the archaeological site validated the initial expectations of the Ephorate on the basis of which they rejected the grant of the planning permission. This led the Local Municipality to appeal this decision to CAC.

The appeal made by the Local Municipality to the CAC provided an opportunity to explore briefly the role of the Central Archaeological Council -and generally of any national heritage advisory council - as mediator in cases where two or more governmental or non-governmental bodies are in dispute. Examining the effectiveness of a heritage state organisation as a mediator will allow the extraction of implications and conclusions regarding the role of mediation in dispute resolution.

The Central Archaeological Council in Greece at the time comprised of an interdisciplinary advisory council belonging in the Hellenic Ministry of Culture (Hellenic Ministry of Culture, 2007). The interdisciplinary committee consisted of a legal advisor, four directors of museums and archaeological services, academic archaeologists, geologists and architects, archaeologists working for the Ephorates and an architect working for the Ministry of the Environment and Public Works. The nature of the committee reveals firstly, the willingness of the Greek state to bridge theory with practice through inviting academics and practitioners and secondly, that interdisciplinarity is still perceived narrowly since only architects, archaeologists, and one geologist are included ignoring the significance of other disciplines such as sociologists, pedagogues and psychologists. Since the majority of the issues with which the CAC deals relate to dispute situations, psychologists, sociologists, communication theorists and negotiators also need to be involved in the committee.

The aim of the CAC as mediator is highlighted on the official website according to which 'It is natural that trends reflecting different approaches regarding the protection of cultural heritage are expressed in terms of the extent of interventions, the absolute or relative protection in relation to other public, social rights (as the right of employment, ownership, transportation, energy, disability access and other public facilities) acknowledged by the constitutional law. Our answer to the dividing and absolute "either this or the other" is the **compromise statement "both this and the other through seeking solutions that are accepted by both parties"**. Our care for our cultural heritage is the common ground on which our approaches are based' [author's translation] (Hellenic Ministry of Culture, 2007).

As I have stressed elsewhere in this thesis, local participation, engagement and involvement is used in heritage management as a means of avoiding or resolving disputes. Similarly, the CAC allows the interested parties to participate in the meetings and together with the advice and guidance of lawyers, they can support their claims and arguments (Hellenic Ministry of Culture, 2007). However, the compromising style that the CAC claims it adopts becomes clouded when reading the next paragraphs of the website, according to which, among the interested parties that participate in the meetings there are some individuals and groups of people who are 'strong-minded (in a negative way), aggressive, rude, uneducated and fanatical' (Hellenic Ministry of Culture, 2007).

Although it is true that some individuals and groups of people can behave aggressively, what an archaeologist needs to do is to examine where such aggressive attitudes originate. I think that negative attitudes of the public constitute the result of long-term abuse of the authority given by law to archaeologists regarding the expropriation of private plots and properties in the name of the 'public good'. A conceptualization also of how archaeology is perceived as 'public good' is totally lacking. Therefore what is really needed is to

move archaeologists' and public mentalities towards an integrative approach to the protection and integration of the past into the present. Since this is a long-term process, archaeologists need to be able to confront the reality of having to deal with, as the CAC refers to them, 'aggressive' individuals. Archaeologists must realise that they need to approach the individuals in a conciliation way and to develop techniques and skills to transform their negative perceptions into positive ones (see chapter 8).

The decision of CAC to preserve the archaeological site which was designated as a protected area generated further tensions and disputes extended to the broader local community. The dispute escalated and the local community reacted negatively to the decision to protect the site for several reasons. The reactions of the local community revealed the importance that the public placed on an open-space and that emphasis on socio-cultural benefits was much greater than the benefits they could get from the preservation of the heritage. However, it is possible that they have not understood the benefits of the preservation of the site due to lack of educational activities. It seems also that the site has not become an integral part of the present that enriches the present and benefits the community.

Despite the general criticisms a compromise was found. The ineffectiveness of the state, bureaucratic mechanism in achieving a satisfying solution led the Archaeological Service to change the initial contending style to an integrative negotiation by suggesting the creation of an *in situ* museum. In view of this, the role of the state as mediator proved insufficient. Integrative negotiation was finally the only solution. This is the first time that a compromise offer was suggested on behalf of the involved parties. There are three main issues raised here. The first issue relates to the reasons why the sixteenth Ephorate changed the contending style to a more compromise one. The second issue relates to the reasons that motivated the Archaeological Service to suggest the solution of an *in situ* museum. A further issue relates to the effectiveness of this solution as a compromise solution.

One of the main driving forces that led to the transformation of the contending style to a compromising one was the general disappointment of the local community regarding the future of the car park and the square. In addition, the creation of *in situ* projects in Greece began to be valued in the 1990s by both the public and the authorities as innovative, evidence of modernisation and development that connects the past with the present. This constituted some of the main reasons for which the sixteenth Ephorate suggested the creation of the *in situ* museum as a compromise solution, in addition to the general tendency of Thessaloniki's authorities to imitate Athens in terms of modernisation and development. The offer was immediately accepted by the Local Municipality mainly due to the fact that the cost had already escalated during the years of debate. This reveals the importance of the 'loss aversion' heuristic according to which a party is willing to take a risk in order to minimise the cost rather than to maximise the gain.

However, this de-escalation phase coincided with the genesis of an internal dispute within the CAC which had previously functioned as mediator. The issue in dispute was the exact location of the *in situ* museum (beneath or above the car park). This dispute resulted partly due to the interdisciplinary and consequently dichotomous nature of the members of the committee.

Dispute resolution

The dispute has been resolved since both the Local Ephorate and the Local authority agreed upon the construction of an *in situ* museum. The *in situ* museum and the car park are still in progress.

6.3. The Archéoforum of Liège, Belgium

This case study has some common characteristics with the example of the Administrative Square. In both squares the long-term excavations and unfinished construction works led to the closure of shops. In both squares the development projects involved the construction of a parking lot for the facilitation of the traffic in the area and, consequently, the rehabilitation of the square. In both cases, the discovered archaeological remains constituted a barrier to the implementation of the development project. Finally, in both cases, after many years, the construction of an *in situ* museum was seen as a compromise. However, there was a significant difference. While in the case of the Administrative Square the public was not interested in the *in situ* conservation of the archaeological site, in the case of the 'Archéoforum', a local society named 'SOS Memoires' fought for the conservation of the archaeological remains.

Historical review

The archaeological site was first discovered partially in 1907-1909 when the local authority undertook the installation of a gas main at the Saint Lambert Square under the supervision of E. Polain (Renson 2004, 13) (Table 7). During the excavations, a Roman hypocaust was discovered that remained accessible to the public from 1910 until the beginning of 1980s (Renson 2004, 15) (see timeline in Table 7).

In 1912, during construction work for the installation of a water-pipe in the square, more archaeological remains were revealed, consisting of Roman remains and a medieval sarcophagus (Renson 2004, 14). In 1929-1930 the expansion of the basement of a shop located on the square led to further archaeological discoveries (Renson 2004, 14). These preliminary surveys had indicated the archaeological significance of the site. As a result, when the local authority decided in the 1960s to rehabilitate the square, archaeologists were expecting the discovery of important archaeological remains, the future of which had to be somehow assured.

The aim of this rehabilitation project was to release the square from the chaotic multiplication of transportation (cars, buses) by reorganising the traffic and transforming the square into a central communication node. Therefore, the rehabilitation project involved the construction of an underground bus station and a parking lot. The initiation and implementation of the project plan took place in the 1970s. The rescue excavations started in 1977 under the supervision of Hélène Danthine, Professor of Archaeology at the University of Liège. As was expected, during the construction of the subway and the car park the continuation of the Roman bath complex was further discovered. In the middle of controversies and delays the excavations at the Saint-Lambert square were continued in 1978 with the financial assistance of the French Community.

Disputing reactions were raised not only by archaeologists but also by a local society – named the 'SOS Memoires' the aim of which was and continues to be the protection of the cultural heritage of the city, and especially the square (Société Royale- le vieux Liège 2003). The name of the society is revealing of the notion of nostalgia and memory discussed in chapter 5 and which will further be examined in this chapter. Protests against the destruction of the remains, initiated after the discovery of the remains in 1977 by the local society 'SOS Memoires', constituted part of a more general dispute context since public involvement in the *St.-Lambert* urban project has often been characterised by disputes, with numerous appeals introduced by local interest groups against new planning permissions and the adoption of plans. The final compromise in 1982 was the removal of the remains from their original site in order to rescue them as a compromise between the archaeologists and the local political authorities.

This compromise was also partly imposed because of changes to the regional planning policy in 1981. In that year, and following the regionalisation of Belgium, urban planning was entrusted to regional authorities, namely the Wallonian region. In 1986, Place St.-Lambert was included into the newly protected historic centre of Liège and the Commission Royale des Monuments, Sites et Fouilles gained an advice competence.

In 1983, Claude Strebelle, an architect, proposed a new scheme that functioned as a reconciliation between urban development and preservation of remains. This resulted in new excavations conducted from 1984 until 1990. The excavations were funded by the Division of Heritage of the Wallon Region (Division du Patrimoine de la Region Wallone) in collaboration with diverse institutes (University of Liège, Archaeological Institute of Liège). The idea of creating an *in situ* museum emerged in 1991.

The excavations continued until 1995 and the *in situ* museum finally opened in 2003. This was also the consequence of intervention by the Minister of Heritage, Robert Collignon, who paid special attention to the efforts of Liège to preserve the traces of its past (Renson 2004, 103).

Table 7 - Timeline of disputes at Archéoforum indicating phases of genesis, escalation, de-escalation and resolution.

Date	Event
1960s	The local authority decided to rehabilitate the square.
1977 Genesis	Rescue excavations started. A Roman bath was found.
1977-1981 Escalation	Disputing reactions arose by local societies and archaeologists.
1981 De-escalation	The removal of the remains was decided.
1983 Resolution	*In situ* museum is suggested as a compromise.
1984-1990 Resolution	Excavations restarted.

Analysis of disputes

Dispute genesis

The initial dispute arose between the archaeologists and the local political authority as in the case of the Administrative Square. However, in this case the historic and symbolic significance of the square and its setting generated public reactions which led to the formation of local societies for the protection of cultural heritage. In this case, not only the goals but also the needs of the parties in dispute were incompatible, an element that led gradually to dispute escalation.

Dispute escalation

The dispute escalation phase extends from 1983 until 1990, when excavations started again in order to create an *in situ* museum. The dispute regarding the protection of the archaeological remains in St. Lambert escalated since general oppositions arose to any development works in this historic place. This implies that when the *in situ* conservation of an archaeological site becomes part of broader confrontations or raises further issues in dispute then disputes escalated. The escalation of the dispute was characterised by protests organised mainly by the local societies.

Dispute resolution

The dispute was finally resolved mainly because an architectural compromise scheme, suggested by the architect Claude Strebelle, proposed the integration of the remains into a museum located beneath the square. This scheme allowed the rehabilitation of the square and the preservation of the remains. A further element that contributed to the resolution of the dispute is related to the fact that the new mayor of the city openly supported the protection of the site. Having assured political support, and consequently economic support, the Archéoforum museum was built and perceived as one of the most innovative and popular museums in Belgium.

6.4. The case of the Mitropolis museum at Naxos, Greece

In contrast to the two previous case studies in which the creation of an *in situ* museum was viewed positively as a solution for resolving disputes that occurred after the accidental discovery of archaeological remains, the case of Naxos shows how the decision to create an *in situ* museum for protecting an archaeological site was viewed negatively by local people.

Historical review

Excavations at the site of the Mitropolis Square at Naxos started in 1982 when the Municipality of Naxos undertook an initiative to create a square in the 'Grotta' area, next to the main port, a project funded by the Hellenic Organisation of Tourism. The aim of this project was the rehabilitation and revitalisation of the area. The excavations were funded by the Archaeological Society of Athens and were supervised by Dr. Vassilios Lambrinoudakis, Professor of Archaeology at the University of Athens and Fotini Zapheiropoulou, director of the twenty first Local Ephorate of Antiquities. The excavations that lasted until 1984 revealed a flourishing town with a fortification wall and workshops dating back to the Mycenaean period (thirteenth – eleventh century BC) and extending to Roman times (first century AD) (PAE 1982, 260-262; 1983, 299-311; 1984, 330-339; 1985, 162-167; 1995, 223) (fig 41).

The fragile condition of the remains required the urgent construction of a temporary shelter which was funded by the Hellenic Organisation of Tourism. In cases where the piles of the shelter were about to damage ancient remains, the remains were recorded, numbered, removed and finally replaced after the installation of the piles of the shelter.

In 1989 the Hellenic Ministry of Culture, the Archaeological Receipts Fund and the Municipality of Naxos undertook the implementation of a project regarding the presentation of the archaeological remains by creating an *in situ* museum. This decision was reinforced mainly by the significance of the site which derives from the fact that it provides a rare example of a burial group, transformed into a shrine for the veneration of heroized ancestors. In addition, the construction of the Mycenaean wall with a stone base three metres wide and mud-brick super-structure constitutes a unique example of Mycenaean architecture on the island of Naxos. The historical significance of the archaeological finds, the fragile nature of the building materials and the importance of the square for local inhabitants necessitated the *in situ* preservation and presentation of the site under a protective shell in the form of an underground *in situ* museum. As Couvelas –Panagiotatou mentions the aim of this museum was two fold. Firstly, it aimed at protecting the archaeological site and, secondly, at enhancing the importance of the square for the citizens (Couvelas - Panagiotatou 2002, 193).

The idea of an *in situ* museum was originally conceived by Manolis Korres, Professor of Architecture at the Polytechnical University of Athens, and Agni Couvelas, architect. The presentation and interpretation of the site was coordinated and directed by Dr. Vasilios Lambrinoudakis, Emeritus Professor of Archaeology at the University of Athens, Olga Philaniotou, archaeologist of the Ephorate of Prehistoric and Classical Antiquities of Cyclades, and Vassiliki Drounga, Professor of Archaeology at the University of Thessaloniki. The local authorities were also actively involved in the project.

The idea of preserving and presenting the archaeological remains *in situ* was not initially welcomed by the local community. Local people opposed the construction of an *in situ* museum as a result of their fear that they might lose the free space of the square. They also perceived that such a modern building did not fit in with the traditional architecture of the island (Naxiologa 2000, 20). However, after the completion of the project, they have come to value the innovative way of presenting and preserving the *in situ* archaeological remains in the present, since the museum has proved to be a popular attraction for visitors who admire this innovative project as this is clearly reflected in the local press and the museum's visitor book.

Analysis of disputes

Dispute genesis

In contrast to the previous case studies in which the creation of an *in situ* museum functioned as a compromise solution after years of delays, the case of Naxos reveals that the creation of an *in situ* museum may not function equally effectively when it is suggested at the beginning of a project. The *in situ* museum was opposed for two reasons. Firstly, the generally negative climate towards archaeologists and

archaeology when they dispute with tourism and economic interests cultivated latent disputes. Secondly, proper information on the nature of the project as a means for raising income and attracting tourists was not disseminated which led to dispute genesis.

Dispute escalation

The latent dispute derived from incompatible goals between the local community and the project initiators evolved into a surface and active dispute. Protests were generated in the area of Mitropolis and local newspapers criticised the project of *in situ* museum pers.comm. 12 December 2006). Therefore, the project initiators started negotiations and, after the implementation of the project, developed activities making them engaged into the archaeology.

Dispute resolution

The dispute was resolved after the local community realised that the *in situ* museum attracts many tourists. This led to the economic revitalisation of the area and many old houses have been transformed to hotels. The acknowledgement of the importance of the museum is also revealed in the visitor book held in the museum.

6.5. Discussion

The analysis of the case studies in this chapter show that in cases where archaeological remains are discovered during public works that aim to improve the quality of citizens' life, public opposition to the *in situ* conservation of the archaeological remains may occur. The main reason for disputes to occur is the perception of local citizens that the socio-economic benefits derived from the implementation of a public project are threatened by the preservation of an archaeological site that occupies a public open-space. Therefore the cultural benefits deriving from the *in situ* conservation of a site are undervalued compared to the socio-economic benefits.

The term 'quality of life' usually refers to the economic status of the citizens. When the term is used within the heritage context, then it usually refers to the economic revitalisation of a local area facilitated by cultural tourism (Council of Europe 1985; ICOMOS 2004, preamble). Associating quality of life with only the economic revitalisation is a narrow approach. Quality of life can also be associated with living within an aesthetic physical environment, living within a historic environment and living within an environment that encourages social interaction, as will be explained below.

The creation of an *in situ* museum as a compromise solution aims at achieving a balance between the socio-economic and cultural benefits. In other words, the role of an *in situ* museum is to ensure the quality of citizens' lives by contributing to the economic revitalisation of the area, ensuring an aesthetic physical environment and encouraging social interaction among the inhabitants. In view of this, it is interesting to examine how an *in situ* museum can balance the socio-economic and cultural benefits and costs and how a heritage manager can persuade the involved parties of the potential benefits that may possibly arise from an *in situ* museum.

It is therefore essential to explore how the cultural benefits of an archaeological site, discovered during a public project and integrated into a museum building, can provide a balance between the socio-economic costs that will derive from its *in situ* conservation and the cultural benefits that will be gained by its *in situ* conservation and presentations. This cost-benefit analysis presupposes an analysis of the significance of a public open-space, located usually in a densely inhabited urban city, for local citizens.

At Mitropolis museum of Naxos and at the Administrative Square the local community reacted negatively regarding the potential of conserving the archaeological remains that were discovered during the rehabilitation of an open-space. The characterisation of the archaeological site at the Administrative Square by the local community as a dead space and a hole that 'attracted mice and snakes instead of tourists' reveals partly the importance that tourism has for the revitalisation of a local area. Similarly, in Naxos, citizens were anxious about a possible economic loss resulting from the possibility of not constructing a square in order to preserve the remains. In the case of Naxos, a tourist island, most of the inhabitants rely on tourism for their annual income. As a result, their fear that the area would remain unexploited for many years caused negative reactions. After they realised that the *in situ* museum contributed to the general revitalisation of the area, encouraging many tourists to visit the site, only then did they appreciate the archaeological value of the site. Their economic interest in the area was greater than its archaeological and symbolic significance. On a tourist island, where heritage has been exploited and commodified in the interest of tourism, the discovery of an archaeological site might have been expected to have been viewed positively by the local people. The question becomes more intriguing since the 'Portara' -the stone gate of a temple of Apollo- is used as the landmark of Naxos and has created a sense of place and shaped a local identity associated with a rich cultural heritage on the island. It seems that open-spaces are of vital importance for local people, especially because squares increase the economic value of place due to their rehabilitation as places hosting activities. Occasionally the enrichment of the space with archaeological remains can be viewed positively.

For local citizens of Thessaloniki at Administrative Square, the archaeological site is a 'dead space' since there is no activity taking place. Gehl has highlighted the importance for people to live within a living city rather than a dead physical environment (1987, 79). Gehl has measured how rapidly the number of pedestrians increases when traffic is reduced and how the increased number of pedestrians enlivens a city (Gehl 1987, 79). In this vein the construction of the parking lot and the square was intended to reduce traffic in the area and enliven it through the presence of shops and other outdoor activities. In view of this, for an *in situ* museum to be accepted/valued it has to function as a place of revival for local people encouraging outdoor activities.

The outdoor activities associated with an open-space can be divided into *necessity, optional and social activities* (Gehl 1987, 13). Necessary activities include compulsory activities such as going to school or shopping (Gehl 1987, 12). Optional activities include activities that people choose to do such as walking or sunbathing. Finally, social activities are the activities that depend on the presence of others in public spaces (Gehl 1987, 14). The quality of the outdoor space will depend on the quality of the above activities which, in turn, is affected by the physical surrounding environment (Gehl 1987, 13). Accordingly, it is natural that the occupation of an open space by an archaeological site that does not encourage any outdoor activities raises negative reactions.

Gehl also emphasises the social role of an open-space between modern buildings in urban centres claiming that an open public space facilitates contact with other people (Gehl 1987, 19) and offers stimulating experiences because 'experiencing people who speak and move offers a wealth of sensual orientation' (Gehl 1987, 23). This implies that *in situ* museums as well as any heritage place, should also function as places that encourage social activities and social interaction by hosting a variety of activities and events that can enrich socialisation. As Emeritus Professor Lambrinoudakis has mentioned from his experience that the Naxos archaeological remains are no longer perceived only as a romantic sense of an ideological, nostalgic past. Archaeological remains nowadays require social interaction with the visitor (Lambrinoudakis 2000, 367).

Although the cases of Naxos and Thessaloniki illustrate the negative attitudes of local people to the preservation of an archaeological site, the case of the Archéoforum at Liège demonstrates the possibility that local societies with a strong sense of historic identity may oppose the implementation of a public project that threatens an archaeological site. The St. Lambert Square in Liège had been attributed in peoples' minds with a highly significant historic and symbolic value. As a result local societies for the protection of heritage opposed the authorities, an opposition that began many years previously before the discovery of the site. In this case quality of life is associated with a symbolic, aesthetic place marked by historic buildings. But this does not apply in densely inhabited areas marked by high blocks of flats. In the first case the scattered archaeological remains reinforce the symbolic, historic identity and therefore improve the quality of life while in the second case the scattered remains reinforce the ugliness of the urban landscape.

As mentioned above, quality of life is also associated with living within an aesthetic physical environment where aesthetics is either associated with the presence of historic or traditional buildings, or with the presence of archaeological monuments that constitute local or national emblems. The importance of an open-public space to contribute to the establishment of an attractive community design and a visually pleasant landscape has also been stressed by town planners and architects (Little 1969, 9). The occupation of an open-space by a dead archaeological site is perceived as contributing to the undermining of the aesthetics of the surroundings in contrast to a nationally or locally valued monument that actually reinforces the aesthetics of the area. The integration of a dead archaeological site into a living modern structure may function as a compromise between different perceptions of aesthetics or may equally raise further debates related to the aesthetics. The issue of aesthetics, as the Naxos case shows, reveals that integrating a modern building into a historic landscape may raise debates which focus primarily on the exterior and interior structure of the museum building. This type of discourse occurs mainly between archaeologists and architects. These issues are also revealed in the visitor book of the museum where some architects registered their disapproval of the architectural solution, the use of bricks in the interior and the simple design of the exterior façade that they felt was hardly recognisable as a museum. Mrs Couvelas, the architect of the museum, defended the building stating that brick was used since it had been the main material found during the excavations. Furthermore, it can easily be distinguished in an aesthetic and 'authentic' way from the remains. Finally, she stated that it creates a dark environment that allows dramatic presentation of the *in situ* finds with proper lighting (Couvelas 1999, 133-38; 2000a, 124-132; 2000b, 64-66). The extent to which scattered archaeological remains are aesthetic is an issue in question. In Thessaloniki the archaeological site of Administrative Square was perceived as an 'ugly' hole while in Liège as an aesthetic one. This depends on the context and the meanings that people attribute to the surroundings.

The issue of integrating aesthetically a museum building into its historic and/or urban environment is a common issue in dispute mainly among architects and town-planners. For instance, in the case of the Montreal Museum of Archaeology and History in Canada where the remains of stone fortifications were discovered during excavation work in the 1980s, a group of architects and urban planners objected to the creation of a high museum building that they felt would spoil the aesthetics of the surrounding urban space

(Brossard 1994, 58). In the case also of the Interpretation Centre of the 'Muralla Punica', Cartagena, Spain – a centre that preserves *in situ* remains of Roman walls and the Post-medieval Pantheon in the basement of the museum building (Miguel Martin Camino, in APPEAR) – there was a dispute between architects and archaeologists. Architects did not agree with the plans for the covering structure which caused delays that negatively affected the conservation of the remains.

The above issues reveal that an *in situ* museum, as any museum building, is perceived as both a physical structure that needs to be aesthetically integrated and as a social structure that needs to reinforce social relations.

Apart from social and physical needs that an open-space and a museum occupying an open-space fulfils, there are psychological needs such as the need for contact, the need for knowledge and the need for stimulation (Gehl 1987, 117). In view of this, a heritage site has to provide an environment that encourages social activity, enhances education and knowledge and offers a stimulating experience. If the museum structure does not fulfil these roles there is the potential for disputes. Furthermore, an *in situ* museum located in an open-space has to engender a 'feeling of security and a stronger sense of belonging to the areas outside the private residence' (Gehl 1987, 61). This can be achieved both inside and outside. Inside, the physical environment of the *in situ* museum should familiarise the visitor with the exhibits. Outside it is essential to create communal spaces at various levels so that movement from small groups and spaces towards larger ones and from more private to the gradually more public spaces can give the feeling of security and sense of belonging (Gehl 1987, 61).

Innovative architecture can lead to structures that project an interior *in situ* conserved site outside to an open-space through mainly the use of transparent material. Using transparent material is an effective way of finding a compromise between *in situ* conservation of underground remains and the rehabilitation of a square. This was revealed in a case study in Atri, Italy where a joint research project was developed by the Archaeological Superintendency for the Abruzzo Region and the Institute for Ancient Topography of Rome University. Among several remains, in the square of the thirteenth century cathedral, very well preserved architectural remains dating to the Roman period were discovered (Scichilone 1986, 310). After study and documentation a decision had to be made regarding the possibility of leaving the excavated structures permanently visible *in situ* rather than backfilling the area and re-establishing the modern pavement in the square. After a complex debate with the local authorities and with the community, the Archaeological Superintendency developed a project for the conservation and the presentation *in situ* of the remains (Scichilone 1986, 310). The conservation project was developed from September 1982 to October 1984, when construction started on the site; all works were due for completion by August 1984. Ultimately the basic idea was not only to preserve the remains *in situ* but also to present them taking into account at the same time the social uses of the square as in the case of Naxos, Thessaloniki and Liège. The project was based on the idea of building four oversized showcases on and around the excavated remains to be permanently displayed, offering a strictly controlled environment (Scichilone 1986, 310).

In general, negative public reactions are reinforced by the fact that the majority of archaeological sites in Greek cities are un-enhanced, occupying open-spaces that could have a function for the future for several years as a result of bureaucratic processes regarding expropriations, or delays in excavations that are prerequisites before the implementation of a public project. As a result, even in cases where the heritage organisations are willing to offer a compromise solution fulfilling the objectives of the parties, there are negative perceptions that occasionally lead to extreme situations. In Crete, for example, the decision by the local Ephorates of Antiquities to integrate some *in situ* conserved mosaics into the new hospital building – resulting in the reduction of the size of the hospital- led the local inhabitants to violent response and attacks against the remains with axes (AD 1987, 558-563). Any public building related to health (such as a hospital), economic revitalisation and tourism (such as a shop centre), quality of life (such as a square or a car park) is perceived as more important than the preservation of an archaeological site. Even projects related to education -an aspect with which the preservation of cultural heritage is strongly associated - may cause debates regarding the dilemma of preserving or not a site. In Spain, for example, the Catalan Central Government and the Municipality of Barcelona proposed in 1996 the construction of the Provincial Library of Barcelona, also known as the Central Library of the City, in the area of the ancient Market of Born (Laporte 2003, 323). Immediately after the initiation of the construction work archaeological remains dating to 1714 were revealed. The remains were very well preserved and provided information regarding life in Barcelona during the eighteenth century. The discovery of the archaeological remains initially caused a debate in the city between those who considered that the project of the library should continue and those who thought that the discovered remains were so important that another plot for the library needed to be found (Laporte 2003, 323). Finally, the architects Enric Sòria and Rafael de Càceres proposed an architectural solution that allowed the coexistence of the library with the archaeological remains (Laporte 2003, 213).

Regarding the effectiveness of *in situ* museums as compromise solutions, the three case studies formulating the major part of this chapter revealed three different attitudes and outcomes. In the case of

the Administrative Square the solution of creating an *in situ* museum beneath the car park and the square was generally accepted as a positive solution despite the economic losses that resulted from the reduction of the available parking places. This positive outcome relied on two main reasons. Firstly, the ten-year delay of the project had caused fears on behalf of the authorities and people that the car park would never be built. Secondly, the suggestion of an *in situ* museum took place within an era in Greece that has been characterised by innovative solutions of integrating archaeological remains into modern structures. The examples of the archaeological remains preserved *in situ* on the stations of the Metropolitan Railway of Athens have been used as an exceptional example and have been followed in various forms as a model in cases where archaeological remains are discovered during the construction of modern buildings. This confirms the theory regarding the diffusion of innovations, a theory that explores the ways in which innovation is communicated through certain channels over time among individuals, groups of people or organisations (chapter 4). The example of the museum on Naxos shows that although the suggestion for an *in situ* museum was an initial plan intended to improve the quality of life, negative public reactions occured. This again can be understood within the broader negative climate towards the local Ephorate of Antiquities, the negative probability of performance (see chapter 3). The implication for heritage managers is that the effectiveness of an *in situ* museum as a compromise solution will also depend on the general perceptions regarding the organisation that initiates an *in situ* project.

A final issue analysed in this chapter is the disagreement among internal parties (intra-organisational disputes). The case of the Administrative Square showed a further miscommunication that arose between the Hellenic Ministry of Culture and the local Municipality regarding the type of structure that would allow the coexistence of the square, the parking lot and the remains. This is common among administrative, governmental organisations as several cases have demonstrated.

So far, the analysis has shown that when the public perceives a public project as more significant than an archaeological site, then disputes occur. This raises a further question. Assessing the criteria of significance placed by the public requires in-depth qualitative research and comparative analyses with criteria of significance they attach to the present. However, some hypotheses can be made if the criteria of significance placed by archaeologists are identified and compared with those of the public.

A systematic research of the *Archaeological Newsletters* in Greece dating back to the 1882 allowed information concerning 267 archaeological sites or remains that have been conserved *in situ* and integrated into modern buildings. The information was organised on a database, which allowed the extraction of conclusions related to the main criteria on which archaeologists justified their decision to conserve *in situ* an archaeological site. These are the topographical significance of the remains (62 examples = 23%) and the state of preservation (54 examples = 20%) (Table 3). Other criteria include the uniqueness of the monuments, the extent to which the remains extent to the adjoining plots, their rarity or representativeness, their monumentality, extensiveness and architectural or historical significance and the extent to which they were consistent with written sources. The extent also to which their *in situ* conservation into the new building was practically feasible was also another criterion. The analysis of data collected from newsletters dating back to the 1880s shows that there is a general stability regarding the importance that archaeologists in Greece attach to the heritage site. Their criteria also do not take into consideration the social significance and impact that the preservation of a site will have on the present community or nation (Table 8; Figure 9).

Figure 9 - Most common types of archaeological remains that are preserved in situ in Greece.

The analysis so far has shown that the public requires the protection of remains of national value, a value associated with the history or symbolism of a place. In contrast to archaeologists who value the well-preserved state of remains (this is actually something that cannot be understood by the public) the monumentality or topographical significance and rarity of a site as important criteria for justifying *in situ* conservation, the public attaches more abstract values to the remains. Regarding the fragmentary state in which a site is usually discovered, its state of preservation, topography, monumentality and rarity/uniqueness cannot really be understood by the public, unless the remains are associated with a glorious, nationally and internationally significant past as was proved by the case studies.

Criteria of significance	Frequency (Number)
Topographical significance	62
Very well preserved	54
Uniqueness	31
Continuation to the adjoining plot	31
Rarity	22
Extensive scale of preservation	22
Monumentality	18
Architectural significance	9
Mosaics are always important!	5
Historical significance	5
Location	4
Representativeness	2
Identification of the site through ancient inscriptions or other sources	2

Table 8 - Criteria of significance according to archaeologists in Greece. The results are based on data collected from the Annual Archaeological Newsletters dating back to 1882.

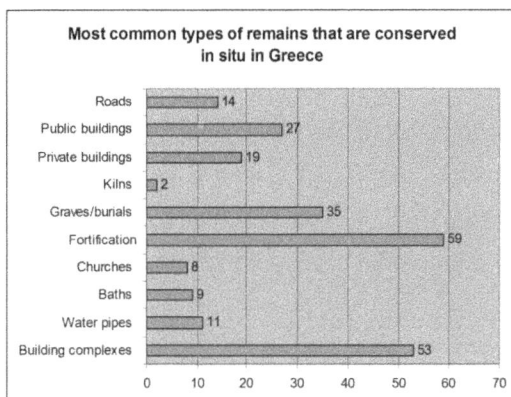

Most common types of remains that are conserved in situ in Greece

Roads	14
Public buildings	27
Private buildings	19
Kilns	2
Graves/burials	35
Fortification	59
Churches	8
Baths	9
Water pipes	11
Building complexes	53

CHAPTER SEVEN: DISPUTE MANAGEMENT AT *IN SITU* MUSEUMS: THE CASE OF THE NEW ACROPOLIS MUSEUM IN ATHENS, GREECE

7.1. Introduction

This chapter is devoted exclusively to the case of the New Acropolis Museum (NAM) since it allows a more holistic examination of the nature of dispute and its management due to the multi-level and multi-faceted disputes that occurred. The particularity of this example derives also from the fact that intensive disputes and debates emerged from the construction of a museum building rather than the creation of a private building. Although this sounds paradoxical, this case reveals that museums are in fact integral components of contemporary socio-political complex systems and therefore they reflect opposing opinions and beliefs expressed by individuals and groups of people. The opponents and supporters of the museum have used, and in many cases abused, the discovery of the archaeological site as a means to fulfil their socio-economic and political interests. Gaining an in-depth knowledge about the complexities inhered in this example has been facilitated through my personal experience as an employee of the NAM and the variety of existing written sources related to the disputes that revolved around this museum.

The core aim of this chapter is the examination of the strategies and tactics that the parties in dispute used in order to achieve their goals. The goal is to explore the effectiveness of the construction of an *in situ* museum as a compromise solution. The previous chapters have showed that the creation of an *in situ* museum functioned as a compromise in the Archéoforum and the Administrative Square. In the case of the Rose Theatre the *in situ* museum provided for the protection of the site but not for the presentation. In the case of Mitropolis Museum at Naxos the decision to construct an *in situ* museum raised oppositions since the museum was to occupy a large part of the open public space. In the case of the NAM, although the decision to create an *in situ* museum was suggested as a compromise for those parties that opposed the destruction of the archaeological site, its construction contributed to the dispute escalation.

7.2. Historical review

Disputes related to the construction of the NAM on the Makriyianni plot, a plot located on the southern slope of the Acropolis Hill, first occurred in the 1970s, when the Prime Minister of Greece gave permission for the construction of a new museum on it (a detailed timeline is included in Table 9).

The initial disputing discourses derived from a disagreement among architects regarding the aesthetic integration of the NAM into the historic landscape

marked by the presence of the Acropolis Hill. This is reminiscent of the Wood Quay case where again the initial debate focused on the integration of a modern building into the historic, urban centre. These discourses gradually became associated with the social impact of the construction of the NAM on the inhabitants of the Makriyianni, whose houses had to be demolished, and with the destruction of the discovered archaeological site in 1997 (Fouseki 2006).

1834-1989: The first attempts to build an Acropolis museum in the proximity of the Acropolis Hill

Since the birth of the Greek State in 1834, the *sacred rock* of the Acropolis and its monuments were transformed into a 'symbolic capital' of democracy and revivalism of Greece (Hamilakis and Yalouri 1996; 1999; Lowenthal 1985, 75-86). The transformation of the Athenian Acropolis into a 'world' as well as a national monument of Greece was mainly the result of the European philhellenism of the nineteenth century (Lowenthal 1988, 727; Lowenthal 1990, 307). The national significance that the Acropolis rock acquired led the Bavarian architect Leo von Klenze to suggest in 1834 the construction of a national archaeological museum on the Acropolis Hill (Philippopoulou-Michaelidou 1998). Due to financial constraints, it was only in 1865 that the construction of the current Museum of the Acropolis, located on top of the Acropolis Hill on the south-eastern corner and next to the Parthenon temple, began designed by the Greek architect Panages Kalkos. Though twice expanded, it has proved to be totally inadequate and inappropriate for housing all the artefacts collected during the excavations on the Acropolis hill due to its limited space both for displaying and for storage. These limitations were exacerbated by the location of the museum on top of the Acropolis Hill, a fact that made further expansion of the museum building impossible.

In 1974, in the aftermath of the fall of the military dictatorship in Greece, an extensive restoration program took place on the Acropolis monuments (Hellenic Ministry of Culture, 1989). As part of this restoration project the then Prime Minister of Greece, Konstantinos Karamanlis, proposed the construction of a new Acropolis museum on the Makriyianni plot which would display the Acropolis artefacts according to modern museological standards. The restoration of classical monuments gained a symbolic significance since it was immediately associated with the restoration of democracy in Greece after the seven year dictatorship and the materialisation of the revival of the glorious spirit and golden age of Greece associated with the 'Golden Age' of Pericles (Yalouri 2001, 89). The Hellenic Ministry of Culture held two national architectural competitions, in 1976 and 1979 respectively, where the Makriyianni plot was suggested as a site for the new museum. However, none of the competitions was successful since the judging committee believed that the architects had not provided sufficient information regarding the stability of the building and its aesthetic integration into the historic landscape.

1989-1997: The international architectural competitions for the construction of a New Acropolis Museum in the Makriyianni plot and the first reactions

On 16 May 1989, the Hellenic Ministry of Culture, then headed by Melina Merkouri, announced a third architectural competition for the construction of the NAM. After the failure of the two previous national architectural competitions she decided to proclaim an international one. This was also partly an attempt to publicise internationally the claim for the repatriation of the Parthenon Marbles and associate this claim with the construction of the NAM which would provide a safe place for the Marbles.

The competitors had to choose from three sites, the Makriyianni area, the site of the Dionysos Restaurant and the Koile site, to the west of the Philopappos hill. The Makriyianni area occupies a building block defined by the Dionysiou Areopagitou, Makriyianni, Chatzichristou and Mitsaion streets, a total surface of 24,150 sq.m. It was agreed that the Ministry of Culture would be permitted to purchase the non-listed buildings on the block in order to facilitate the construction of the NAM. The listed buildings that could not be demolished due to their historical value at this site were:

a) The Centre for the Acropolis Studies: this used to be the first military hospital (1834-1928) of the independent Greek nation and had been constructed by the Bavarian architect Wilhem von Weiler (Figure 10) (Bamiatzis 1996). It is commonly referred to as the Weiler building and is currently being used as the Centre for Acropolis Studies.

Figure 10 - Weiler Building, Makriyianni plot. (Photograph: Kalliopi Fouseki, 20/07/2002).

b) The small church of Saints 'Anargiroi' (Healer Saints) located on the north-west corner of the Centre for Acropolis Studies (Figure 11).

Figure 11 - Church of Saints Anargiroi, Makriyianni plot. (Photograph: Kalliopi Fouseki, 20/07/2002).

c) The *neoclassical* building located on the north-east corner of the block, now called the 'House of Makriyianni', named after General Makriyiannis, a hero of the Greek War of Independence, who lived in this house during the mid-nineteenth century (Figure 12).

Figure 12 - House of Makriyianni plot. (Photograph: Kalliopi Fouseki, 20/07/2002).

Each of the areas had several difficulties which would complicate the construction of the NAM. Firstly, the proximity of the Makriyianni plot to the Acropolis Hill and the Acropolis Station of the Metropolitan Railway restricted the surrounding space and did not allow the construction of parking facilities. This area also is densely inhabited which, as will be shown below, led to expropriations of the surrounding flats and raised several disputes. The proximity of the plot to the Acropolis Hill indicated, as will also be presented, the expected discovery of significant archaeological remains. Furthermore, the presence of the listed historic buildings restricted even more the available space for the museum building. Finally, since the plot initially belonged to the Ministry of Defence the transferral of ownership to the Hellenic Ministry of Culture would have necessitated a time-consuming, bureaucratic process. Despite these disadvantages, the Makriyianni plot provided a visual contact with the

Acropolis Hill. The supporters of this plan also believed that the construction of the museum would lead to the general revitalisation of the area (Hellenic Ministry of Culture 1990, 58-59).

The Koile site also provided visual contact with the Acropolis Hill and its monuments and also provided enough space for parking facilities. However, it was estimated that here too important archaeological remains were lying underneath which would have complicated the construction of the museum (Hellenic Ministry of Culture 1990, 58-59). The Dionysos restaurant site also had the advantage of providing visual contact with the Acropolis Hill. However, again there was the expectation of archaeological discoveries and there was a lack of parking facilities as a result of the pedestrianisation of the surrounding area according to the Unification of Archaeological Sites programme (Hellenic Ministry of Culture 1990, 58-59).

In view of the above difficulties, several academics and architects proposed alternative sites for the construction of the museum. However, none of these sites lacked disadvantages. For example, the Professor of Classical Archaeology, Nikos Stambolidis, suggested that the plot located next to the 'Theseion' Metropolitan Railway Station was an ideal place for the museum since there was no need for expropriations and no possibility for archaeological discoveries. This site also provides visual contact to the Acropolis Hill and since the surface of the plot is steep, the view of the surrounding blocks of flats is obscured (*To Vema*, 30/07/2000). However, there were some disadvantages including the increased cost that the removal of the railway lines necessitated and the lack of parking facilities. Another site suggested by a team of students at the Technical University of Athens, was the 'Kerameikos site' an area also located in the proximity of the 'Theseion' Metro Station. This site again provided a visual contact to the Acropolis Hill but it had a high potential of archaeological discoveries and was lacking parking facilities (*To Vema*, 02/04/1989). The Greek architect Christos Papoulias suggested an innovative and challenging idea to build a new Acropolis Museum into the Acropolis Rock (*To Vema*, 05/12/1999). This idea not only provided visual contact to the Acropolis Hill but also did not disrupt the aesthetics of the surrounding landscape and did not require any expropriations. However, there were static problems related both to the stability of the building and the stability of the surrounding monuments.

As a result, the Central Archaeological Council (CAC) decided to conduct the new architectural competition in two main stages according to the European Directive (92/50/EEC). The first stage involved choosing the location, studying the development of the selected area (proposals for traffic circulation and parking areas) and including the present Acropolis Museum and the Centre for Acropolis Studies in the functions of the NAM. This competition was completed in April 1990 with awards going to twenty-four studies of which ten

were selected to proceed to the second stage. The second stage involved the selection of the design of the NAM. The first prize was awarded to the Italian architects M. Nicoletti and L. Passarelli on 10 November 1990 whose design was located in the Makriyianni area (Hellenic Ministry of Culture 1990, 11).

The decision to build the NAM in the Makriyianni area provoked reactions by the Greek Association of Architects and the local inhabitants who denounced the museum construction to the Supreme Judicial Council. The Council decided to cancel the project in September 1993 (decision no: 2137, 24-09-1993) (*Ta Nea*, 25/11/93; *To Vema*, 03/11/1996; *Eleftherotypia*, 10/03/2002). The decision was based on the argument that the competitors' submissions were opened by the Greek Technical Committee rather than the International Evaluation Committee, as the guidelines of *UNESCO* (1956) regarding the conduct of international competitions require (*Ta Nea*, 25/11/93; *Eleftherotypia*, 10/03/2002). The main claim of the architects was that the high, modern building on this site would have spoiled the aesthetic and historic character of the Attican landscape. Local inhabitants whose blocks of flats had to be demolished reacted against the proposal for the NAM using similar arguments. Their main interest though was saving their flats from expropriation. Opposition to the construction of the museum in the Makriyianni plot was also voiced by international architects who again believed that the design of Nicolletti and Passarelli did not respect the Acropolis Hill (*Ta Nea* 24/07/1997). Bernard Tschumi, the winner of the second competition (analysed later in the chapter) was one of these international architects.

In view of these difficulties, the 'Melina Merkouri Foundation', a private organisation with the main objective of securing the funding and construction of the NAM was founded in 1995 (*Ta Nea*, 18/08/1999). At the same time the Greek Parliament established the Organisation for the Construction of the New Acropolis Museum (OANMA) as a private legal entity supervised by the Minister of Culture (Law 2260/1994; Papachristos 2004, 442).

1997-1999: Disputes that occurred after the discovery of archaeological remains

The archaeological excavations on the Makriyianni plot started in 1997 and revealed a significant Early Christian settlement dating to the seventh century AD as well as remains dating to even Prehistoric times (*Ta Nea*, 14/05/1998). Among the finds, dating from the prehistoric to the Ottoman period, the most important are four large ancient building complexes with well preserved walls and two roads of the Roman and Early Christian period. Two of the building complexes of the later Roman times were destroyed after the sixth century AD while some of their spaces were reused as workshops. In the middle Byzantine era large sections of the area were demolished and replaced by a larger ceramics workshop. A third building complex dating to the later Roman period and surrounded by a colonnade was converted into storage rooms for agricultural use during the Ottoman occupation. The fourth complex is a cold-water Roman public bath (*Ta Nea*, 18/08/1999).

1999-2002: The second international architectural competition

The archaeological significance of the discovered remains relies on the fact that they enrich the limited knowledge of the development of the city of Athens to the south side of the Acropolis after the raids of 267 AD and the destruction of the city by the Slavs in 582 AD (*Ta Nea*, 18/08/1999; OANMA 2006). The disputes that occurred in relation to the preservation of the discovered archaeological site led the Ministry of Culture to the decision to establish an archaeological committee to evaluate the significance of the new archaeological finds (Papachristos 2004, 446). The issue of *in situ* conservation or destruction of the archaeological remains was discussed in detail by the Central Archaeological Council (CAC) on 12 October 1999, which decided that the new archaeological finds should be preserved and integrated into the new museum since they constituted unique remains of the seventh century AD (Papachristos 2004, 446; *To Vema*, 25/07/1999; *Ta Nea*, 18/08/1999; 14/10/1999). It is important to stress at this point that the creation of an *in situ* museum was perceived by CAC as the ideal solution for ensuring the continuation of the project without opposing reactions. However, this hope never materialised. The reactions of the Association of Greek Architects became even stronger when the Hellenic Ministry of Culture decided to announce a second international architectural competition aimed at building a new museum on the same plot. The architects retained their initial position that the plot was inappropriate because of the archaeological remains and the continuation of the archaeological excavations (*Ta Nea*, 02/06/2000). Similarly, the Citizens' Movement kept repeating that the location of Makriyianni area was inappropriate due to the archaeological interest of the area (*To Vema*, 20/05/2000). They also interpreted the insistence of the Greek government to build the museum before the Olympic Games of 2004 as an abuse of the cultural heritage for commercial purposes (*To Vema*, 30/07/2000). The British and Greek newspapers (*The Guardian* 15-07-2002) as they did in 1999 after the discovery of the archaeological site, published detailed articles relating to the destruction of the remains on the Makriyianni plot (*Eleftherotypia*, 20/04/2002; *Ta Nea*, 17/07/2002). In April 2002 the Greek International Council on Monuments and Sites (*ICOMOS*), drew up a list of archaeological sites endangered by construction projects related to the Olympic Games which included the Makriyianni area (*Eleftherotypia*, 06/09/2002).

The above oppositions clearly revealed that the *in situ* museum was not perceived as an ideal solution for saving the archaeology but as a means that reinforced its destruction and damage. The main reason was the fact that the *in situ* preservation of the archaeological remains fulfilled the expectations and claims only of those groups that emphasised the archaeological significance of the site. Other groups with other interests such as economic, political or academic and scientific used the destruction of the site as a means to achieve deeper interests.

The creation of an *in situ* museum was promoted by Professor Dimitrios Pandermalis, the president of OANMA, as an effective way of linking the past with the present and of integrating the archaeological remains and the historic buildings of the Makriyianni area into the museum complex. He asserted that 'the visitor will pass through the remains of the daily human life of the Byzantine and Roman periods and eventually will be elevated to the godly world of the archaic and classical periods' (*Eleftherotypia*, 18/07/2002). He therefore emphasised the notion of innovation, curiosity and sense of place, some of the key characteristics of *in situ* museums that were analysed in chapter 4. However, the general negative climate did not allow the estimation of the innovative approaches to the museum building at that time.

Despite the oppositions, the second international architectural competition was completed in 2001 and the first prize was awarded to architects Bernard Tschumi and Michalis Fotiadis.

The criteria for the construction of the NAM as defined in the international competition had been as follows:

- Integration of the approximately 2,200 square meters of the archaeological remains of the third, fourth and seventh centuries AD into the museum building.
- Replication of the natural light and atmospheric conditions of the original location on the Acropolis for the exhibits within the museum.
- The achievement of a balance between the museum's architecture and that of the Acropolis Hill, the Weiler building and the façade of the neighbouring Acropolis Metro Station.
- Capacity for visitors to view the Parthenon frieze and the Acropolis simultaneously (OANMA, 2001).

2003–2005: Athens 2004 Olympic Games and national elections: their effect on continuation of the museum's construction

In July 2003, inhabitants of the area, representatives of ICOMOS and architects to this council made again appeals to the Supreme Judicial Council according to which the museum plans did not include any provision for the protection of the site (*Ta Nea*, 17/07/2003; *To Vema*, 08/06/2003). The Supreme Judicial Council ordered that construction of the museum be interrupted temporarily while requesting evidence from OANMA that the construction was not destroying the significant ancient remains. OANMA's evidence that the museum had been modified in such a way that it protected the archaeological site allowed the continuation of the project (*Ta Nea*, 28/07/2003). The inhabitants though did not use only legal procedures for preventing the implementation of the project. During this period, police officers requested the inhabitants to leave their flats. However, the local inhabitants replied aggressively and endeavoured to prevent the policemen from entering their flats. Their refusal was based on the fact that the amount of compensation had not yet been dealt with (*Ta Nea*, 17/07/2003). Two more inhabitants of the same block of flats were arrested for breach of the peace by the police because they were demonstrating against their demolition (*Eleftherotypia*, 25/07/2003).

In 2003, Mr. Petros Tatoulis (member of the Conservative Party [Nea Democratia] in opposition) accused members of the CAC and architects of the international committee who had approved the museum plan, of destroying a significant archaeological site (*Ta Nea*, 27/07/2004). His appeal to the Supreme Court of Appeal (Arios Pagos) became known when he was appointed as Vice-Minister of Culture after his party won the elections in March 2004. His appeal provoked reactions by both the Association of Archaeologists of the Hellenic Ministry of Culture and the Greek Communist Party (KKE) (*Eleftherotypia*, 17/03/2004; 11/05/2004).

In March 2004, the Supreme Judicial Council decided to halt the construction works for the museum (decision no: 130-2004) after appeals made by the inhabitants and the architects that the 'red zone of the archaeological site', the part that was suggested to be preserved, was actually under threat (*Ta Nea*, 11/03/2004). The President of the Supreme Judicial Council, Mr. Pikramenos, rejected the appeals since he claimed that the 'red zone' was adequately protected but expressed doubt as to the legality of the architectural competition since Mr. V. Chandakas, Director of Restoration, Museums and Technical Works, was simultaneously a member of the OANMA council and of the CAC, which was responsible for approving the museum building. Moreover, the CAC had approved the plan for the museum building to be taller than the neoclassical Weiler building, at that time an illegal measure. However, Law 2912/2001 permitted the museum building to be five metres taller than the Weiler building (*Ta Nea*, 15/03/2004; 17/03/2004; 20/03/2004).

Table 9 - Timeline of disputes at the New Acropolis Museum indicating phases of dispute genesis, escalation, de-escalation and resolution.

Date	Event
1976	1st national architectural competition for the
	construction of the NAM.
1979	2nd national architectural competition for the construction of the NAM.
16 May 1989	1st international architectural competition for the construction of the NAM.
04/1990	The outcome of the competition was the construction of the museum on the Makriyianni plot.
04/1990 Genesis	This decision provoked reactions by architects, archaeological and local inhabitants. They denounced the decision to the Supreme Judicial Council.
09/1993 Escalation	The Supreme Judicial Council requested the interruption of the project.
1995 De-escalation	The 'Melina Merkouri Foundation' and the Organisation for the Construction of the New Acropolis Museum are being established as an attempt to restart museum construction works.
1997 De-escalation	Excavations started on the Makriyianni plot.
1998 Escalation	An important early Byzantine settlement was discovered.
1998 Escalation	Oppositions were generated at national and international level including the British Museum.
1998 Escalation	Local inhabitants appealed again to the Supreme Judicial Council. Their claim was that archaeological remains were destroyed and that a high building in historic setting was about to be built.
1998 Escalation	The Supreme Judicial Council interrupted the excavation works for further investigations. (**1st interruption of excavations**)
1998 Escalation	The Supreme Court of Appeal however decided that no problems existed regarding the construction of the museum.
12/10/1999 Escalation	The CAC decided the creation of an *in situ* museum on the same plot.
1999 Escalation	This decision caused further reactions by architects, local societies and archaeologists.
2001 Escalation	Despite the reactions a second international competition was announced.
2002-2003	Local inhabitants, ICOMOS

Escalation	and the Supreme Judicial Council appealed against the museum since the museum was destroying the remains.
2002-2003 Escalation	The Supreme Judicial Council interrupted the excavations for further investigation. (**2nd interruption**)
2002-2003 Escalation	In the meantime, inhabitants resisted in evacuating their flats and were fighting with police officers.
03/2004 Escalation	The Supreme Judicial Council, after appeals, again order the interruption of excavations in order to examine the extent to which the remains were destroyed. However, it was proved that the site was appropriately protected.
03/2004 Escalation	A further appeal to the Supreme Court of Appeal was made by opposition political parties.
2007 Resolution	The museum will be built and some of the flats have already been demolished.

7.3. Analysis of disputes

Introduction

In the case of the NAM three main dispute phases can be distinguished: the phase of pre-existing disputes, the phase of disputes that occurred before the discovery of the archaeological remains and the phase related to disputes that occurred after the discovery of archaeological remains. The analysis of the disputes in this book will deal extensively with the second phase although the role of pre-existing disputes and issues in dispute in the escalation and climax of the dispute are also examined. However, since the book deals with *in situ* conservation of archaeological remains into modern structures, the second phase will be analysed more thoroughly. The above phases can be divided into four main sub-phases (four sub-networks). The initial network (1990-1995) consisted of the Hellenic Ministry of Culture, which later was replaced by the Organisation of the Construction of the New Acropolis Museum and the Greek Association of Architects. What linked the involved parties into this complex network was initially the symbolic significance of the historic landscape marked by the presence of the Acropolis Hill and the Parthenon (network 1). Many of the claims and objectives were based on the extent to which the modern building would disrupt the aesthetics and the symbolism of the classical monuments of the Acropolis Hill. The initial network was gradually enlarged with the participation of more parties after the discovery of the archaeological site which caused

further disputes and reactions. The first opposing parties were the British Museum, archaeologists (mainly academics), the Citizens' Movement and the local inhabitants whose houses had to be expropriated (network 2: 1997-1998). While the disputing reactions were becoming more intensive, third parties (CAC) endeavoured to achieve a compromise by the suggestion of the creation of an *in situ* museum (network 3: 1999-2000). This solution not only wasn't accepted by all parties but also generated further reactions including reactions by ICOMOS. Within this negative climate and close to the national elections of 2004 the opposing political parties started accusing the NAM of destroying the archaeological site (network 4: 2003-2005).

Dispute genesis and dispute escalation

In the previous chapters dispute genesis and dispute escalation have been examined as two separate sections since the transition phase between the two stages was clearer than in this case. In this case study the stage of dispute genesis evolved very rapidly to the stage of escalation due mainly to the pre-existence of issues in dispute in the past. Therefore, the two stages are co-examined in the same section.

In accordance to the analysis of the previous chapters, this section analyses the interrelated dispute key elements that cultivated and intensified the disputes in the case of NAM.

The interrelated dispute elements that played a significant role in dispute genesis and escalation are:

- ❑ Further issues in dispute ↔ Type of level
- ❑ Further issues in dispute ↔ Number of parties involved
- ❑ Power ↔ Parties
- ❑ Style (problem-solving) ↔ Probability of Performance
- ❑ Actions ↔ Behaviours
- ❑ Behaviours ↔ Powers
- ❑ Behaviours ↔ Commonalities

Further issues in dispute and type of level/number of parties:

The case study showed that, as in the case of Wood Quay (chapter 5) when international bodies and organisations are concerned about other issues in dispute (apart from the issue of preserving *in situ* an archaeological site) then unavoidably a dispute acquires international dimensions (see the intervention of UNESCO, British Museum and ICOMOS in the case of NAM) In addition, the more issues in dispute exist in a dispute situation the more parties are involved in the dispute and the more complex the dispute becomes.

Power and parties

The involved parties in the disputing discourses regarding the construction of the NAM can be divided into two main categories. The first group includes those who support the construction of the NAM. This is indicated by a variety of reasons such as the repatriation of the Parthenon Marbles, winning elections and raising political profile. The second consists of those who oppose the museum construction. In both groups heritage organisations and political parties are involved since the publicity that the issue acquired raised political concern as in the case of Wood Quay. The heritage organisations that supported the museum construction were two independent private organisations (Melina Merkouri Foundation and the Organisation for the Construction of the NAM) that had been created to facilitate and carry forward the construction of the museum, a scheme initially started by the Hellenic Ministry of Culture. The Central Archaeological Council is mainly a governmental body and therefore its decisions on archaeological issues of major importance, are strongly affected by the political party in power at the time. However, the British Museum at an international level and the Hellenic ICOMOS at a national level denounced the destruction of the archaeological site. Of course, the main driving force behind the British Museum's stance was the use of the destruction of the site to justify their refusal to repatriate the Parthenon Marbles. A group of architects and archaeologists who were not working for OANMA and the Makriyianni excavations also opposed the construction of the NAM, each group for completely different reasons. The local voice was represented mainly by the local inhabitants whose houses had to be expropriated and the Citizen's movement.

The most powerful parties were the political parties that affected public opinion strongly through the use of the media. Also UNESCO intervened importantly in order to preserve the most important of the archaeological remains, and the inhabitants who collaborated with ICOMOS and the association of architects using the media to prevent the construction of the NAM. The figure also shows that there are more powerful opposing parties than supporting ones, and this, was one of the reasons why the construction of the NAM was not completed on time. The constant assessment of the power of the involved parties is an essential step in the dispute management process. The assessment should take into consideration external and internal factors and requires a constant dialogue with the involved parties.

The complexity of the disputes over the NAM derived also from the fact that the objectives or claims of each party are multiple and intermixed. The protection of the archaeological site was often used as a means for the fulfilment of further goals. This is not a new phenomenon but it becomes complicated when the

variety of the parties and their goals is so heterogeneous.

Styles/behaviours and powers/actions/ probability of performance

The style that each party adopted in the disputes depended on his/her power and the probability of performance towards OANMA (probability of performance has been defined in chapter 3 as the extent to which a party believes that the negotiator will realise his/her compromising offer). The parties opposed to the creation of the museum maintained their contending dispute style until the end of the process while OANMA endeavoured to adopt a more negotiative, compromising style in the middle of the disputing discourse, which unfortunately did not succeed. Low probability of performance on behalf of the governmental bodies and lack of trust discouraged any negotiation.

Commonalities and styles

Despite the fact that there were common goals that could have possibly constituted a common ground for developing a compromise solution, the competitive and aggressive styles of the parties in dispute did not allow them to recognise these common needs and goals. These goals were mainly the construction of a new museum that could have forced the British government to lend the Parthenon Marbles for the Olympic Games and the protection of the discovered antiquities. A common goal between the local inhabitants and OANMA was the economic revitalisation of the Makriyianni area.

The commonality of the goals could have been reinforced by the obligatory passage points through which most of the involved parties, including the opponents and the supporters of the NAM, had to go. These are the legal procedures that resulted from the appeals of the opponents. Legal processes caused delays and increased the cost for the NAM. They were costly and time-consuming for the opponents as well. However, it proved to be an unavoidable obligatory passage point since it was perceived by the opponents as the only means to achieve their goals.

Actions/offers and styles

Litigation, arbitration and mediation were among the first means and tactics that the opposing parties to the construction of the NAM used in order to achieve their goals. As shown in the previous chapters, the above strategies constitute common choices for those parties that have high aspirations of their goals and needs. These parties usually adopt a competitive style and endeavour to use any possible means for achieving their goals ignoring any risk, time and cost. This becomes very clear after the decision of the Hellenic Ministry of Culture to construct a modern museum building in the vicinity of the Acropolis Hill. The Greek Association of Architects denounced this decision to the Supreme Judicial Council on the basis that the museum would spoil the aesthetics of the landscape and would constitute a sacrilege. The opposition of the architects was used by the local inhabitants whose houses were to be expropriated in order to oppose the decision to construct the museum. The opponents ignored the cost in both money and time cost since they valued their goals more highly. The Hellenic Ministry of Culture decided to establish a private organisation, OANMA, to deal with the effective resolution of the dispute and to accelerate the construction of the museum. This was deemed necessary due to the ineffectiveness of the bureaucracy of the state so that a central committee with legal experts who could handle the complex situation could be established. Therefore, the OANMA's role was also to function as a mediator and negotiator among the involved parties. It is characteristic that the first president of the OANMA was a lawyer with experience in international organisations. The discovery of the archaeological remains reinforced the initial reactions of the architects and brought into the network more opposite parties rendering the debate more complex.

The discovery of the archaeological remains and their partial destruction was used by many parties as a means to legitimise their initial opposition and to achieve their main interests. This is one of the main reasons for which the decision of the Ministry of Culture to construct an *in situ* museum failed. The problem was not limited to the preservation of the archaeological site. The reasons for the dispute were much more complex. The *in situ* museum could provide for the protection of the site but could not secure the aesthetic integration of a modern structure into the historic landscape and the avoidance of the expropriations of private property. The main actions taken by the opponents were generating negative publicity through media, raising the issue on a global level, judicial appeals.

Dispute resolution

The museum is under construction and the expropriations and demolitions of the flats are still in process. Debates and tensions, to a lesser extent, still exist. The most recent debate relates to the governmental decision to destroy a building dating back to the 1930s located next to the museum building. The aim of the demolition relates to the aesthetic enhancement of the surroundings of the museum. The executive committee of the World Archaeological Congress urged the former Minister of Culture, Mr. Voulgarakis, 'not to consent to removing the designation of 17 Dionysiou Areopagitou Street, Athens, as a building-monument. It is an important example of 1930s Art Deco architecture, and a testament to the recent material and cultural memory of

Greece' (Zimmerman, 2007). The building has been declared as a scheduled monument by the Ministry of Urban Development (YPECHODE) in 1978, and a "work of art" by the Hellenic Ministry of Culture in 1988. Zimmerman continues that, although the significance of the NAM is recognized internationally, 'one of the most important features of the landscape of the Athenian Acropolis is its character as a palimpsest of human activity from ancient times to the present. It is this multi-temporal material culture that is valued by archaeologists and the public the world over. The demolition of this building, a monument of high aesthetic, historical, and mnemonic value, will harm and degrade this sense of diachronic cultural development, and will devalue the Acropolis and its New Museum, as well as the Athenian Cultural Heritage as a whole' (YPECHODE; see also Fouseki 2007).

7.4. Discussion

This section analyses the arguments of both the opponents and the supporters of the construction of the museum, focusing on the use of the discovered archaeological site as a means to legitimise their positions and, consequently, to fulfil their main objectives and interests. In order to understand the opposition to or support for the construction of the NAM in relation to the archaeological remains, it is essential to understand the contradictory values that different parties placed on the broader context within which the archaeological remains were discovered. This context is determined by the archaeological remains that were found on the Makriyianni plot (Early Christian settlement), the Acropolis Hill and its monuments to which the museum provides visual contact and on the Parthenon Marbles with the repatriation of which the museum is associated. The occasion of the Athens 2004 Olympic Games also played an extra role regarding the construction of the museum.

Political uses of archaeological heritage in the case of the NAM: a game of political power

This chapter uses the term 'political use' in order to refer to the ways in which archaeological heritage is used in the reinforcement of the power of the political parties and to legitimise the British Museum's arguments for refusing to return the Parthenon marbles to Greece.

The NAM was promoted as a symbol of national pride and was used as a means to reinforce political power by the Socialist Party that supported its construction. The same attitude was adopted regarding the conservation of the archaeological site where the construction of an *in situ* museum was promoted as an innovative way of combining the past with present needs and was used as a means to reinforce political power and to gain votes from those opposing the destruction of the site. It is also interesting to see how political actions of the two main political parties, namely the Socialist and the Conservative party, changed or reformed these responses according to the circumstances and then to compare the sequence of these actions with similar case studies such as the Rose Theatre and the Wood Quay.

Although, the focus is the analysis of the political uses of the discovery of the archaeological site at the Makriyianni plot and the decision to construct an *in situ* museum, it is essential to examine this specific issue within the broader socio-political context within which the construction of the NAM took place. This context, as mentioned above, was marked by the association of the museum with the repatriation of the Parthenon marbles, the proximity of the building to the Acropolis Hill, and the organisation of the Athens 2004 Olympic Games.

In the case of the NAM, two main groups can be distinguished in terms of political uses or abuses. The first group consists of the two main, and opponent, political parties, which are the Socialist (PASOK) and the Conservative party (Nea Democratia). These parties used the partial destruction of the Early Christian remains as an argument to legitimise or de-legitimise the construction of the museum, respectively. The second group consists of representatives from the British Museum and the OANMA. The British Museum, opposing the repatriation of the Parthenon Marbles, accused OANMA of destroying significant archaeological remains. In view of this, the following tensions/disputes can be determined. Firstly, there is a national, micro-level dispute between the political parties, and secondly a macro-level, international debate. At a certain point, these levels become intermixed and the national opponents of the museum use the international condemnation of the project as an argument and vice versa.

At a micro-level, the NAM constituted a basic instrument for the Socialist party to reinforce its power within the national borders. This acquired even greater significance a few months before the national elections of 2004 and the subsequent holding of the Athens 2004 Olympic Games. After the national elections, and the dominance of the Conservative Party, the policy of the latter was reshaped and became supportive of the construction of the NAM stressing that the main priority of the government was the repatriation of the Parthenon Marbles (while initially the conservative party was opposing the construction of the NAM on the Makriyianni plot).

At a macro-level, the NAM constituted the response to doubts raised by the British Museum about Greece's ability to fulfil its role as a guardian of its heritage, a claim that was reinforced after the discovery of the archaeological site and its partial destruction. The debate about repatriating the Parthenon Marbles ended in an inter-organisational meeting which assessed

which of the two museums would be the most appropriate place, in terms of safety. This debate took on further dimensions after the revelation of the damage to the Parthenon sculptures in the British Museum during the 1930's (*The Guardian*, 29/11/1999) and the theft of an Archaic marble head from the British Museum in 2002 (*The Guardian*, 6/08/2002). Therefore, the partial destruction of the archaeological site at the Makriyianni plot was used by both the British Museum and the British media in order to reinforce their assertions concerning the inability of Greece to safeguard its heritage. An article published in the *Guardian* entitled 'Drills and axes ravage ancient Greek site' (15/07/2002) stated that 'In Greece's haste to build up a museum so magnificent that Britain will finally bow to its demand to return the Parthenon marbles in time for the 2004 Olympic Games, authorities have begun destroying a unique archaeological site at the foot of the Acropolis'. On the other hand, the NAM and the Greek state, by suggesting the construction of the *in situ* museum aimed not only to emphasise their ability to safeguard their heritage but also their capability of being a modern and developed state. This again reveals the constant attempts by the Greek nation to stress their 'honourable profile' (Mouliou 1996) and to counter any patronising attitude by foreign powers as expressed through the ownership of national heritage (Yalouri 2001, 83).

It is interesting to explore how the Greek State has attempted to resolve this debate. The current Greek policy is that of negotiation aiming to achieve a compromise. As a result, the Greek Government has suggested sharing the Parthenon sculptures with the British Museum (BM) by housing the Parthenon marbles in the NAM, while the title of ownership would remain with the BM. The former Minister of Foreign Affairs, Mr. Georgios Papandreou, stated that 'This is something we want, to move from controversy to building a partnership conceptualising this problem, a *win-win situ*ation for both Greece and Britain. I think we can both do something which is very important for world culture, around the time of Olympic Games, and this would be high visibility for Britain and high visibility for British culture' (*The Guardian*, 06/06/2000). He continued 'The Parthenon Hall with the restituted Parthenon Marbles in 2004 will demonstrate leadership and vision not just in the field of cultural heritage protection and management, but in the broader domain of international cultural relations and cultural diplomacy' (Papandreou, 2000).

His statement reveals that the Greek government had adopted the so-called integrative negotiation process – analysed in chapter 3- trying to define the commonalities between the British Museum/UK government and the NAM/Greek state, on the basis of which an agreement might have been achieved. It becomes obvious from this proposal that what the Greek government considers a powerful element for negotiating is the British Museum's desire to acquire more archaeological exhibits and retain the ownership of the marbles. However, the value of the Parthenon Marbles seems to be perceived by the British Museum as being irreplaceable.

Another interesting issue is the use of heritage as a means of international diplomacy. Mr. G. Papandreou emphasised that the restitution of the Parthenon marbles would have served as evidence of a superior British cultural policy and of a good relationship between the two countries. He also threatened that, in the event that the sculptures were not returned, British cultural policy would be regarded in a negative way internationally because the Parthenon Hall would be left empty. The aim of the former and current Greek governments was to emphasise the British refusal to return the Marbles through their symbolic absence and through the physical presence of the Parthenon temple, achieved by its proximity to the NAM.

The Greek policy was contradictory. On the one hand, the Greek government aimed to achieve a compromise through collaboration with the British Museum. On the other hand, it adopted a 'threatening' policy by claiming to leave the Parthenon Hall empty as a means of applying pressure. These contradictory actions and attitudes are a repeated pattern seen also in the case of Wood Quay where the 'Friends of Medieval Dublin' started negotiations with the developers while organising at the same time protests and massive gatherings.

The British Museum, on the other hand, has for some decades emphasised its role as representative of international cultural policy and foreign affairs arguing that 'the existence of the Parthenon marbles at the museum functions as the best ambassador for Greece regarding also the fact that it is visited by over six million people per year (The Conservative Party 1996; Wilson 1985).

Unavoidably, the discourse between the two museums, and occasionally, the two nations, evolves into a game of power. The repatriation of the Parthenon Marbles to Greece would constitute an emblem of political and national power. The retention of the marbles by the British Museum also constitutes proof of its power and dominance. Both opponents use a variety of means in the form of threats and accusations. The discovery of the archaeological site is damaging for the NAM and the creation of an empty Parthenon Hall is damaging for the British Museum. The win-win situation that the Greek state attempted to achieve failed ultimately because the discovery of the archaeological remains provided the British Museum with a new means to defame the NAM.

The NAM as a national and international symbol

The construction of the NAM has been imbued with symbolic values that derive from the various meanings that different parties have placed on the NAM, the

Acropolis Hill and the discovered archaeological site at national and international level. This section explores the main motivations and expected outcomes of each of the involved parties, the means they used in order to achieve their objectives, and their aspirations and values towards the archaeological site that was finally preserved *in situ*.

For the supporters of the NAM, the latter was viewed as a means for the repatriation of the Parthenon marbles and as an attempt to raise the local claim for the repatriation of the Parthenon marbles into a global issue (Yalouri 2001). Therefore, its construction unavoidably acquired a national significance, and the NAM itself constitutes a national emblem and vision. The exhibition of the replicas of the Parthenon Marbles in the Acropolis Station, next to which the NAM is being constructed, functions as a constant reminder of the local claim for the restitution of the Parthenon sculptures. As the head of the 'METRO's' art committee, Triantafyllia Lagoudakou said 'This is a silent protest that speaks for us all. This subway station sends a message to the thousands of commuters and tourists who will use this station every day: The Parthenon Marbles should be returned to their homeland' (*The Guardian*, 16/11/2000). The symbolic significance that the NAM acquires through its association with the demand for the repatriation of the Parthenon marbles became even greater when the museum construction was associated with the Athens 2004 Olympic Games. The revival and restitution of the Olympic Games, following the national humiliation resulted by the refusal of the global community to grant the 1996 ('Golden') Olympics to Greece, gained a special value symbolising the 'celebration of Hellenism in its complete restitution' (Yalouri 2001, 86). Therefore, the completion of the NAM before the Olympic Games was promoted as a national vision aimed at bringing the Parthenon Marbles back to Greece. As a result, both the NAM and the revival of Olympic Games, were viewed as representations of the glorious Hellenic spirit (Yalouri 2001, 86).

While the opponents accused OANMA of being destroyer of archaeological heritage, the creation of an *in situ* museum designed to integrate parts of the archaeological site into the museum has been perceived by its supporters as an emblem of progress and development and as an innovative way of linking the 'glorious past' with a revived, glorious present. The museum was also viewed as evidence of the establishment of an 'honourable profile' and of Greece's capability to safeguard its national and international heritage (Boniface and Fowler 1993, 104). The promotion of the NAM as a symbol of development is inseparable from the general development public projects that have taken place in Greece, especially in Athens, over the last ten years. The association of technological progress with the revival of a glorious past represented by the Parthenon marbles, the Acropolis Hill and the Athens 2004 Olympic Games, seems to be a common phenomenon.

For instance, Otto, the first King of the independent Greek State (1834-1862), was among the people who promoted the revival of the Olympic Games (which was achieved later in 1896) in association with a general development of the city (Dimitriadoou 2001, 44). Similarly, the current policy of the Greek government involves significant environmental and cultural development projects to which the NAM is linked. Among the most important are the construction of the Acropolis Metro Station (Vlassopoulou et al., 2000), the Unification of Archaeological Sites in Athens (Papageorgiou, 2000), and the extensive conservation and restoration works on the Acropolis Hill (Hellenic Ministry of Culture, 1989).

The 'honourable profile' that the Greeks have attempted to establish through recent development projects associated with the promotion of ancient culture, reveals the constant attempt of the Greek nation to assert its position in the global arena. This has also been characterised by Yannis Hamilakis as the representation of 'a new image of modern and civil Europeanisation' when he refers to the case of the underground metro stations (Hamilakis 2001, 36). Therefore, the project of the NAM has been viewed as an international symbol since it is linked with the internationally valued Parthenon Marbles.

For the opponents of the NAM, the discovery of the archaeological remains and their partial destruction as well as the construction of a high, modern building close to the 'sacred' rock have been perceived as threats to the national vision, which is the repatriation of the Parthenon marbles. Since this national vision is also a sacred one, both the destruction of the archaeological site and the museum building itself have been characterised as national sacrilege. The 'Citizen's Movement' opposed the construction of the NAM at the Makriyianni area arguing that its construction would lead to the destruction of the archaeological finds. They stressed that 'it is unbelievable that the CAC and the Ministry of Culture act in such an authoritative manner causing the Greek as well as the global reaction against the construction of the NAM and spoiling greatly these significant elements of our cultural heritage' (*Kathimerini*, 4/04/2002). Furthermore, they claimed that 'we will have the paradox of having a museum, which even though it is intended to preserve and present the ancient relics, will however be constructed over them, leading to their destruction' (*To Vema*, 20/05/2001). 'This will constitute a powerful argument for the British Museum to refuse the repatriation of the Parthenon Marbles' (*Eleftherotypia*, 03/08/2001). According to their arguments the role of the NAM seems paradoxical to them since the main aim of a museum institution should be the conservation and presentation of the archaeological finds rather than their destruction. Moreover, they emphasise the negative impact that this may have at international level regarding the national claim for the repatriation of the Parthenon marbles. Thus, the national profile and image in the global arena

constitutes an issue that raises concern among the Greeks. The fact that the Early Christian and Roman remains are considered significant elements of Greek culture, although they are not monumental remains of 'glorious' classical times, also reveals that the archaeological value of the site is empowered by its location in the vicinity of the Acropolis. In fact, their demand that the archaeological finds be conserved is mainly a claim for the protection of the slopes of the 'sacred rock'. It is the significant archaeological value of the Acropolis monuments, with which the NAM is associated, that has led the 'Citizens Movement' to protest against the museum's construction.

The opponents of the NAM also associated its construction with the consumption connotations derived from the organisation of the Athens 2004 Olympic Games. Within general negative perceptions of the Olympic Games, viewing them in a commercial light the NAM has also been perceived by its opponents as a tourist attraction that detracts from the national visions and meanings of the Acropolis Hill, the Parthenon and the Marbles.

The NAM as a symbol of sacredness and sacrilege

The construction of the NAM has been viewed as a symbol of sacredness and sacrilege by its supporters and opponents respectively. Statements including words such as desecration and sacrilege are characteristic (Hamilakis and Yalouri 1999; Yalouri 2001). These perceptions depend either on specific objectives, interests or motivations, or on unconscious, more emotional driving forces of the involved interested parties. The following exploration of sacred/sacrilege connotations is based on the systematic analysis of statements derived both from newspaper articles and public web forums.

The levels at which the notion of sacredness and sacrilege can be distinguished refer to the following thematic axes. Firstly, the NAM is perceived as a symbol of sacrilege when viewed as a building that spoils the aesthetics of the cultural landscape that is marked by the presence of the Acropolis Hill and the Parthenon. In this chapter, this is conventionally called the **sacrilege of aesthetics.** Secondly, the NAM is perceived to be a structure that destroys significant archaeological remains, and therefore is viewed as a symbol of **archaeological sacrilege**, mainly by archaeologists and the Citizen's Movement. Thirdly, the NAM as an idea is perceived to be a symbol of national sacrilege since it is regarded as being incapable of fulfilling the main national demand for the repatriation of the Parthenon marbles. Finally, since the construction of the NAM requires the demolition of an Orthodox church located on the Makriyianni plot, it is associated with the concept of **religious sacrilege.**

Simultaneously, the NAM is viewed as a symbol of sacredness. Firstly, the museum is perceived by its supporters as a means of enhancing the **sacredness of**

aesthetics through allowing visual contact of the Parthenon marbles with the Acropolis Hill and the Parthenon. Secondly, it is promoted as an innovative museum type that successfully integrates the discovered archaeological remains in the form of an *in situ* museum. In this way it enhances the **'sacredness' of archaeology.** Thirdly, it is perceived as being an effective way to achieve the local demand for the repatriation of the Parthenon marbles, at the same time constituting a proof of Greece's ability to safeguard properly its cultural heritage (**national sacredness).** Fourthly, the NAM incorporates an Orthodox church into the general building complex of the plot, although it was initially scheduled for demolition **(religious sacredness).**

The following sections explore thoroughly each of the above thematic axes and determine the driving forces which cultivated the above perceptions, and which should have been taken into consideration had a dispute management strategy been prepared for this site.

After the establishment of the Greek state in 1830, the Acropolis was imbued with sacredness whose purity and aesthetics had to be protected. The aesthetics refer both to the surrounding landscape marked by the presence of the Parthenon and the Acropolis monuments and to the characterisation of the Acropolis Hill as a work of high art (Yalouri 2001,149).

The 'purification' of the Acropolis by the removal of recent, vernacular buildings and buildings later than the Classical period of Athens started as early as in 1835 transforming the Acropolis and its landscape into a monumental place in time and space (Caftanzoglou 2000; 2001; Hamilakis and Yalouri 1996; Petrakos 1997; Yalouri 2001, 153). This process is associated with the 'perceptions of purity and pollution, which characterise many religious systems of thought' (Hamilakis and Yalouri 1999, 118). A similar 'purification' took place in the case of the NAM where the surrounding blocks of flats had to be demolished in order to plant trees.

However, the construction of a modern tall building in the proximity of the Acropolis Hill has been perceived by both the architects and the 'Citizen's Movement' as an aesthetic sacrilege since it will disrupt the view to the Acropolis, that must remain dominant, and will spoil the character of the landscape (*Eleftherotypia* 19/02/2002). Words such as desecration or sacrilege have often been used by protestors in order to oppose the construction of the building on the slopes of the Acropolis Hill. A characteristic event, revealing this contention, occurred during the presentation of the design of the NAM by Bernard Tschumi at the Hellenic Ministry, when two people raised panels with the following text written in English and Greek: '(A) Museum in Makriyianni (is) sacrilege. It destroys antiquities (and) antagonises the massiveness of the Parthenon' (*Eleftherotypia* 19/02/2002).

The use of the word desecration [*hybris* in Greek] indicates the sacredness with which the Acropolis monuments are imbued and therefore any building close to them is considered profane. The same notion also refers to the destruction of the archaeological site which will be analysed below. Similar contentions have been expressed in the past, a fact that reveals that some values are diachronic and repeated. A characteristic example is the discussion that arose about the position of the Law Megaron to have been built by Alexandros Nikoloudis in 1931 on the same plot in the Makriyianni area. The obstruction of the view to the Acropolis due to the 60 m. high dome raised international concern, which finally led to the withdrawal of the plans (Mpiris 1995, 306-308).

The notion of aesthetics results not only from the sacred connotations with which the Acropolis monuments are imbued but also from the perception of these monuments as works of high art. On this basis, a debate regarding the appropriate display of the marbles in the museum context has arisen between the British Museum and the NAM as sacrilege in terms of aesthetics. The supporters of the NAM argue that the Duveen gallery of the British Museum is misleading since it gives a misleading idea of the size, shape and colour of the Parthenon and its sculptures by its rearrangement in a false symmetry and the use of coloured spotlights which exaggerate the shadows (in Skeates 2000, 34). In contrast, it has been argued that the Parthenon Hall of the NAM, having the dimensions of the Parthenon frieze and allowing the Attic light through the transparent walls of different types of glass, will constitute the appropriate place for the marbles. This will permit the promotion of the aesthetic value of 'whiteness' that is attributed to the Acropolis monuments legitimising the ownership of the Parthenon marbles since the real 'whiteness' of the marbles can only be found under the 'Greek sun' and in the Attic landscape (Yalouri 2001, 184). In view of this, their display at the British Museum makes them inauthentic. Two further notions are associated with the aesthetics here. Authenticity, original context and 'whiteness' are closely related to the notion of aesthetics and these are indirectly related to the notion of sacredness, since if 'whiteness' and 'authenticity' are considered by the supporters of the NAM as essential prerequisites of aesthetics, and aesthetics a prerequisite of sacredness, then the intermix of the above elements affects perceptions. In reply, the British Museum emphasises a further dimension that is related to the aesthetics, that of the integral and comparative art. Representatives from the British Museum argue that the Parthenon marbles are an integral part of the museum because only as a whole do they allow a comparative study with the rest of the collections. In view of this, their sense of aesthetics can be revealed and understood wholly, since the scholars will have the chance to compare and recognise their unique value through this comparison (The British Museum, 1997).

A further notion associated with aesthetics is that of the original context, which partly relates to the notion of the authenticity, although it also has a more spatial meaning, in addition to a conceptual one. In detail, the supporters claim that the location of the NAM in the vicinity of the Acropolis rock as a central part of the Unification of the Archaeological Sites will provide 'a true sense of the aesthetics' of the Parthenon marbles that can be understood only in their original historical and cultural context (Papandreou, 2000). The argument that the Parthenon marbles will regain their 'true sense of aesthetics', if they are exhibited at the NAM, implies that the British Museum presents an inauthentic view of the Parthenon marbles since they are isolated from their historic context. Here the role of the museum in creating a cultural context is obvious (Macdonald, 1996, 8). The NAM not only constitutes part of the historical context in which the Parthenon marbles were created but also creates a contemporary context in which the authenticity and meaning of the sculptures will be presented.

The above debate reveals the subjectivity of the notion of 'aesthetics' and 'sacredness', which have been used appropriately for achieving specific purposes. In any case, the important element in this debate is to examine how heritage managers can assess subjective perceptions (not excluding their own subjective perceptions), how can then modify them – if necessary- and how can they manage them.

Similar contentions, revealing the 'sacredness' with which the Acropolis monuments are imbued, are often expressed by archaeologists. In a discussion I had with an academic of prehistoric archaeology at the University of Athens he argued that what happens in the Makriyianni area is a sacrilege. According to this, not only is the view disrupted but also important archaeological finds are destroyed. According to same informant, the sacrilege committed upon the landscape is based on the archaeological destruction of the site (pers. comm., 2002). A similar concept of sacredness is expressed in a dialogue between Eleana Yalouri and an archaeologist, who mentions that 'The Acropolis is not a public space. It is a place, which was made for worship. It also has a character of worship as reference point for Hellenism today' (Yalouri 2001, 163-164). To the author's remark that the Acropolis is no longer part of a living religion he replied 'A religion never dies, it changes form, but it does not die' (Yalouri 2001, 163-164). The unchangeable religious character emphasised by the archaeologist can be explained by the fact that for Orthodox Christianity once a place is sacred it remains so and its sacredness cannot be undone (Stewart 1998, 8-9). Thus, the long tradition of the Acropolis as a cult site is not erased in people's minds and consciousness.

The concept of sacredness is also related to the national symbolism that the Acropolis has for the Greek nation (Yalouri 2001, 142). Similarities between nationalist imagining and religious ideology have been pointed out by various authors (Yalouri 2001, 142; see also Eriksen 1993, 107-108; Gellner 1983, 56; Herzfeld 1992, 34-39). If the NAM as a national symbol is imbued with these notions of sacredness or sacrilege, then consequently the discovered archaeological heritage is imbued with similar connotations.

At a local level, apart from the group of inhabitants who are obliged to leave their houses, there was another local group in the Makriyianni district who opposed the destruction of the Orthodox church, devoted to Saint Georgios the 'Trophy- holder' located on the Makriyianni plot. This church is still in use not only as an ecclesiastical place but also as a memorial to events of the Greek Civil War (the so-called 1944 Confrontation in particular). Eventually, the OANMA requested permission from the Archbishop of Greece to demolish the church. The agreement was to transform the adjusting *neoclassical* building, that used to be the cooking facilities (refectory) of the military hospital and of the Barracks, into a church (*Ta Nea*, 28/07/2000).

Another earlier church is devoted to the healer Saints, 'Agioi Anargiroi', and was erected next to the hospital after the departure of the Bavarian King Otto in 1862. Due to its association with the historic military hospital, the church was preserved and incorporated into the museum complex.

Opposition by the religious community to cultural projects that affect or alter Christian churches constitutes a quite frequent phenomenon in Greece. This is the result of the two facets of Greek identity, classical Hellenism and Byzantine Christian Orthodoxy (Herzfeld 1987, 111), as well as the fact that the Church in Greece plays a leading role in guarding Greek national interests together with the state (Yalouri 2001, 139). In view of this, the NAM must function not only as a link between past and present but also as the link between Byzantine and Classical civilisation. Therefore, Byzantine archaeological remains will be integrated into the classical past and the two orthodox churches will constitute integral parts of the museum complex. Occasionally, the conservation of the archaeological or 'pagan' past disputes with the interests of the church, and usually the public opposes any attempt to preserve archaeological remains *in situ* where the conservation requires demolition or alteration of a church.

The values and meanings analysed above are inseparable from economic profits derived mainly from tourism and the financial support of the European Union. Tourism constitutes one of the most important financial resources for Greece, while at the same time contributing to the financial support of the Archaeological Receipts Fund, responsible for the conservation of Greek archaeological sites. In view of this, it seems that the commodification of the antiquities is a necessary evil (Tunbridge and Ashworth 1996, 59; Yalouri 2001, 103).

The association of the NAM with tourism development was viewed from two contradictory perspectives. Although tourism could constitute a meeting point of the local-global relationship through the immediate and personal contact of the local people with the tourists (Clifford 1997, 213-219), it is often criticised by the Greek nation. It is viewed as a threat to the local-national identity since it is associated with the homogenisation, consumption and commodification associated with the phenomenon of globalisation. On the other hand, tourism is considered to be the 'ambassador' of Greek heritage particularly by the Greek state accomplishing the national mission of promoting Greek heritage internationally (Yalouri 2001, 135).

The association of the NAM with the Athens 2004 Olympic Games was considered to be on the one hand a 'touristic fiesta' (*Eleftherotypia*, 07/04/2002), while on the other it was thought to provide, a unique opportunity to promote Greek heritage internationally. Representatives of the 'Citizen's Movement stressed that: 'The Ministry of Culture must decide if it desires (or is able) to link the NAM with the Olympic Games of 2004. It has to be clarified that the NAM constitutes a building that will exist for us…, a building that we do not construct for whatever foreigners but for ourselves, our city, Athens, and the Parthenon sculptures as well as the sculptures of the other temples' (*To Vema* 30/07/2000). In this statement commodified associations of the NAM and Olympic Games are implied. The 'whatever foreigners' represent the tourists-travellers as consumers rather than the tourists-travellers as pilgrims (Yalouri 2001, 135). The tourists who came for the Olympic Games and would possibly visit the NAM are not accepted by Greeks as consumers of culture since any appropriation of the NAM and the Olympic Games, symbols of the Hellenic spirit, is equal to appropriation of national identity.

More recent historic buildings in Greece are valued not only for their architectural significance but also for their association with recent historic events related to the independence of the Greek state in 1830. Despite the fact, that the following years were marked by constant periods of wars, Greek people aim to commemorate the military events on any occasion. In view of this, the construction of the NAM has sometimes been viewed as a threat to the historic buildings, commemorating nineteenth century events. Consequently, the destruction of the archaeological site that demonstrates the continuity of history from the ancient archaeological past is viewed as part of a general attempt to destroy and remove recent memories.

In detail, along with the archaeological remains, the area also has historical value associated with the history of the Greek State after its independence that is reflected in the preserved neoclassical buildings of the nineteenth century.

The *neoclassical* building, currently used as the Centre for the Acropolis Studies, was the first military hospital in Greece and one of the first monumental buildings of the independent Greek State. The medical function of the building was indicated by placing a statue of the ancient healer deity 'Asklepeios' on the façade (*Kathimerini,* 26/03/1989). General Makriyiannis, who became the owner of the plot in 1833, ordered its construction in 1834 to the Bavarian architect Wilhem von Weiler (Bamiatzis 1996).

In addition to its architectural significance the building is of special historic value as well. During its function as a military hospital (1834-1930) it contributed to the development of Greek medical science. Many heroes of national disputes from several periods received medical treatment in that hospital (Bamiatzis 1996). In view of this, the 'Society of Friends of the Museum of Hellenic Medicine' suggested that the military hospital be transformed into a museum of the history of Greek medicine. Therefore, the society opposed the integration of the building into the NAM (Bamiatzis 1996) where according to Mrs. Mendoni, then General Secretariat of the Ministry of Culture, it would function as a visitor centre (*Ta Nea*, 18/08/99).

In 1930 the military hospital was transformed into the Gendarme's Barracks and was associated with the Greek Civil War. In particular, on the 1st December 1944, a violent confrontation took place in the Makriyianni area between members of the communist and conservative parties (Istoria tou Ellinikou Ethnous 1999, 101-107). Today there is a memorial plaque to the casualties of the Gendarmes' Barracks placed on the front side of the orthodox church of Saint Georgios.

Another *neoclassical* building located in the Makriyianni area is the so called 'House of Makriyianni' on the northeast side of the plot. This building housed the nurses of the military hospital (*Kathimerini, 26/03/1989*). It will be preserved as a typical example of the neoclassical architecture that flourished in Athens. However, there were other neoclassical buildings surrounding the Makriyianni plot that had to be demolished provoking oppositions to the museum's construction since the neoclassical architecture retains the romantic spirit of old Athens, that commemorates a 'glorious' past. The neoclassical buildings had to be demolished in order to enhance aesthetically the surroundings of the museum through the plantation of trees. The demand for the conservation of old structures expressed a desire for the retention of a romantic, innocent past.

The presence of archaeological remains within a surrounding historic context can function as a link of an absent, unfamiliar and remote past with the more recent, familiar historic past. If it is accepted that recent historic events and the surviving buildings with which they are associated engender memories and feelings of familiarity then, the archaeological past, as a link to the recent past, can also be familiar and cause oppositions to its destruction. Also, the ancient past is an evidence of continuity of history and therefore unavoidably and unconsciously contributes to the reinforcement of national identity in Greece as well as the universe.

There was a local group of people who supported the construction of the NAM due to significant economic benefits derived from tourism as well as the revitalisation of the area. There was also a significant part of the local community that opposed its construction. This group consisted of inhabitants whose houses, surrounding the Makriyianni plot, were to be expropriated. On 1st October 1996, the inhabitants, 150 families in total, requested that the decision of the Supreme Judicial Council to construct the NAM on the Makriyianni plot be reversed (*To Vema*, 18/05/1997). Their arguments focused on the traffic problems that would be caused by the construction of the museum arguing at the same time that the NAM functioned as the representation of commodification and tourism.

Reactions against expropriations of houses in the vicinity of the Acropolis took place in 1833 when Athens was proclaimed the capital of the newly formed Greek State. In May 1832, Stamates Kleanthes and Edward Schaubert were requested to draw up the New City Plan including the city's fortification wall, ancient remains and the monuments of the medieval period and Turkish domination (Dimitriadou 2001, 31). The expropriations of land for the opening of roads, the forming of open areas, and the creation of a large archaeological zone around the Acropolis were viewed positively by Athenians who were willing to offer their properties to the State, governed then by the Bavarian King Otto (AD 1929, 1-28). However, the financial inability of the Greek State to pay compensation for the expropriated property changed the initial willingness of the citizens to offer their properties for the conduct of excavations. This led the Government to ask the architect Leo von Klenze to draw up a new plan which was accepted on 18 September 1834 (Travlos 1993, 238).

This story was repeated at the Makriyianni area and indicates that there are stable values, unchangeable over time. The fear of loss of property as well as the feeling of displacement led the local community to resist the construction of the NAM. An inhabitant of the area said in a local meeting: 'According to the law our houses must be demolished for the common benefit. However, I cannot understand what the meaning of the common benefit is since none of the inhabitants accepted the state decision'. Since their demand to retain their homes proved insufficient in persuading the government, they used more powerful arguments to try to block the construction of the NAM in the area, such as the destruction of the archaeological site of Makriyianni or future traffic problems and air pollution caused by the increase in tourism. The dislocation of the local inhabitants (Bender 2001, 8) could not be easily accepted either by

the local community or by the Citizen's Movement. Newspaper articles with titles such as 'When the Ancient Greeks move away the Modern Greeks' (*To Vema*, 16/12/1990) or 'The museum uproots 150 families' (*Epikairotita*, 30/11/1990) indicate the social impact on contemporary Greek society. Among the participants at a meeting of the local community, that took place on 19 June 2002 at the Makriyianni district, to discuss how to prevent the construction of the NAM in the Makriyianni area, an inhabitant said that: 'I think that the only solution to our problem is to hang big panels on our balconies writing in capitals "REFUGEES IN OUR OWN COUNTRY" (see also Pathfinders 2006). Another inhabitant also declared that: 'We have spent a lot of years in this area and we are emotionally tied to this site'. These words reveal the feeling of displacement dominating the inhabitants. Their removal from the place is equal to 'movement' of their memories associated with it. An architect and historian who suggested the use of an industrial building as an alternative to the Makriyianni district said: 'What right do we have to underestimate these blocks of flats that might be of special architectural or historical value in the future? Did anybody consider the landscape that has shaped for decades by the presence of these blocks of houses and tied to the memories of people who used to walk around the area?' (*To Vema*, 19/09/1991). People are emotionally tied to the buildings they live in and the scenes and memories created by these (Ashworth et al., 2005). What people remember of the past fashions their sense of community and determines their allies, enemies and actions (Alcock 2002, 1). In the case of the Makriyianni area, an inhabitant of the area, filmed and took pictures of the on-going archaeological excavation from his balcony in order to present this evidence to national and global communities of the 'archaeological destruction' that is taking place on the site. At the same time, the police was often called to stop the on-going excavation. Videos of the on-going excavation were sent to national and universal press agencies. The local community of the Makriyianni area used its personal or collective memories and experiences so as to form a sense of belonging and the notion of loyalty to the surrounding place (Lovell 1998; Schama 1995; Tilley 1994). This sense of belonging as a way of remembering is used for creating collective identities and placing political claims on territory (Lovell 1998).

7.5. Final comment

To sum up, the dispute around the construction of the NAM was based on opposing views along the possible ways of promoting the significance of the Acropolis monuments and of achieving the repatriation of the Parthenon marbles. The NAM was considered on the one hand to be an instrument for national reinforcement in a global context and compelling justification for the repatriation of the Parthenon marbles leading also to an increase in economic profits, while on the other hand it was denounced as a touristic fiesta and a means of aesthetic, historic and archaeological disruption of the Attic landscape. Within this framework, the discovery of the Byzantine archaeological remains and their partial destruction could easily be used as an argument against the construction of the NAM in this specific area, and consequently against the commodification of culture and tourist homogenisation. The tourism and economic exploitation of any archaeological site, especially a site of national importance is partly viewed as sacrilege, and this affects unavoidably the protection or perception of the archaeological site discovered in the Makriyianni plot.

The case of the NAM covers a broad range of disputes and the issue of *in situ* conservation was examined within this broad framework. The next chapter concludes with a comparative analysis of the presented case studies identifying the common behavioural patterns of the parties in dispute and enriching the suggested dispute management process with further guidelines.

CHAPTER EIGHT: CONCLUSION

8.1. Introduction

The book provides an innovative approach to the examination of the nature of dispute and its management. The adoption of an inter-disciplinary approach not only facilitates the formation of a dispute management model that can be used by heritage managers as a basis for resolving disputes but it also highlights one of the main arguments of the book that an **interdisciplinary approach is needed in the management of disputes both in theory and in practice.**

Two main notions related to the emergence and resolution of dispute have been emphasised, that have been ignored or neglected in the heritage management theory. These are the notion of **interdependence** and the notion of the **probability of performance.** The notion of interdependence refers to the extent to which two or more dispute elements are strongly interrelated and therefore any change to one element will unavoidably affect the other. The interrelated elements are presented in detail in section 8.2. The notion of negative probability of performance (what the other party thinks of the main negotiation party as regards his/her willingness to meet the party's needs) is of crucial importance in the context of heritage. Heritage managers are usually directly involved and therefore they cannot function as neutral mediators. Hence, the perceptions of the other parties depend on the extent to which a heritage manager can indeed meet their needs plays a crucial role. In Greece negative attitudes towards the Archaeological Service are very common as the latter is strongly associated with bureaucracy and authoritarianism. This derives to a great extent from the fact that the service is an agency of the state. The impression of authoritarianism derives from an attitude of superiority common to many archaeologists who are responsible for rescue excavations and decision-making not to engage or interact with other interested parties. The power of law authorises and empowers them to act as guardians of cultural heritage (and consequently as guardians of the common public good), but can also cause suspicion and negativity among other people

In view of the above two notions –the notion of interdependence and the notion of negative probability of performance – the book suggests a series of interrelated elements and examines techniques for altering negative perceptions concluding with a suggested operational dispute management model that can be used by heritage managers during their negotiation transactions with the involved parties in a dispute (section 8.5). The formation of the operational dispute management model has been based on the descriptive dispute management model that was suggested in chapter 3. What differentiates the operational model from the descriptive one is the fact

that each step is enriched with specific guidelines and tactics. The proposed guidelines are based on the examination of both the key dispute elements and their interrelationships at the stage of dispute genesis, escalation and resolution discussed in the case studies. The examination and comparison of the key dispute elements has revealed repeated patterns (constants). The repeated patterns are important for predicting a dispute situation. A series of variables by which the constants may be affected is also presented. The identification of the constants and variables has made it possible to develop the guidelines included in the steps of the operational dispute management model (8.5).

8.2. Dispute genesis

Individual dispute elements

The individual dispute elements that contribute to dispute genesis as well as to dispute escalation (section 8.3) are the nature of the project, power, positions, identities, ownership, further issues in dispute and frames.

The nature of the development project must be considered to see whether it is to play a role in dispute genesis. In the case of a museum project disputes may arise since a museum institution is perceived by the public to be an institution aimed exclusively at protecting national heritage. Therefore, any threat to an archaeological site by the construction of a museum building tends to be perceived as a paradoxical and irrational phenomenon. The extent to which strong disputes will arise also depends on the significance of the museum itself in the public's minds.

Dispute theorists (see Pruitt and Rubin 1986) maintain that one of the main sources of dispute is the imbalance of power. However, the book shows that balanced power also leads to disputes (Administrative Square, NAM, Wood Quay). This indicates that disputes are generally a game of power during which two or more parties either own power and want to reinforce their positions or endeavour to obtain power using the media, judicial appeals to supreme judicial councils or seeking interventions by international organisations. Although the sources of power may differ (including in large part) financial power in the case of developers, authority conferred by law in the case of the Archaeological Services and the power of media in the case of the public) the result is the same. When two or more parties of equal strength are in dispute then integrative negotiation is not initially an option (see section 8.3.2.).

The main position that raised general disputes especially in cases of private projects was the demand that excavations had to be completed by a specific deadline (NAM, Rose, Wood Quay). Setting deadlines for the completion of an excavation is interpreted by the parties that are interested in the preservation of the site as total destruction of the site. This mainly occurs in cases where nationally important monuments –often also of international significance- are under threat (Wood Quay, Rose Theatre, NAM). In the case of public projects a decision that the archaeological site should be preserved *in situ* has also caused negative reactions by the public. As explained thoroughly in chapter 6, the preservation of an archaeological site can be perceived as a threat to other socio-economic benefits (Naxos, Administrative Square).

In addition, when local identities associated with the feeling of belonging and personal memory are threatened by national and international identities associated with more materialistic interests (mainly economic), then disputes arise (NAM, Administrative Square).

There are also differences between state ownership of a plot/property and an archaeological site, and state ownership in general (NAM) as well as with private ownership.

Other issues in dispute in the past or present also constitute a frequent source of dispute. Some of these issues include the aesthetic integration of a modern building into a historic-urban and nationally valued landscape/space (Wood Quay and NAM), the environmental impact in the broader area (Administrative Square, Archéoforum, NAM); and the retaining of private properties (NAM).

Mismatches in frames lead to disputes. Parties talking about salary may be likely to use outcome frames while parties talking about relationships may be likely to use characterization frames. For instance, a developer talking about a dispute over the integration of an archaeological site into a modern building can be talking about the *in situ* museum (substantive frame), his/her preferences of how the *in situ* museum will look or which parts of the site will be preserved (an outcome frame), how much input the archaeological service should be able to have in determining what happens to the plot of his/her private property (a procedural frame) as well as whether he/she views the involved groups and individuals favourably or unfavourably (a characterisation frame). This reveals that two or more negotiators may be talking to each other from different frames, from different perspectives and points of views. Mismatches may relate to the type of frame, the content in the same frame or the level of abstraction. In contrast, when frames match, the parties are more likely to focus on common issues and a common definition of the situation (see further analysis, section 8.2.).

Interrelated elements that lead to dispute genesis

This section identifies a series of interrelationship pairs that lead to dispute genesis. Most of the hypothetical assumptions are followed by guidelines which will be incorporated into the final dispute management model.

First interrelationship pair: Nature of project ↔ Types of disputes

The types of dispute that usually occur after the decision to create a modern building or complex within a historic centre (NAM, Wood Quay, Rose Theatre) include external disputes caused by architects and archaeologists who are concerned with the aesthetic integration of the modern structure into the landscape, the environmental impact that the building may have on the local area and the unavoidable destruction of the archaeological heritage (NAM, Archéoforum, Rose Theatre, Wood Quay). In the case of a public development project (Naxos, Administrative Square, Atri, Market of Born) both internal and external disputes may occur related to the ways in which socio-economic benefits can be combined with cultural ones.

Second interrelationship pair: Values/needs attached to the site ↔values and needs attached to the project

If the **values** and **needs (constants)** attached to the discovered archaeological site are incompatible (variable) with the **values** and **needs** attached to the project then disputes will arise unless the parties realise that they actually share *common needs*. The guideline derived from this hypothetical assumption is the necessity for a heritage manager/negotiator to assess the common needs and distinguish them from incompatible goals and interests. The operational model suggests specific ways for assessing these needs and summarises some of the needs that the parties in dispute had in the case studies but failed to recognise because they adopted a highly contending style.

Third interrelationship pair: Number & power of the parties involved in a dispute ↔ Type of disputes

If the **parties (constant)** involved in the dispute are **multiple and powerful** then external disputes will most probably arise unless the *disputes that occurred in the past have been resolved* (variable). This requires the ability to assess the current and potential parties involved in the dispute situation as well as their power and how this evolves.

The case studies showed that when international bodies and organisations are concerned with other issues in dispute (apart from the issue of preserving *in situ* or not an archaeological site) then unavoidably a dispute gains international dimensions (see the intervention of the National Museum in Wood Quay and the intervention of UNESCO in the case of NAM).

Fourth interrelationship pair: Nature of the project ↔Further issues in dispute

If the **nature of the project (constant)** was and/or is still associated with **further issues in dispute** (constant) then disputes will most probably arise until *these issues have been resolved* (variable). The implication derived from this assumption is that gathering background information of the pre-existing disputes is essential. The use of a timeline suggested by Fisher et al (2005, 20) can prove to be very useful.

Fifth interrelationship pair: Frames, goals and issues in dispute

The choice of goals and the choice of frames are strongly interactive, and the existence of one will rapidly produce evidence of the other (Lewicki et al. 1999, 41). Specific frames may be likely to be used with certain types of issues. Therefore an extra interrelationship pair is the type of **issue in dispute** (constant) with the **type of frame (constant)**. Accordingly if the parties adopt an outcome frame then the issue in dispute will most probably relate to financial issues or gaining political power (developers and local authorities).

8.3. Dispute escalation

The analysis showed that disputes escalated due to the interrelationship of two or more key individual dispute elements which are described thoroughly below.

First interrelationship pair: Type of offer ↔Probability of performance

If the party that makes the **offer (constant)** has a negative **probability of performance (constant)** then disputes will escalate *unless the offer is being suggested after repeated delays and increased costs (variable)*. For instance, in the case of NAM the offer to announce an architectural competition for an *in situ* museum was not successful partly because it did not achieve other goals, interests and needs that had not been assessed adequately as well as because the Hellenic Ministry of Culture and CAC is negative. Similarly, in the case of the Rose Theatre, the decision to preserve the archaeological remains *in situ* did not lead to the resolution of the disputes. The demand for *in situ* preservation evolved into a demand for *in situ* presentation. The implication derived from the above is that a heritage manager/dispute manager needs to assess the probability of performance.

Second interrelationship pair: Behaviours ↔Positions of third parties /arbitrators + goals/needs

The position of **third parties** who function as arbitrators who do not meet the **needs** of the parties will generate **contending styles** *unless the parties feel that they cannot afford any further losses in terms of costs and money*. For instance, in the case of NAM the decision by the Supreme Judicial Council in 2003 that the museum was protecting the area led to fights and protests with the archaeologists. Also, it was only after seven years of debate that the decisions of the judicial

bodies were accepted by the local inhabitants. This implies that a heritage manager needs to introduce negotiation immediately since litigation and arbitration that are often reliant on the law are time-consuming.

Third interrelationship pair: Behaviours ↔ Actions

If the parties adopt **competitive styles (constants)** then they will most probably immediately seek for **arbitration/litigation (constants)** and **distributive negotiation (constant)** rather than integrative negotiation *unless a mediator intervenes beforehand (variable)*. This implies that it may be useful to hire a mediator at the first signs of dispute before it escalates, although time and budget restrictions may not allow this. Depending on the situation, a heritage manager could function as mediator as long as he/she is not directly involved in the dispute situation.

Fourth interrelationship pair: Actions ↔ Level of power

As mentioned above equally powerful parties will adopt a **contending style (constant)** and be unwilling to initiate an **integrative negotiation (constant)** simply because they believe that they do not share any common goals and interests with the partner in dispute. Those parties that do not possess high political or legal power (authority) will endeavour to reinforce their power by adapting different strategies and different styles (see FMD at Wood Quay, Rose Theatre Trust) combining negotiation, compromise solutions (tours), open public meetings and judicial appeals.

Fifth interrelationship pair: Type of compromise offer ↔ Type of the dispute

If the **compromise offer (constant)** that a party suggests does not fulfil the core **needs (constant)** of the involved parties then disputes will escalate *unless the offer is suggested after many years of dispute*. For example, in the case of NAM the announcement of architectural competitions generated further disputes because of the **scale/type and level of dispute (national and external),** the **power of the parties** (high power) and **the incompatibility of needs, values and goals**. This requires the assessment of *common needs* (variable).

Sixth interrelationship pair: Stage of dispute ↔ Type of offer

If the dispute has reached the **stage of crisis (constant)** then usually a **compromise offer (constant)** is being suggested by one or more parties. The outcome though will depend on the extent to which *some of the parties are very powerful and therefore not interested in cultivating long-term relationships*.

Seventh interrelationship pair: Type and level of dispute ↔ Mediation (actions) + Type of parties

If a dispute generates massive negative public reactions and protests then politicians intervene as mediators [Wood Quay, NAM, Rose Theatre]. Usually, representatives of government departments adopt a neutral attitude while political parties tend to favour a specific party involved in a dispute situation (NAM, Wood Quay). The case often is that the opposing party supports negative public reactions to a heritage project (see conservative party at NAM or Labour party at Wood Quay). National heritage organisations (for example National Monuments Advisory Council at Wood Quay or Central Archaeological Council in Thessaloniki) also function as mediators trying to reconcile the different interests and objectives.

Eighth interrelationship pair: Stage of dispute ↔ Type of dispute

Another common pattern is that after a temporary post-dispute situation internal disputes occur (Wood Quay: disputes within the City Council, Thessaloniki: disputes within the CAC).

8.4. Dispute resolution

There are three main interrelationship pairs that lead to dispute resolution. These are the nature of project and type of offer, the issue in dispute and type of dispute, and styles/behaviours and stage of dispute.

Nature of project ↔ Type of offer

If the project relates to the construction of a **museum building** then usually the compromise offer to create an *in situ* **museum** will be more easily accepted by the parties in dispute (Aboa Vetus, NAM, Guildhall Roman Amphitheatre) unless *technical (mainly financial and static reasons) reasons will not allow their preservation or unless this solution does not satisfy the needs of the general public (see Naxos).* This implies that the advantages of the creation of an *in situ* museum should be highlighted early and also that an *in situ* museum should accommodate the unexpressed, less obvious needs (see chapter 6).

Issue in dispute ↔ Type of dispute

Reactions related to the aesthetic integration of a building usually lead to redesigning the building using new material or lowering it, a compromise usually found to be acceptable [Wood Quay, NAM]

Styles/behaviours ↔ Stage of dispute + effectiveness of mediation/arbitration

If the dispute has gone through the **stage of crisis** two or more times then it is more likely that the initial **contending style** will be transformed to a more compromising one. This of course depends strongly on the ineffectiveness of previous strategies and methods. The example of the Administrative Square of Thessaloniki shows clearly how the contending style of the local political authority and the archaeological service was gradually transformed to a more compromising style because of the yearly delays and the increased costs resulting from the long-term negotiations between the authority and the archaeological service.

8.5. Operational dispute management model

This section follows the structure of the dispute management model presented in chapter 3. Each step of the descriptive model is enriched with specific guidelines (what should be done) and tactics (how it should be done) that have derived from the identification of constants and variables (Table 10). A brief analysis then follows.

Preventing disputes (step I)

Guidelines: In order to prevent dispute occurrence heritage managers should:
- ❑ gather background information on pre-existing disputes
- ❑ gather background information on similar projects and disputes in the country or other countries
- ❑ make a list of the actual and potential interested parties
- ❑ gather background information concerning the relationships of the parties with each other

Tactics/Tools: Heritage managers could avoid disputes if they:

- ❑ assess the parties' perceptions of the project, the heritage organisation and/or the potential discovered archaeological site by organising focus-groups and face-to-face interviews (see the example of Jorvik Viking Centre) (chapter 5).
- ❑ actively engage the potential interested parties in the process from the initial stage of the project

Analysis: indicators of potential disputes

As mentioned in chapter 3 preventing the emergence or escalation of a dispute requires the ability to identify 'clues and signals clearly' and to treat the conditions that create disputes (Fisher et al 2005, 104). This raises two main questions. Firstly, what are the possible clues and signals of a dispute in the heritage sector? Secondly, how can these be identified and assessed?

The indicators of a potential dispute include the pre-existing disputes in the past and the perceived incompatibility of goals and needs. In the case of Wood Quay and the NAM the pre-disputes were related to the aesthetic integration of a modern building into its urban-historic landscape. The recurrence of disputing discourses may be explained by the inherent tendency of human beings to recycle historic events or by the tendency of academics to recycle discourses from the past, since in both cases these disputing discourses were initiated by academics and journalists. The perceived incompatibility of goals and needs requires assessment of the perceptions of the actual and potential interested parties. It can be revealed that while the parties at this stage perceive they have incompatible goals, they may realise that their goals and needs are compatible. Generally, a heritage manager needs to identify the latent disputes that as mentioned in chapter 3, exist when goals are incompatible but behaviours are compatible.

Preventing a dispute or, at least predicting a dispute, is crucial and should constitute an integral step in the overall management plan of a site, even in cases in which disputes are not obvious.

A useful tactic for preventing disputes is the active engagement of potential parties and the assessment of their perceptions and views of a project at the initial stage of planning as well as gathering information about the past. In the case of the Jorvik Viking Centre, for example, the prior assessment of the general public's perceptions towards the preservation of the archaeological heritage endangered by the construction of a modern building led to avoidance of external disputes.

Table 10 - The operational dispute management model.

Preventing disputes (step I)

❑ Gather background information on pre-existing disputes.
❑ Gather background information on similar projects and disputes in the country or other countries.
❑ Make a list of the actual and potential interested parties.
❑ Gather background information concerning the relationships of the parties with each other.
❑ Assess the parties' perceptions of the project, the heritage organisation and/or the potential discovered archaeological site by organising focus-groups and face-to-face interviews.
❑ Engage the potential interested parties in the process from the initial stage of the project.

Framing the problem (step II. 1)

❑ Assess parties' perceptions of the profile of the heritage organisation and its managers and

their willingness to meet their needs (probability of performance).
❑ Assess the parties' perceptions of the estimated costs and benefits derived from their involvement in the dispute.
❑ Use psychoanalytical tools and techniques or consultation by psychologists regarding the assessment and where appropriate the modification of the negative perceptions of the parties.
❑ Use persuading techniques in order to convince the parties of the existing gains in finding a compromise solution.

Gathering background information (step II, 2.1.)

❑ Gather background information on pre-existing disputes, the parties involved in the dispute and their negotiation styles.
❑ Use the tool of timeline to assess what individuals or groups of people think of a dispute that occurred in the past, a current dispute or a dispute that may occur in the near future.

Analysing the dispute situation: type, level, and scale of dispute (step II, 2.2.)

❑ Assess **continually** the evolution of a dispute situation by examining how the types, levels and scales of a dispute change throughout the time. This will allow the prevention of dispute escalation and its ultimate resolution.
❑ Use the tool of pyramid for analysing the multi-level disputes. This analysis will allow the exploration of dispute escalation from a local to a national and from a national to an international level.

Identifying the parties and assessing their power (step II, 2.3.)

❑ Make a list of the actual and potential parties that are involved in a dispute situation.
❑ Attribute the level of power to each of the parties indicating clearly how and why the power changed.
❑ Use the tool of dispute mapping (Fisher et al. 2005, 22).

Identifying the sources of dispute (step II, 2.4.)

❑ Assess incompatible goals and disputes (II, 2.4.1), incompatible behaviours (II, 2.4.2.) and further issues in dispute (II, 2.4.3) in order to generate alternative offers which can accommodate the maximum of the above goals, transform contending behaviours and resolve further actual or potential issues in dispute.
❑ Use the tool of onion for visualising comprehensively the existing incompatible

goals and behaviours (Fisher et al. 2005, 27).

Identifying commonalities (step II, 2.5.)

❑ Identify some common needs which usually underlie the positions and goals which are common.
❑ Persuade the involved parties that they actually share common interests and needs (modify perceptions).
❑ Create an agenda of shared items.

Generating alternative options (step II, 3)

❑ Assess the common needs, heritage managers should generate alternative options on the basis of the above needs.
❑ Generate a list of issues in dispute. The parties can then trade off among those issues so that one party achieves a highly preferred outcome on the first issue and the other person on the second issue (Lewicki et al 1999, 119).
❑ Organise meetings of the interested groups in which participants think of as many solutions as possible.
❑ Distribute a questionnaire to the interested parties asking them to list all the possible solutions.
❑ Develop communication techniques in order to ensure that their messages will be transmitted clearly.

Developing a negotiation strategy (step III)

❑ Develop an integrative negotiation strategy in order to reinforce long-term relationships with the involved parties.
❑ Use 'manageable' questions (Nierenberg 1976, 125-126).
❑ Choose the appropriate form of listening.
❑ Adopt a 'role reversal' way of interaction.

Making a compromising offer (step III, 1.1.) on the basis of the losses and gains derived from an offer (step III, 1.2. –1.5.)

❑ Develop a series of alternative offers.
❑ Start with the offer that is closer to his/her reservation points and then gradually move to the offer that is closer to the other party's reservation points.
❑ Use effective communication and persuasion techniques as needed.

Resolving the disputes (step III)

❑ Ensure that external disputes have been resolved. This also requires that internal disputes have been prevented.
❑ Find compromise solutions that can accommodate the disputing and diverse points

of views.

Framing the problem (step II. 1)

Guidelines: In order to assess how the parties frame the problem heritage managers should:

❑ Assess parties' perceptions of the profile of the heritage organisation and its managers and their willingness to meet their needs (probability of performance).
❑ Assess the parties' perceptions of the estimated costs and benefits derived from their involvement in the dispute.

Tactics/Tools: Heritage managers could assess the frames by:

❑ Using psychoanalytical tools and techniques or consultation by psychologists regarding the assessment and where appropriate the modification of the negative perceptions of the parties.
❑ Exercising techniques in order to convince the parties of the existing gains in finding a compromise solution.

Analysis: techniques of modifying perceptions

Modifying perceptions requires first the assessment of perceptions. Both assessment and modification of perceptions can be facilitated by the Transactional Analysis method (TA) (see, Goldman and Rojot 2003, 154; Harris 1969; James and Jongeward 1971).

The Transactional Analysis method analysed in chapter 3 has some important implications. Being aware of which ego state a party in negotiation or dispute adopts, guides the main negotiator (in this case the heritage manager) in terms of how to respond and communicate his/her alternative offer. Initially, it is good for a negotiator to adopt an adult ego state. According to this ego state the negotiator adopts a mild facial expression, speaks clearly and is relaxed. The way he/she should explain his/her alternative offers will be explanatory, descriptive and interrogatory. This adult ego state should cause a similar response and stimulus of the other party which is essential if an agreement is to be achieved. If the negotiator is also interested in ensuring a good long-term relationship with the involved parties in dispute then it is imperative that he/she adopts the nurturing parent ego state as well.

Gathering background information (step II, 2.1.)

Guidelines

❑ Heritage managers should gather background information on pre-existing disputes, the parties involved in the dispute and their negotiation styles.

Tactics: Heritage managers could gather background information by:

❑ using the tool of timeline to assess what individuals or groups of people think of a dispute that occurred in the past, a current dispute or a dispute that may occur in the near future.

Analysis:

The aim of using timelines – graphics that show events plotted against time (Fisher et al. 2005, 20-21) is to get an in-depth understanding of public perceptions of a dispute situation that existed in the past. This is essential since people often have different histories and 'people on opposing sides of the dispute may note or emphasise different events, describe them differently, and attach contrasting emotions to them' (Fisher et al. 2005, 20-21). This was clearly shown in the case of the NAM. The supporters viewed creation of the new museum as a symbol of sacredness that would lead to the repatriation of the Parthenon marbles and the opponents viewed the museum's construction as a symbol of sacrilege leading to the destruction of the archaeological site. A timeline actually created by the interested parties can prove to be particularly useful, since it will allow people to learn about each other's history and perceptions of the dispute situation (Fisher et al. 2005, 21). The use of the timeline not only makes the involved parties understand each other's perceptions but also identifies which events are more important for each side. This will help the negotiator to develop a series of alternatives based on commonalities.

Analysing the dispute situation: type, level, and scale of dispute (step II, 2.2.)

Guidelines:

❑ Heritage / dispute managers should assess **continually** the evolution of a dispute situation by examining how the types, levels and scales of a dispute change throughout the time. This will allow the prevention of dispute escalation and its ultimate resolution.

Tactics: The above guideline can be achieved by:

❑ Using the tool of pyramid for analysing the multi-level disputes. This analysis will allow the exploration of dispute escalation from a local to a national and from a national to an international level.

Identifying the parties and assessing their power (step II, 2.3.)

Guidelines:

❑ Heritage managers should make a list of the actual and potential parties that are involved in a dispute situation.
❑ They should also attribute the level of power to each of the parties indicating clearly how and why the power changed.

Tactics: Heritage managers could assess constantly the powers of the parties by:

❑ using the tool of dispute mapping (Fisher et al. 2005, 22)

Analysis:

Dispute mapping is a technique for representing graphically a dispute situation. This graphic places the parties in relation both to the problem and to each other (Fisher et al. 2005, 22). This tool provides a visualisation of the relationships between parties in dispute. The information usually included in the mapping includes a summary of the parties involved in a dispute situation, a description of the relationships between all these parties and how these can be represented on the map, issues in dispute and position of the disputing parties. A 'pyramid' or 'multi-level' triangles can be used as a tool for showing levels of hierarchy the parties in a dispute situation (this tool is particularly useful for multileveled disputes) (Fisher et al. 2005, 32, 60). During this step it may be useful to use the tool of mapping the dispute situation (Fisher et al. 2005, 22-25).

Identifying the sources of dispute (step II, 2.4.)

Guidelines:

❑ A heritage manager should firstly assess incompatible goals and disputes (II, 2.4.1), incompatible behaviours (II, 2.4.2.) and further issues in dispute (II, 2.4.3) in order to generate alternative offers which can accommodate the maximum of the above goals, transform contending behaviours and resolve further actual or potential issues in dispute.

Tactics:

❑ It would be useful if heritage/ dispute managers used the tool of onion for visualising comprehensively the existing incompatible goals and behaviours (Fisher et al. 2005, 27).

Analysis:

The tool of onion is again a graphic that is used in order to illustrate the positions, the underlying interests and needs. It is imperative to illustrate the relation of positions, needs, and interests, since, depending on the dispute situation, needs may be hidden. Fisher et al. (2005, 28) rightly mention that 'in a situation of dispute and instability …people may look at the more collective and abstract level of interests and base their actions on these' rather than on their needs. They continue saying that 'when those interests are under attack, they may take up and defend a position that is still further removed from their needs' (Fisher et al. 2005, 28). However, the analysis of the case studies showed that if a compromise needs to be established, then the offers need to meet the deeper, sometimes unconscious needs. Positions and interests that look diverse and incompatible may inhere compatible needs. Therefore, it is essential to identify those needs and distinguish them from positions and interests.

Identifying commonalities (step II, 2.5.)

Guidelines: In order to find a compromise offer and resolve the dispute, heritage managers should:

- ❑ Identify some common needs which usually underlie the positions and goals which are common.
- ❑ Persuade the involved parties that they actually share common interests and needs (modify perceptions).

Tactics: Heritage/dispute managers could persuade the other parties of the fact they share common needs by:

- ❑ Creating an agenda of shared items.
- ❑ Using persuasive techniques (see above Transactional Analysis).

Generating alternative options (step II, 3)

Guidelines:

- ❑ Having assessed the common needs, heritage managers should generate alternative options on the basis of the above needs.
- ❑ They also should generate a list of issues in dispute. The parties can then trade off among those issues so that one party achieves a highly preferred outcome on the first issue and the other person on the second issue (Lewicki et al 1999, 119).

Tactics: Heritage managers could generate alternative options by:

- ❑ Organising meetings of the interested groups in which participants think of as many solutions as possible.
- ❑ Distributing a questionnaire to the interested parties asking them to list all the possible solutions.
- ❑ Developing communication techniques in order to ensure that their messages will be transmitted clearly.

Developing a negotiation strategy (step III)

Guidelines:

- ❑ Heritage/dispute managers should develop an integrative negotiation strategy in order to reinforce long-term relationships with the involved parties.

Tactics: How could heritage managers improve the communication with the involved parties in dispute in order to avoid misunderstandings?

- ❑ by using 'manageable' questions (Nierenberg 1976, 125-126)
- ❑ by choosing the appropriate form of listening
- ❑ by adopting a 'role reversal' way of interaction

Analysis:

Questions can be divided into two main categories: the manageable and unmanageable (Nierenberg 1976, 125-126). Manageable questions are clear and prepare the other person's thinking for further questions and generate thoughts while manageable questions cause difficulty and consequently anger. Negotiators should use open-ended questions inviting the other to think. The questions should also be low emotionally but ascertain at the same time how the other party feels (see detailed examples of questions in Nierenberg 1976, 125-126).

Active listening refers to the form of listening during which the receivers rephrase or restate the sender's message in their own language (Lewicki et al. 1999, 167). Active listening in a negotiation transaction should be characterised by a greater emphasis on listening than speaking; responding to personal rather than abstract points such as feelings, beliefs and positions; following the other rather than leading him/her to a specific point and responding to the feelings of the other (Athos and Gabarro 1978).

In my opinion the other two main forms of listening – passive listening (receiving the message without providing feedback) and acknowledgement (maintaining eye contact) are also important, especially at the beginning of a negotiation transaction since a negotiator can cultivate a positive climate and gradually gain the trust.

Another important technique for communicating and negotiating effectively is role reversal by which negotiators repeat the positions of the other party in order to convince them that they have understood their positions (Johnson 1971; Rapoport 1964; Walcott et al. 1977).

Making a compromise offer (step III, 1.1.) on the basis of the losses and gains derived from an offer (step III, 1.2.- 1.5.)

Guidelines

- ❑ A series of alternative offers should be developed by the involved parties.
- ❑ The negotiator needs to start with the offer that is closer to his/her reservation points and then gradually move to the offer that is closer to the other party's reservation points.

Tactics

- ❑ Effective communication techniques are needed.
- ❑ Effective persuasion techniques are needed.

Resolving the disputes (step III)

Guidelines:

- ❑ Heritage managers should ensure that external disputes have been resolved. This also requires that internal disputes have been prevented

Tactics:

- ❑ Heritage managers can avoid internal disputes by finding compromise solutions that can accommodate the disputing and diverse points of views

Analysis:

Internal disputes seem generally to be unavoidable, especially in interdisciplinary projects. Therefore, while interdisciplinarity facilitates innovation and innovation leads eventually to reputation and recognition (thereby unifying the initial disputes) it is also a source of dispute.

8.6. The importance of integrating a dispute management model into the heritage management process

Chapter 3 depicted how a dispute management model fits into the broader heritage management process. The importance of integrating the model into the overall heritage management plan relies on the fact that it provides a basis for a heritage manager to predict, plan 'and hopefully avoid or resolve potential and existing disputes'. The model is general and flexible so that it can be adapted to every site specifically. This model is above all a starting point for considering and revisiting tactics, techniques and skills that a heritage manager needs to possess. The perception of many archaeologists that they are the most capable in managing an organisation dealing with the

archaeological heritage is one of the reasons why they ultimately fail to deal effectively with dispute situations. Heritage managers need to develop their skills in communication and negotiation.

8.7. Limitations and further areas for research

This book has demonstrated that the creation of a generic dispute management model is highly important for the field of heritage management because of the existing gap in the relevant literature regarding the development of dispute management strategies. The suggested model can be used by heritage managers as a tool in developing a strategy for avoiding and resolving disputes that occur during the implementation of a heritage project. This model can function as an essential element of the commonly used heritage management models that have been employed so far on national and international levels. The contribution is particularly important since these models do not provide systematic guidelines based on theoretical approaches to dispute management and analysis of disputes within the heritage sphere.

However, as with any model, there are certain limitations which need to be taken into consideration during the development of a dispute management strategy in any particular situation. The identification of these limitations sets the framework for the development of further areas of research (see following section).

One of the first limitations is the question of the applicability of the model worldwide. The suggested model is generic insofar as it provides a starting tool for managing future dispute which is designed to assist heritage managers across the world. Bearing in mind that each country has its own cultural, administrative and institutional contexts and specificities, any model of generic guidelines can only be valid when it is adopted within the special circumstances of each case and situation.

A potential further area of research could be the exploration of the applicability of this model to an even wider context by enriching it with more case studies and extending it to dispute situations other than those generated by the discovery of archaeological remains during modern development.

A further limitation is the fact that the in-depth analysis of the New Acropolis Museum forms the basis of this model with analysis of elements and information from other case studies used predominantly to broaden and illuminate a wider range of issues. The primary aim was to identify commonalities in dispute outcomes rather than to focus on dispute driving forces. Naturally, this was imposed by both the lack of detailed information regarding the case studies (see chapter 2, methodology) and by the fact that each site, each group of people, each dispute situation and each individual are unique and therefore mapping common driving forces is a risky process. For the purposes of this book the selection of a case study that provided a range of information wide enough for the development of the model was deemed important. Owing to the fact that the assessment of the driving forces is an integral and crucial step of dispute management, a future challenge could be the elaboration and improvement of the suggested model in this direction.

An additional limitation and, simultaneously an interesting but large area for further research, is the political role of the heritage manager in the operation of the model and the ethical issues involved. This issue gains additional gravity since the model authorizes the heritage manager to use persuading techniques and psychoanalytical tools in order *to convince* the parties in dispute that they have common interests and *to modify* their negative perceptions of each other. Although any negotiation transaction involves, to a great extent, a conscious or unconscious attempt to modify the perceptions and beliefs of other parties, it is imperative that this is implemented within an ethical code. Any organization and agency, whether public or private, should clearly define the ethical principles that underline heritage management practice including dispute management strategies.

Finally, the suggested model is based on the assumption that negotiation transaction seeks the identification of common interests and goals which can constitute a common ground. This is the main principle of the integrative negotiation process, one of the four types of negotiation that were analysed in chapter 3. As mentioned in chapter 3, I consider the integrative negotiation to be the most applicable and compatible with heritage management strategy. The adoption of this strategy occasionally requires the heritage manager to compromise more than he/she is willing to do. However, there are cases in which common goals do not exist and cannot therefore be identified. In these cases, future research could examine the potential of distributive negotiation as a potentially useful way forward, and of course, there are other possibilities that might prove helpful such as mediation and arbitration techniques.

8.8. Ways forward

The book suggests a generic dispute management model that can be used by heritage managers as a tool for managing disputes in the heritage sector. Regarding the fact that every case is unique, the methodology that every negotiator/heritage manager needs to adopt is the one elucidated in this book. A negotiator/heritage manager should first gather as much information as possible on pre-existing and current disputes, observe the evolution of the dispute situation, identify the constants and variables and then develop a negotiation strategy. The ultimate aim is to transform a distributive

negotiation to an integrative one which means that the parties in dispute need to be persuaded that common needs and goals actually exist. This requires a total transformation of the negative profile that the Greek Archaeological Service and/or other services have among the public, otherwise the parties in dispute cannot be persuaded that the archaeologists are really interested in meeting their needs. There is mistrust.

Interdisciplinary workshops would be particularly useful if psychologists, communicators, politicians, sociologists, economists and heritage managers or archaeologists participated in the process and provided seminars on negotiation transactions with dispute parties. Areas including techniques of persuasion, communication, assessment of frames and cognitive heuristics need to be further researched since the role of cognitive heuristics is vital in decision-making and in negotiation.

Above all, it is important that heritage managers who are concerned with the effective management of a heritage organisation need to understand the importance of negotiating and communicating effectively with the involved parties in dispute. Developing local engagement activities and involving the interested parties in planning is not enough. What is needed is a constant assessment before, during and after the implementation of a heritage project of the feelings, needs, positions, interests of the actual and potential disputes as well as a constant assessment of how the feelings, needs and positions alter.

REFERENCES

AD (Archaeologikon Deltion): *Αρχαιολογικόν Δελτίον, [Archaeological Newsletter]*

Addyman, P.V., 1990. Reconstruction as interpretation: the example of the Jorvik Viking Centre, York. In: P. Gathercole and D. Lowenthal (eds). *The Politics of the Past. One World Archaeology.* London: Unwin Hyman, 257-264.

Addyman, P. and Gaynor, A., 1984. The Jorvik Viking Centre: an experiment in archaeological site conservation. *International Journal of Museum Management and Curatorship,* 3, 9-18.

Adler, P.A. and Adler, P., 1994. Observational techniques. In: N.K. Denzin and Y.S. Lincoln (eds). *Handbook of qualitative research.* London: Sage Publications, 377-392.

Aggleton, J. P. and Waskett, L., 1999. The ability of odours to serve as state-dependent cues for real-world memories: Can Viking smells aid the recall of Viking experiences? *British Journal of Psychology*, 90,1-7.

Alcock, S.E., 2002. *Archaeologies of the Greek past: Landscape, monuments and memories.* Cambridge: Cambridge University Press.

Alderfer, C.P., 1980. The methodology of organisational diagnosis, *Professional Psychology,* 11, 459-468.

Alexopoulos, G., 2000. *Aboa Vetus & Ars Nova Museum: a statement of significance.* Unpublished essay for the optional undergraduate course 'Management of Archaeological Sites'. Athens: Department of History and Archaeology, University of Athens.

Alexopoulos, G., 2007. Development of the concept of cultural heritage on Mount Athos: Past and Present. In: S. Grabow, D. Hull and E. Waterton (eds). *Which Past, Whose Future: Treatments of the Past at the start of the 21st Century',* BAR International SERIES 1633. Oxford: Oxbow Books, 75-84.

Allison, J., 1999. Self-determination in cultural resources management: indigenous peoples; interpretation of history and of places and landscapes. In: P. J. Ucko and R. Layton (eds). *The archaeology and anthropology of landscape. Shaping your landscape* London: Routledge, 264-283.

Amason, A.C. 1996. Distinguishing the effects of functional and dysfunctional conflict on strategic decision making: Resolving a paradox for top management teams. *Academy of Management Journal,* 39, 123-148.

Anyon, R., 1991. Protecting the past, protecting the present: cultural resources and American Indians. In: G. S. Smith and J. E. Ehrenhard (eds). *Protecting the past.* Baton Rouge, FL: CRC Press, 215-222.

Anyon, R., Ferguson, T.J. and Welch, J.R., 2000. Heritage management by American Indian Tribes in the Southwestern United States. In: F.P. McManamon and A. Hatton, (eds). *Cultural resources management in contemporary society. Perspectives on managing and presenting the Past.* London: Routledge, 120-141.

Aplin, G., 2002. *Heritage: identification, conservation, and management.* South Melbourne: Oxford University Press.

Apostolakis, G.E. and Pickett, S.E., 1998. Deliberation: Integrating analytical results into environmental decisions involving multiple stakeholders, *Risk Analysis,* 18 (5), 621-634.

Archiseek 2007. *Irish architecture.* Retrieved on 17/07/2007 from World Wide Web:www.irisharchitecture.com/buildings_ireland/dublin/southcity/quays/wood/wood.html

Aslan, Z., 1997. Protective Structures for the Conservation and Presentation of Archaeological Sites. *Journal of Conservation and Museum Studies* 3, 1-8.

Ashworth, G.J., Graham, B. and Tunbridge, J.E. (eds), 2005. *Senses of place: senses of time.* Aldershot: Ashgate.

Athos, A.G. and Gabaro, J.J., 1978. *Interpersonal behavior: Communication and understanding in relationships.* Englewood Cliffs, NJ: Prentice Hall.

Atkinson, P. and Delamont, S., 2005. Analytic perspectives. In: N.K. Denzin and Y.S. Lincoln (eds). *The SAGE handbook of qualitative research* (3rd ed.). London: SAGE, 821-840.

Avrami, E., Mason, R. and De la Torre, M. (eds), 2000. *Values and heritage conservation. Research report.* Los Angeles: The Getty Conservation Institute.

Baillie, R., 2002., The Billingsgate Bath House - London's Roman Secret Retrieved on 15/01/2006 from World Wide Web: http://www.colas.freeserve.co.uk/context/50jan2002/billingsgate.html

Bamiatzis, G., 1996., Σύνταγμα Μακρυγιάννη [*my own translation:* Makrigianni Gendarme's Barracks]. In: *Ιστορία Εικονογραφημένη*, September 1996, 114-119.

Bateman, N., 2000. *Gladiators at the Guildhall: the story of London's Roman amphitheatre.* London: Museum of London Archaeology Service.

Bazerman, M. and Neale, M., 1992. *Negotiating rationally*. New York: Free Press.

Bell, V.R. 2013. The politics of managing a World Heritage Site: the complex case of Hadrian's Wall. *Leisure Studies*, 32, 115-132.

Bender, B., 1993. *Landscape: politics and perspectives*, New York: Berg

Bender, B., 2001. Introduction: Landscape-Meaning and action. In: B. Bender and M. Winer, (eds). *Contested landscapes: Movement, Exile and Place*. Oxford-New York: Berg, 1-18.

Berelson, B.R., 1952. *Content analysis in communication research*. Glencoe, Illinois: Free Press.

Berne, E. 1972. *What do you say after you say hello? The psychology of human destiny*. New York: Grove Press.

Bertrand, I. and Hughes, P., 2005. *Media, research, methods. Audiences, institutions, texts*. Basingstoke: Palgrave Macmillan.

Biddle, M., 1989. The Rose reviewed: a comedy (?) of errors. *Antiquity*, 63 (241), 753-760.

Blain, J. and Wallis, R. 2007. *Sacred sites: contested rites/rights*. Brighton: Sussex Academic Press.

Boniface, P. and Fowler, P.J (eds), 1993. *Heritage and tourism in the 'global village'*. London and New York: Routledge.

Boylan, P.J., 1993. *Review of the convention for the Protection of Cultural Property in the Event of Armed Conflict: The Hague Convention of 1954*. Paris: UNESCO.

Breglia, L., 2006. *Monumental ambivalence: the politics of heritage*. Austin: University of Texas Press.

Brossard, J.G., 1994. Pointe - a- Gallière, Musee d' Archeologie et d' Histoire de Montreal. La conservation de sites archeologiques de A a Z.' in Vestiges archéologiques, la conservation in situ : actes du deuxième Colloque international de l'ICAHM, Montréal, Québec, Canada, 11-15 octobre 1994 / [organisé par] Comité international de gestion du patrimoine archéologique de l'ICOMOS Ottawa : ICHAM publications, 55-61.

Brown, L.A., 1981. *Innovation diffusion: a new perspective*. New York: Methuen, G (N).

Burton, J.W., 1990. Human Needs Theory. *Conflict: Resolution and Prevention*. London: Macmillan, 36-48.

Burton, J.W., 1991. Conflict Resolution as a Political System' in Volkan, V., Julius, D., Montville, J.V.,

(eds.), *The Psychodynamics of International Relationships: Concepts and theories, Volume II: Unofficial Diplomacy at Work*, 82-83, Lexington, MA, Lexington Books.

Butler, B., 2001. Return to Alexandria: Conflict and contradiction in discourses of origin and heritage revivalism. In: R. Layton, P.G. Stone and J. Thomas (eds). *Destruction and Conservation of Cultural Property*. London and New York: Routledge, 55-74.

Caftanzoglou, R., 2000. Profane Settlement: Place, Memory and Identity under the Acropolis, *Oral History*, 28(1), 43-51.

Caftanzoglou, R., 2001. The Shadow of the 'Sacred Rock': Contrasting discourses of place under the Acropolis. In: B. Bender and M. Winer (eds). *Contested landscapes: Movement, Exile and Place*. Oxford-New York: Berg, 21-35.

Cairns, E., 1994. *A welling up of deep unconscious forces: psychology and the Northern Ireland Conflict*. Coleraine, Centre for the Study of Conflict: University of Ulster.

Callon, M., 1986. *The sociology of an actor-network: The case of the electric vehicle*. Basingstoke: Palgrave Macmillan.

Campbell, D.T., 1967. Stereotypes and the perception of group differences, *American Psychologists*, 22, 817-829.

Carman, J., 2002. *Archaeology and heritage: an introduction*. London, New York: Continuum.

Carman, J, 2005. *Against cultural property: archaeology, heritage and ownership*. London: Duckworth.

Cernea, M., 2001. Economic benefits and poverty reduction through cultural heritage preservation, in The World Bank, *Cultural heritage and development: a framework for action in the Middle East and North Africa*. Washington: The World Bank, 41-55. Retrieved on 15/09/2005 from World Wide Web: http://lnweb18.worldbank.org/mna/mena.nsf/Attachments/Orientations/$FILE/14938.pdf

Chamberlain, K., 2004. *War and cultural heritage : an analysis of the 1954 Convention for the Protection of Cultural Property in the Event of Armed Conflict and its two Protocols*. Leicester : Institute of Art and Law.

Champion, M., 2000. *Seahenge: a contemporary chronicle*. Aylsham: Barnwell's Timescape.

Cheshire, J. D. and Feroz, E. H., 1989. Allison's models and the FASB statements no's 2, 5, 13 and 19.

Journal of Business Finance and Accounting, 16 (1) 119-130.

Chippindale, C. 1989. Editorial, *Antiquity*, 63 (240), 411-420.

Christodoulakos, G., 1993. Προβλήματα προστασίας και ανάδειξης ανασκαφών μέσα στη σύγχρονη πόλη: παράδειγμα τα Χανιά [*my own translation:* Problems of protection and promotion of excavations in a modern city: the example of Chania] in *Νέες πόλεις πάνω σε παλιές* [new cities above old one] *Conference at Rhodes, 27-30 September, 1993*. Athens: Eptalofos, 471-473.

Clark, K. (ed.), 1999. *Conservation plans in action: proceedings of the Oxford conference*. London: English Heritage.

Clark, K. 2001. *Informed conservation. Understanding historic buildings and their landscapes for conservation*. London: English Heritage.

Clarke, H. 2004. C*arrickmines: the lessons of wood quay* [From Sunday Tribune (Sunday 17 October 2004), originally written for conference on Carrickmines] Retrieved on 17/10/2004 from World Wide Web: http://fmd.ie/carrickmines/041017-lessons-of-wood-quay.html).

Cleere, H.F. (ed.), 1989. *Archaeological Heritage Management in the Modern World One World Archaeology 9*. London: Unwin Hyman.

Clifford, J. 1997. *Routes: Travel and Translation in the late twentieth century*, Cambridge, Mass: Harvard University Press.

Cohen, M. D., March, J. G. and Olsen, J. P., 1972. A garbage can model of organizational choice, *Administrative Science Quarterly*, 17, 1-25.

Cosier, R.A. and Dalton, D.R., 1990. Positive effects of conflict: a field assessment, *International Journal of Conflict Management*, 1, 81-82.

Council of Europe, 1954. *European cultural convention*. Retrieved on 20/09/2007 from World Wide Web: http://www.conventions.coe.int/Treaty

Council of Europe, 1975. *Declaration of Amsterdam.* Congress on the European Architectural Heritage. Retrieved on 08/11/2015 from World Wide Web: http://www.getty.edu/conservation/publications_resources/research_resources/charters/charter22.html

Council of Europe, 1985. *European Convention of the Protection of the Archaeological Heritage of Europe.* Retrieved on 16/05/2005 from World Wide Web: www.conventions.coe.int/Treaty/en/Treaties/Html/066.htm

Council of Europe, 1992. *European Convention of the Protection of the Archaeological Heritage of Europe (Revised)*. Retrieved on 16/05/2005 from World Wide Web: www.conventions.coe.int/Treaty/en/Treaties/Html/066.htm

Couvelas–Panagiotatou, A., 1999. Επιτόπιο μουσείο Νάξου [*my own translation:* In-situ Museum of Naxos] Αρχιτεκτονικά θέματα [*my own translation:* Architectural issues*], 33, 133-138.

Couvelas– Panagiotatou, A. 2000a. Επιτόπιο μουσείο Νάξου [*my own translation:* In-situ Museum of Naxos] ΚΤΙΡΙΟ [BUILDING], 124,124-132.

Couvelas–Panagiotatou, A. 2000b. Museum Naxos, *The Architectural Review*, 1236, 64-66.

Crawley, J. and Graham, K., 2002. *Mediation for Managers: Resolving Conflict and Rebuilding Relationships at Work.* London: Nicholas Brealey Publishing.

Creamer, H., 1990. Aboriginal perceptions of the past: the implications for cultural resource management in Australia. In: P. Gathercole and D. Lowenthal (eds). *The politics of the past. One World Archaeology*. London: Unwin Hyman, 130-140.

Crooks, J., 1995. Monumental Headache, *Building Magazine*, 8, 45-50.

Daes, E-I., 1997. *Protection of the heritage of indigenous people*. New York: United Nations.

Darvill, T., 1995. Value systems in archaeology. In: M.A. Cooper, A. Firth, J. Carman and D. Wheatley (eds). *Managing archaeology*. London: Routledge, 40-50.

Deeben, J., Groenewoudt, B.J., Hallewas, D.P. and Willems, W.J.H., 1999. Proposals for a practical system of significance evaluation in archaeological heritage management, *European Journal of Archaeology*, 2 (2), 177-199.

De la Torre, M. (ed.), 2002. *Assessing the values of cultural heritage*. Los Angeles: The Getty Conservation Institute.

De la Torre, M. (ed.), 2005. *Heritage values in site management: four case studies*. Los Angeles: The Getty Conservation Institute.

Demas, M., 2002. Planning for conservation and management of archaeological sites: a value-based approach. In: J.M. Teutonico and G. Palumbo (eds). *Management planning for archaeological sites: an international workshop organised by the Getty*

Conservation. Los Angeles: Getty Conservation Institute, 27-56.

Denzin, N.K. and Lincoln, Y.S., 2005. Introduction: The discipline and practice of qualitative research. In: N.K. Denzin and Y.S. Lincoln (eds). *The SAGE handbook of qualitative research* (3rd ed.), London: SAGE, 1-33.

Deutsch, M., 1977. *The resolution of conflict.* New Haven, CT: Yale University Press.

Dimakopoulos, I., 1997. *Protective Shelters in the form of a tumulus: Vergina: an Underground Archaeological and Museological Site in the form of a Crypt.* Athens: Greek Archaeological Receipts Fund.

Dimitriadou, E., 2001. Νεοκλασσική Αθήνα: Η γέννηση μιας ευρωπαϊκής πρωτεύουσας, [*my own translation:* Neoclassical Athens: The birth of a European capital] *Corpus*, 31, 28- 46.

Dougherty, J.E. and Pfaltzgraff, R.L., 1981. *Contending theories of international relations.* New York: Harper and Row.

Dreliosi, A. and Filimonos, M., 1993. Διατήρηση μνημειακών συγκροτημάτων στη Ρόδο: τα οικόπεδα Φώκιαλη – Ψαίνου – Κωσταρίδη [*my own translation :* Preservation of monumental complexes at Rhodes: the plots of Phokiali–Prasinou and Kostaridi] in *Νέες πόλεις πάνω σε παλιές* [new cities above old one] *Conference at Rhodes, 27-30 September, 1993,* Eptalofos, Athens, 433-439.

Druckman, D., Broome, B.J. and Korper, S.H., 1988. Value differences and conflict resolution: facilitation or delinking? *Journal of conflict resolution*, 32, 489-510.

Druckman, D. and Zechmeister, K., 1973. Conflict of interest and value dissensus: propositions in the sociology of conflict, *Human Relations,* 26, 449-466.

Eccles, C. 1990, *The Rose Theatre*, Nick Hern Books: London.

Eleftherotypia: Greek daily newspaper

Endere, M.L., 2002. *Management of archaeological sites and the public in Argentina.* Unpublished PhD thesis: University of London.

English Heritage, 2000. *Stonehenge world heritage site management plan.* London: English Heritage.
Retrieved on 13/12/2006 from World Wide Web: http://www.english-heritage.org.uk

Epikairotita: Greek Newspaper

Eriksen, T.H., 1993. *Ethnicity and Nationalism: Anthropological Perspectives*, Chicago: Pluto Press.

Ethnos: Greek daily newspaper

Feilden, B.M. and Jokilehto, J., 1998. *Management guidelines for world cultural heritage sites.* 2nd edition. Rome: ICCROM.

FEK (Φύλλο ελληνικής κυβερνήσεως) *[Governmental newsletters]*

Firenze by Net 2007. *Firenze by net.* Retrieved on 23/04/2007 from World Wide Web: www.mega.it/ita/gui/monu/buc.htm

Fisher, R., Ury, W., and Patton, B., 1991. *Getting to yes: Negotiation agreement without giving in,* (2nd edition). New York: Penguin.

Fisher, S., Abdi, D.I., Ludin, J., Smith, R., Williams, S. and Williams, S., 2005. *Working with Conflict: skills and strategies for action.* London: Zed Books.

Flick, U., 2002. *An introduction to qualitative research.* (2nd ed.) London: SAGE

Fontana, A. and Frey, J.H., 2005. The interview: from neutral stance to political involvement in N.K. Denzin and Y.S. Lincoln (eds.) *The SAGE handbook of qualitative research* (3rd ed.), London: SAGE, 695-727.

Fouseki, K. 2006. Conflicting discourses on the construction of the New Acropolis Museum: Past and Present, *European Review of History*, 3 (4), 533-548.

Fouseki, K. 2007. Developing and Integrating a Conflict Management Model into the Heritage Management Process: The case of the New Acropolis Museum in Grabow, S., Hull, D. and Waterton, E. (eds.) *Which Past, Whose Future: Treatments of the Past at the start of the 21st Century*, BAR SERIES 1633. Oxbow Books: Oxford, 127-136.

Fouseki, K. 2008. Discerning the evidence of 'in-situ museums' in Greece, in Menozzi, O., Di Marzio, M. L., and Fossataro, D. (eds.) *SOMA 2005 Proceedings of the IX Symposium on Mediterranean Archaeology, Chieti (Italy), 24-26 February 2005. BAR SERIES 1793.* Oxford: Oxbow Books, 447-454.

Freeman, R.E., 1984. *Strategic management: a stakeholder approach.* Boston: Pitman.

Fuery, P. and Fuery, K., 2003. *Visual cultures and critical theory.* Oxford, UK: Oxford University Press.

Galtung, J., 2005. Peace studies: a ten points primer. Paper presented in the conference on 'Peace studies in China' held at Nanjing University, 4-6 March 2005. Retrieved on 16/10/2006 from World Wide Web: www.transcend.org/t_database/printarticle.php?ida=53 6.

Gehl, J., 2001. *Life between buildings: using public space*. Translated by Jo Koch, 5th edition. Copenhagen: Danish Architectural Press.

Gehl, J. and Gemzøe, L., 1996. *Public spaces, public life*. Translated by Karen Steenhard. Copenhagen: Danish Architectural Press and the Royal Academy of Fine Arts, School of Architecture.

Gehl, J. and Gemzøe, L., 2003. *New city spaces*. 3rd edition. Copenhagen: Danish Architectural Press.

Gellner, E., 1983. *Nations and Nationalism,* Oxford: Blackwell

Goldman, A. and Rojot, J.C., 2003. *Negotiation: Theory and practice*. London: Kluwer Law International.

Goyder, J. 1992. Scheduling Monuments: The Rose Theatre Case, *International Journal of Cultural Property*, 1(2): 353-358.

Graham, B., Ashworth, G.J., Tunbridge, J.E., 2000. *A geography of heritage: power, culture and economy*. London: Arnold.

Greenberg, R. M. (ed), 1997. *Parks Canada: archaeology and aboriginal partners*. Retrieved on 15/09/2005 from World Wide Web: http://crm.cr.nps.gov/issue.cfm?volume=20&number=04

Graf, H., 2006. *Networks in the innovation process : local and regional interactions*. Cheltenham: Edward Elgar

Guthrie, C., 1999. Better settle than sorry: the regret aversion theory of litigation behaviour, *University of Illinois Law Review*, 1, 43-90.

Hadrian's wall country, 2002. *Management plan 2002-2007*. Retrieved on 10/08/2007 from World Wide Web: www.hadrians-wall.org

Haiman, F.S., 1951. *Group leadership and democratic action*. Boston: Houghton Milffin.

Hall, C.M. and McArthur, S., 1996. The Human dimension of heritage management: different values, different interests, different issues. In: C.M. Hall and S. McArthur (eds). *Heritage management in Australia and New Zealand*. Oxford: Oxford University Press, 2-21.

Hamad, Ahmad, A., 2005. The reconceptualisation of conflict management, *Peace, conflict and development: an interdisciplinary journal*, 7. Retrieved on 14/09/2006 from World Wide Web: http://www.peacestudiesjournal.org.uk

Hamilakis, Y., 2001. Antiquities Underground, *Antiquity,* 75, 35-36.

Hamilakis. Y. and Yalouri, E., 1996. Antiquities as symbolic capital in modern Greece, *Antiquity*, 70, 117-129.

Hamilakis, Y. and Yalouri, E., 1999., Sacrilizing the past: the cults of archaeology in modern Greece, *Archaeological Dialogues,* 6 (2), 115-159.

Hammer, W.C. and Organ, D.W., 1978. *Organisational behavior: An applied psychology approach*. Dallas, TX: Business Publication.

Harper, D. 2005., What's new visually? in N.K. Denzin and Y.S. Lincoln (eds.), *The SAGE handbook of qualitative research* (3rd ed.). London: SAGE, 747 – 762.

Harris, T.A., 1969. *I'm Ok-You're OK: a practical guide to transactional analysis*. New York: Harper and Row.

Haynes, I., Sheldon, H. and Hannigan L. (eds), 2000. *London Underground: the archaeology of a city*. Oxford: Oxbow Books.

Haworth, R., 1984. The modern annals of Wood Quay. In: J. Bradley (ed), *Viking Dublin Exposed: The Wood Quay saga*, 16-37. Dublin: The O'Brien Press.

Hefferman, T.F., 1988. *Wood Quay: The Clash over Dublin's Viking Past*. Austin: University of Texas Press.

Hellenic Ministry of Culture, 1989. *International Meeting for the Restoration of the Acropolis Monuments (1989) 3rd International Meeting for the Restoration of the Acropolis Monument*: Athens, 31 March-2 April 1989 – proceedings Athens: Hellenic Ministry of Culture, Committee for the Preservation of the Acropolis Monuments.

Hellenic Ministry of Culture, 1990. *The New Acropolis Museum: An International Competition*, Athens: Hellenic Ministry of Culture.

Hellenic Ministry of Culture, 2007. *Central Archaeological Council*. Retrieved on 13/07/2007 from World Wide Web: www.yppo.gr/0/kas

Herzfeld, M., 1992. *The Social Production of Indifference: Exploring the Symbolic Roots of Western Bureaucracy*, New York: Berg

Hine, C.M., 2000. *Virtual ethnography*. London: SAGE.

Hodder, I. and Doughty, L. (eds), 2007. *Mediterranean prehistoric heritage: training, education and management*. Cambridge: McDonald Institute for Archaeological Research.

Howard, P., 2003. *Heritage: management, interpretation, identity*. London, New York: Continuum.

ICAHM, 1996. *Archaeological remains in situ conservation. Proceedings of the second ICAHM international conference. ICOMOS International Committee on Archaeological Heritage Management, Montréal, October 11-15, 1994*. Ottawa: ICAHM.

ICOM (International Council of Museums), 2001. *Development of the Museum Definition according to ICOM statutes (1946-2001)*.
Retrieved on 20/09/2007 from World Wide Web: http://icom.museum/hist_def_eng.html

ICOMOS (International Council of Museums and Monuments), 1990. *Charter for the Protection and Management of Archaeological Heritage*. Retrieved on 09/04/2005 from World Wide Web www.international.icomos.org/e_archae.htm

ICOMOS (International Council of Museums and Monuments) 2013. *Burra charter*. ICOMOS: Australia Retrieved on 10/06/2015 from World Wide Web: http://australia.icomos.org/publications/charters/

ICOMOS (International Council on Monuments and Sites), 2004. *ICOMOS Ename charter for the interpretation of cultural heritage*. Retrieved on 27/05/2006 from World Wide Web: www.enamecharter.org

Intriligator, M.D., 1982. Research on conflict theory: analytic approaches and areas of application, *Journal of Conflict Resolution*, 26 (2), 307-327.

Istoria Ellinikou Ethnous, 1999. Η σύγκρουση του Δεκεμβρίου 1944 [*my own translation:* The Battle of the December 1944], in *Istoria Ellinikou Ethnous, volume 16,* [History of the Greek Nation]Athens: Ekdotiki Athinon, 101-107.

James, N. 2000. Presenting history: development and failure in work. *Antiquity*, 74 (286): 744-745.

James, M. and Jongeward, D., 1971. *Born to win: transactional analysis with gestalt experiments*. Reading, MA: Addison-Wesley.

Jehn, K.A, 1997a. A qualitative analysis of conflict types and dimensions in organisational groups, *Administrative Science Quarterly*, 42, 530-557.

Jehn, K.A., 1997b. To agree or not agree: The effects of value congruence, individual demographic dissimilarity, and conflict of workshop outcomes.

International Journal of Conflict Management, 8, 287-305.

Jick, T.D., 2006. Mixing qualitative and quantitative methods: triangulation in action'. In: A. Bryman (ed.), *Mixed methods, vol. II*, London: SAGE: 217-254.

Johnson, D.W., 1971. Role reversal. A summary and review of the research, *International Journal of Group Tensions*, 1, 318-334.

Jones, G.R., George, J.M. and Hill, C.W.L., 1998. *Contemporary management*. Boston, Mass: Irwin/McGraw-Hill.

Kerr, J., 1996. *The conservation plan: a guide to the preparation of conservation plans or places of European cultural significance* (4th edition). Australia: National Trust of Australia (NSW).

Kirk, J.K. and Miller, M.L., 1986. *Reliability and validity in qualitative research*. London: SAGE

Klamer, A. and Zuidhof, P.W., 1999. Values of cultural heritage: merging economic and cultural appraisals. In: *Economics and heritage conservation: a meeting organised by the Getty Conservation Institute, December 1998, Getty Centre*. Los Angeles: Getty Conservation Institute, 23-61.

Kokkou, A., 1977. *Μέριμνα για τις αρχαιότητες στην Ελλάδα και τα πρώτα μουσεία* [*my own translation:* Care for Greek antiquities and the first museums] Athens: Hermes.

Korn, R., 1990. *Visitor Surveys: A user's manual*. Washington, D.C: American Association of Museums.

Krippendorf, K., 1980. *Content analysis: an introduction to its methodology*. Thousand Oaks, London: SAGE.

Krustanov, G., 1981. Problems of cultural monuments' preservation connected with the construction of the Sofia underground, *Monumentum*, 23-24. Retrieved on 07/07/2006 from *23-24* World Wide Web: www.international.icomos.org/ monumentum/vol23-24/vol23-24_15.pdf

Lambrinoudakis, V., 2000. Η αναγκαιότητα της διαχείρισης των αρχαιολογικών χώρων: η εμπειρία της Νάξου και γενικότερες σκέψεις. [*my own translation:* The necessity to manage archaeological sites: the experience of Naxos and general thoughts], in Étienne, Roland (ed) *Les Politiques de l' Archéologie du milieu du XIXe siècle à l'orée du XXIe. Colloque organisé par l'École française d'Athènes à l'occasion de la célébration du 150e anniversaire de sa fondation. Discours prononçés à l'occasion du 150e anniversaire de l'EFA*. Champs Helléniques Modernes et Contemporains: Études sur la société grecque moderne et contemporaine. Athens: École Française d'Athènes (in Greek), 363-370.

Lansaw, P. 1983. The Wood Quay [Dublin] question [discoveries and controversy], *Archaeology* 37 (5): 80

Laporte, A., 2003. La estimación dels visitants: entre la ciencia y la magia. El caso de los restos arqueologicos del Born de Barcelona in Museu d' Història de la Ciutat, Institut de Cultura. Ajuntament de Barceloma (eds) *II Congreso Internacional sobre Musealización arqueológicos: Nuevos Conceptos y Estrategias de Gestión y Communicación, Barcelona, 7,8,9 D' Octubre de 2002.* 323-328. Barcelona: Ajuntament de Barcelona.

Latour, B., 1987. *Science in action: how to follow scientists and engineers through society.* Milton Keynes: Open University Press.

Latour, B., 2005. *Re-assembling the social: an introduction to actor-network-theory.* Oxford: Oxford University Press.

Layton, R., Stone, P.G., and Thomas, J. (eds), 2001. *Destruction and conservation of cultural property.* London: Routledge.

Lewicki, R.J., Saunders, D.M. and Minton, J.W., 1999. *Negotiation*, (3rd edition). United States of America: McGraw – Hill Companies.

Likert, R. and Likert, J.G., 1976., *New ways of managing conflicts*, New York: McGraw- Hill.

Litterer, J.A., 1966. Conflict in organisation: A re-examination, *Academy of Management Journal,* 9, 178-186.

Little, C.E., 1969. *Challenge on the land: open space preservation at the local level.* Oxford: Pergamon.

Longuet, I. and Vincent, J-M., 2001. France., In: . Pickard (ed). *Policy and law in heritage conservation.* London and New York: Spon Press, 92-112.

Lovan, W.R., Murray, M. and Shaffer, R. (eds) 2004. *Participatory governance: planning, conflict mediation and public decision-making in civil society.* Aldershot: Ashgate.

Lovata, L. M., 1987. Behavioural theories relating to the design of information systems. *MIS Quarterly*, 11(2), 147-149.

Lovell, N., 1998. Belonging in Need of emplacement?' In: N. Lovell (ed). *Locality and Belonging.* London – New York: Routledge. 1-24.

Loverdou -Tsigarida, K., 1988. Νέα ανασκαφικά ευρήματα στην κρύπτη του ναού του Αγίου Δημητρίου Θεσσαλονίκης [*my own translation:* New

archaeological finds from the Crypt of St. Dimitrios in Thessaloniki], Το Αρχαιολογικό Έργο στη Μακεδονία και Θράκη, 2, 257-270.

Lowenthal, D., 1985. *The Past is a Foreign Country.* Cambridge: Cambridge University Press.

Lowenthal, D., 1988. Classical antiquities as national and global heritage, *Antiquity*, 62, 726-735.

Lowenthal, D., 1990. Conclusion: archaeologists and others. In: P. Gathercole and D. Lowenthal (eds) *The Politics of the Past,.* London: Unwin Hyman. 302-315.

Lyles, M. A. and Thomas, H., 1988. Strategic problem formulation: Biases and assumptions embedded in alternative decision-making models, *Journal of Management Studies*, 25 (2), 131-145.

Lynch, B. 2013. Special Issue: Working through conflict in museums: museums, objects and participatory democracy. *Museum Management and Curatorship* 28 (1): 1-128.

Macdonald, S., 1996. Theorizing Museums: Introduction, in S. Macdonald and G. Fyfe (eds) *Theorising Museums: Representing identity and diversity in a changing world*, Oxford; Cambridge: Blackwell: The Sociological Review. 1-18.

Mack, R.W. and Snyder, R.C., 1957. Analysis of social conflict: toward an overview and synthesis, *Journal of Conflict Resolution*, 1, 212-248.

Markham, A., 1998. *Life on-line: researching real experience in virtual space.* Wlanut Creek, CA: Altamira.

Marsden, P.V., 1968. Roman house and bath at Billingsgate, *London Archaeologist,* 1 (1), 3-5.

Martin, F.X., 1984. Politics, public protest and the law, in J. Bradley (ed), *Viking Dublin Exposed: The Wood Quay saga*, 38-67. Dublin: The O'Brien Press, 38-67.

Maslow, A., 1943. A theory of human motivation. *Psychological review*, 50, 370-396.

Mason, R. and Avrami, E., 2002. Heritage values and challenges of conservation planning. In: J.M. Teutonico and G. Palumbo (eds). *Management planning for archaeological sites: an international workshop organised by the Getty Conservation.* Los Angeles: Getty Conservation Institute, 13-26.

Merriman, N., 2000. *Beyond the Glass Case: the past, heritage and the public.* London: Institute of Archaeology, University College London.

Mikelakis, M., 2002. Επιτόπιο Μουσείο Νάξου [*my own translation:* In – situ museum of Naxos] *Corpus*, 36, March 2002, 20-24.

Miles, D. and Brindle, S., 2005. *Case study: The Rose Theatre, Bankside, London*. Paper presented in the APPEAR conference organised by the Committee for the regions in Brussels, in October 2005.

Millar, S., 2007. Stakeholder and community participation, in A. Leask and A. Fyall (eds), *Managing World Heritage Sites*. Oxford: Elsevier BH. 37-54.

Minissi, F., 1961. Protection of the mosaic pavements of the Roman villa at Piazza Armerina (Sicily), *Museum*, 14, 128-132.

Monjoie, S., 2005. 'Etude de cas : L' Archéoforum de Liège, Belgique'. Unpublished paper presented in the APPEAR conference, October 2005, Belgium.

Montville, J., 1991. Track two diplomacy : the arrow and the olive branch : a case for track two diplomacy, in V.D. Volkan, M.D.J., Montville and D.A., Julis (eds), *The psychodynamics of international relations , vol.2, Unofficial diplomacy at work*, Massachusetts : Lexington, 161-175.

Morley, I.E. and Stephenson, G.M., 1977. *The Social Psychology of Bargaining*, Willmer Brothers Limited, Birenhead: UK

Mouliou, M., 1996. Ancient Greece, its classical heritage and the modern Greeks: aspects of nationalism in museum exhibitions, in J.A. Atkinson, I. Banks and J. O'Sullivan, (eds) *Nationalism and Archaeology: Scottish Archaeological Forum,*. Glasgow: Cruithne Press, 175-199.

Municipality of Thessaloniki, 2007. Retrieved on 15/07/2007 from World Wide Web: http://www.thessalonikicity.gr/

Murray, E.J., 1968. Conflict, I: Psychological aspects, in D.L. Sills (ed), *International encyclopedia of the social sciences, volume 3*. New York: Crowell and Macmillan, 220- 226.

Mpiris, K. 1995. The city of Athens from the 19th to the 20th century [my own translation] (*Αι Αθήναι από του 19ov εις τον 20ov αιώνα*)

Museu d' Història de la Ciutat, Institut de Cultura and Ajuntament de Barcelona, 2003. *II Congreso internacional sobre musealización arqueológicos: nuevos conceptos y estrategias de gestión y communicación, Barcelona, 7,8,9 D' Octubre de 2002*. Barcelona: Museu d' Història de la Ciutat, Institut de Cultura. Ajuntament de Barcelona.

Myers, D., Smith, S.N. and Shaer, M. 2010. *A didactic case study of Jarash Archaeological Site, Jordan: Stakeholders and Heritage Values in Site Management*. Los Angeles: The Getty Conservation Institute.

Nafziger, J., 2004. A Blueprint for Avoiding and resolving Cultural Heritage Disputes, *Art, Antiquity and Law*, 3, 3-20.

National Trust, 2002. *The creation of a statement of significance*. Retrieved on 29/11/2004 from World Wide Web: http://www.nationaltrust.org.uk/environment/html/features/papers/creation01.htm

National Trust, 2003. *Guidelines on the preparation of a statement of significance*. Retrieved on 29/11/2004 from World Wide Web: http://www.nationaltrust.org.uk/environment/html/peo_com/papers/signif01.htm

Naxiologa, 2000. Αρχαιολογικός χώρος πλατείας Μητροπόλεως: Η παρεξηγημένη κληρονομιά μας [*my own translation:* archaeological site of Mitropolis square: our misunderstood heritage] in Naxiologa, 2, 20-22.

Nierenberg, G., 1976. *The complete negotiator*. New York: Nierenberg and Zeif Publishers.

Nicholson, M., 1970. *Conflict analysis*. London: English Universities Press.

Nightingale, D., 1974. Conflict and conflict resolution, in G. Strouss, R.E. Miles, C.C. Snow and A.S. Tannenbaum (eds), *Organizational behavior: Research and issues*, Madison, WI: Industrial Relations Research Association, 141-163.

OANMA, (Organisation for the Construction of the New Acropolis Museum) 2001., *The New Acropolis Museum: The International Competition*, Athens: Organization for the Construction of the New Acropolis Museum.

OANMA (Organisation for the Construction of the New Acropolis Museum) and First Ephorate of Prehistoric and Classical Antiquities, 2006. *To Μουσείο και η ανασκαφή* [my own translation: The Museum and the excavations], Athens: OANMA.

Oikonomou, G. and Georgiou, A.K., 2000. *Ποσοτική ανάλυση για τη λήψη διοικητικών αποφάσεων* [my own translation: Quantitative analysis for decision-making process], Athens: Benou.

Office of the Deputy Prime Minister, 2003. *Participatory planning for sustainable communities: international experience in mediation, negotiation and engagement in making plans*. London: Office of the Deputy Prime Minister.

O' Keefe, P.J., 2000. Archaeology and human rights, *Public archaeology*, 1, 181-194.

Orton, C. 1989. A tale of two sites, *London Archaeologist*, 6, 59-65.

Osborne, M.J., 2002. *A course in Game Theory,* The MIT Press: Cambridge, London, Massachusetts.

PAE (Πρακτικά Αρχαιολογικής Εταιρείας) *[Archaeological Newsletters]*

Papachristos, N., 2004. Η περίπτωση του Νέου Μουσείου Ακρόπολης *[my own translation:* The case of the New Acropolis Museum in Greek], in E. Trova (ed), *Η πολιτιστική κληρονομιά και το δίκαιο [my own translation:* cultural heritage and law],. Athens and Thessaloniki: Sakkoula, 437-449.

Papageorgiou, L., 2000. The Unification of Archaeological sites of Athens. The birth of an archaeological park?, *Conservation and Management of Archaeological Sites,* 4(3),177-84.

Papandreou, G., 2000. *Papandreou argues for the Return of the Parthenon Marbles,* Memoranda submitted by the Government of the Hellenic Republic and by the Melina Merkouri Foundation: Examination of Witness, Monday, 5 June 2000.
Retrieved on 08/08/2002 from World Wide Web:
http://www.papandreou.gr/June_2000/gpap_argues_ma rbles_En_05062000.html

Pathfinders, 2006. *Forum on the New Acropolis Museum* Retrieved on 12/12/2006 from World Wide Web:
http://homepages.pathfinder.gr/kalel/Press.htm

Pearson, M. and Sullivan, S., 1995. *Looking after heritage places. The basics of heritage planning for managers, landowners and administrators.* Melbourne: Melbourne University Press, 126-186.

Pelled, L.H., Eisenhardt, K.M. and Xin, K.R., 1999. Exploring the black box: An analysis of work group diversity, conflict, and performance, *Administrative Science* Quarterly, 44, 1- 28.

Petrakos, V., 1982. *Δοκίμιο για την αρχαιολογική νομοθεσία [my own translation:* Essay on the archaeological legislation], Hellenic Ministry of Culture–Archaeological Receipt Fund.

Philippopoulou-Michaelidou, E., 1998. *Melina Merkouri Foundation: The Museum of Acropolis,* Hellenic Ministry of Culture. Retrieved on 18/07/2002 from World Wide Web:
http://www.culture.gr/4/41/411/e41105.htm

Pickard, R. (ed), 2001. *Policy and law in Heritage conservation.* London: Spon

Post, J.E., Preston, L.E. and Sachs, S., 2002. *Redefining the corporation: stakeholder management and organisational wealth.* Stanford, Calif: Stanford University Press.

Pred, A., 1984. Place as historically contingent process: Structuration theory and timegeography of becoming place. *Annals of the Association of American Geographers,* 74, 279-297.

Prastakos, G., 2003. *Διοικητική Επιστήμη: Λήψη επιχειρησιακών αποφάσεων στην κοινωνία της πληροφορίας* [my own translation: *Management science: decision-making in the information* society]. Athens: Stamoulis.

Protopsaltis, E. G., 1967. *Ιστορικά έγγραφα περί αρχαιοτήτων και λοιπών μνημείων της ιστορίας κατά τους χρόνους της Επαναστάσεως και του Καποδίστρια [my own translation:* Historical documents about antiquities and the rest of historic monuments during the Revolution period and the times of Kapodistria], Athens.

Pruitt, D.G. and Rubin, J.Z., 1986. *Social conflict: escalation, stalemate and settlement.* New York: Random House.

Putnam, L. and M. Holmer, 1992. Framing, Reframing, and Issue Development, in L., Putnam and M.E., Roloff (eds.), *Communication and Negotiation,* Newbury Park, CA: SAGE. 128-155.

Pwiti, G., 1996. Let the ancestors rest in peace? New challenges for cultural heritage management in Zimbabwe. *Conservation and Management of Archaeological Sites* 1(3), 151-160.

Rahim, M.A. and Bonoma, T.V., 1979. Managing organisational conflict: a model for diagnosis and intervention, *Psychological reports,* 44, 1323-1344.

Rahim, A.M., (ed), 2001. *Managing conflict in organisations,* 3rd edition. London: Quorum Books

Rapoport, A., 1964. *Strategy and conscience.* New York: Harper and Row.

Rascón Marqués, S. and Méndez Madariaga, A. 2000 (eds), *Ciudad, arqueología y desarrollo: La musealización de los yacimientos arqueológicos: actas del 1er congreso internacional ciudad, arqueología y desarrollo. Alcalá de Hanares, 27 al 29 de Septembre de 2000.* Consejería de Educación de la Communidad de Madrid, Ayuntamiento de Alcalá de henares, Museum d'Historia de la Ciutat de Barcelona.

Reimann, C., 2001. Assessing the state-of-the-art in conflict management: reflections from a theoretical perspective, in A. Austin, M. Fisher and N. Ropers (eds.), *Berghof handbook for conflict transformation.* Berlin: Berghof Research Centre for Constructive Conflict Management in Austin. Available at: Retrieved on 02/03/2003 from World Wide Web http://www.berghofhandbook. net/articles/reimann_handbook.pdf.

Renson, A., 2004. *Archéoforum de Liège: une ville retrouve ses racines* . Belgium : Institut de Patrimoine de Wallon.

Richardson, B. and Richardson, R. 1989. *Business Planning: An approach to strategic management,* London: Pitman.

Richardson, L. and St Pierre E.A., 2005. Writing: a method of enquiry. In: N.K. Denzin and Y.S. Lincoln (eds). *The SAGE handbook of qualitative research* (3rd ed.), London: SAGE, 957-978.

Rogers, E.M., 1995. *Diffusion of innovations*. 4th edition. New York: The Free Press.

Rosney, B., 1984. Occupation diary, In J. Bradley (ed), *Viking Dublin Exposed: The Wood Quay saga*. Dublin: The O'Brien Press, 68-93.

Ross, R.S. and Ross, J.R., 1989. *Small groups in organisational settings*. Englewood Cliffs, NJ: Prentice-Hall.

Rowsome, P., 1996. The Billingsgate Roman house and bath – conservation and assessment, London. *Archaeologist*, 7, 415–423.

Saaty, T.L., 1990. The analytic hierarchy process in conflict management, *International Journal of Conflict Management*, 1, 47-68.

Schadla – Hall, R. T., 1984. Slightly looted: a review of the Jorvik Viking Centre. *Museums Journal*, 84, 62 – 64.

Schama, S., 1995. *Landscape and memory*, London: Harper Collins Publishers.

Schelling, T.C., 1960. *The strategy of conflict.* Cambridge, MA: Harvard University Press.

Schmidt, H., 1988. *Schutzbauten*. Stuttgart: Theiss.

Scichilone, G., 1986. The site of the Cathedral at Atri: a case study of in situ conservation of archaeological remains' in ICCROM Preventive Measures during Excavation and site Protection, 6-8 November Conference. Italy: Sintesi Grafica s.r.l., 309-318.

Seeden, H., 1990. Search for the missing link: archaeology and the public in Lebanon. in P. Gathercole and Lowenthal, D., (eds), *The Politics of the Past*. One World Archaeology. London: Unwin Hyman, 141-159.

Sheldon, H., 1990. The Museum of London and the Rose, *Antiquity,* 64 (243), 286-288.

Sheurich, J.J., 1995. A postmodernist critique of research interviewing, *Qualitative Studies in Education*, 8, 239-252.

Skouris, P. and Trove, E., 2003. *Προστασία αρχαιοτήτων και πολιτιστικής κληρονομιάς* [*my own translation: Protection of antiquities and cultural heritage*], Athens: Sakkoula.

Silverman, D., 2005a. *Interpreting qualitative data: methods for analysing talk, text and interaction.* (2nd ed.). London: SAGE.

Silverman, D. 2005b. *Doing qualitative research: a practical handbook.* (2nd ed.). London: SAGE

Simms, A., 1984. A key place for Dublin, past and present, in J. Bradley (ed), *Viking Dublin Exposed: The Wood Quay saga*, Dublin: The O'Brien Press: 154-163.

Simon, H., 1965. *Administrative behaviour: a study for decision-making process in administrative organisation*, 2nd ed , New York: Free Press, Collier – MacMillan.

Simpson, L. 2014. Heritage outrage: Wood Quay. *History Ireland*. 22(2): 46.

Siouti, G., 2004. Η προστασία του φυσικού και πολιτιστικού περιβάλλοντος από τη Νομολογία: Σύγκρουση αγαθών ή αειφόρος προστασία του χώρου; [*my own translation:* The protection of the natural and cultural environment from the Case law/juripridence: 'Collision' of goods or an eternal protection of the space?' in E. Trova (ed), *Η πολιτιστική κληρονομιά και το Δίκαιο* [*my own translation:* The Cultural Heritage and the Law] 81-94. European Public Center-Sakkoula: Athens – Thessaloniki.

Skeates, R., 2000. *Debating the archaeological heritage*. London: Duckworth.

Smith, C.G., 1966. A comparative analysis of some conditions and consequences of interorganisational conflict, *Administrative Science Quarterly,* 10, 504-529.

Smith, L., 2004., *Archaeological theory and the politics of cultural heritage*. London: Routledge.

Société Royale- le vieux Liége 2003. Retrieved on 12/04/2005 from World Wide Web: http://www.vieuxliege.be

Stake, R.E., 1978. The case study method in social inquiry, *Educational Researcher*, 7 (2), 5-8.

Stake, R.E., 2005. Qualitative case studies in N.K. Denzin and Y.S. Lincoln (eds.),. *The SAGE handbook of qualitative research* (3rd ed.). London: SAGE, 443-466.

Start, D., 1999. Community archaeology. Bringing it back to local communities. In: G. Chitty and D. Baker (eds). *Managing historic sites and buildings.*

Reconciling presentation and preservation. London: Routledge, 49-60.

Stewart, C., 1998. Who owns the Rotonda ? Church vs. Greek State, *Anthropology Today,* 3-9.

Stovel, H., Stanley-Price, N. and Killick, R. (eds), 2005. *Conservation on living religious heritage: papers from the ICCROM 2003 Forum on Living Religious History: conserving the sacred.* Rome: International Centre for the Study of the Preservation and Restoration of Cultural Property.

Stroebe, W., Kruglansky, Aa.w., D. Bar-Tal, M. Hewstone, M. (eds), 1988. *The social psychology of intergroup conflict: Theory, research and applications,* New York: Springer- Verlag.

Ŝtulk, J., 2001. Czech Republic. In: R. Pickard (ed). *Policy and law in heritage conservation,.* London and New York: Spon Press. 41-72

Supreme Council of Ethnikoi Hellenes, 2007. Retrieved on 30/08/2007 from World Wide Web: www.ysee.gr

Sullivan, H., 1984. Monitoring visitor use and site management, in H. Sullivan (ed) *Visitors to Aboriginal sites: access, control and management: Proceedings of the 1983 Kakadu workshop.* Canberra: Australia National Parks and Wildlife Service, 43-53.

Sullivan, S., 1997. A planning model for the management of archaeological sites, in M. De la Torre (ed) *The conservation of archaeological sites in the Mediterranean region. An international conference organised by the Getty Conservation Institute and the J. Paul Getty Museum, 6-12 May 1995.* Los Angeles: Getty Conservation Institute, 15-26.

Tasia, A., 1993. Η σωστική ανασκαφή της ΙΣΤ' ΕΠΚΑ στην πλατεία Διοικητηρίου [*my own translation:* Rescue excavations of the 16th EPKA at Administrative square] Το αρχαιολογικό έργο στη Μακεδονία και Θράκη, 7, 329–341.

Tasia, A., Zola, Z., Bachlas, A. and Stagkos, A., 1996. Το ανασκαφικό έργο της ΙΣΤ' Εφορείας στο Διοικητήριο [*my own translation:* The archaeological work of the 16th Ephorate at Adminstrative Building] Το αρχαιολογικό έργο στη Μακεδονία και Θράκη (10 A-B), 545 – 557.

Ta Nea: Daily Greek liberal newspaper

Tedeschi, J.T., Schlenker, B.R. and Bonoma, T.V., 1973. *Conflict, power and games: The experimental study of interpersonal relations.* Chicago: Aldine.

Teutonico, J.M. and Matero, F. (eds), 2003. *Managing change: sustainable approaches to the conservation of the built environment: 4th Annual US/ICOMOS*

International Symposium organised by US/ICOMOS, Program in Historic Preservation of the University of Pennsylvania, and the Getty Conservation Institute, Pennsylvania, April 2001. Los Angeles: Getty Conservation Institute.

The British Museum, 1997. *The Sculptures from the Parthenon: a statement from the British Museum.* Retrieved on 08/08/2002 from World Wide Web: http://www.thebritishmuseum.ac.uk/gr/debate.html.

The Conservative Party, 1996. *The Parthenon Sculptures,* Retrieved on 16/08/2002 from World Wide Web:
www.uk.digiserve.com/mentor/marbles/consrv.htm

The Guardian: British daily newspaper

The Rose Theatre Trust, 2006. *The Rose.* Retrieved on 23/09/2007 from World Wide Web: http://www.rosetheatre.org.uk/

Thessaloniki Politon, 2006.
Retrieved on 13/07/2006 from World Wide Web: www.thessalonikipoliton.gr

Thomas, K.W., 1992. *Conflict and negotiation processes in organisations,* in M.D., Dunnette and L.M., Lough (eds.), *Handbook of industrial and organisational psychology,* 3, 2nd edition, Chicago: Rand-McNally, 651-717.

Thomas, J.M. and Bennis, W.G., 1972. *The management of change and conflict: selected readings.* Harmondsworth: Penguin.

Tilley, C., 1994. *A Phenomenology of Landscape: places, paths and monuments,* Oxford and Providence, RI: Berg.

Tiverios, M., 2005. [*my own translation:* 'The archaeological finds are buried again'. To Vema 05/06/2005.
Retrieved on June 2005 from World Wide Web: http://tovima.dolnet.gr/print_article.php?e=B&f=14481&m=B61&aa=1

To Vema: Daily Greek Newspaper

Travlos, I., 1993. *Poleodomiki Exelixis Athinon apo ton Proistorikon Chronon mexri ton Arxon tou 19ou aionos* [*my own translation:* Urban Planning development from the prehistoric times until the beginning of the 19th century]Athens:KAPON.

Tribe, D., 1993. *Negotiation,* London: Cavendish Publishing Limited

Turner, J.C., Hogg, M.A., Oakes, P.J., Reicher, S.D. and Wetherell, M.S. 1987. *Rediscovering the social group: a self-categorisation theory.* Oxford: Blackwell.

Tunbridge, J.E. and Ashworth, G.J., 1996. *Dissonant heritage: The management of the past as a resource in conflict*. Chichester: WILEY.

Truscott, M. and Young, D. 2000. Revising the Burra Charter: Australia ICOMOS updates its guidelines for conservation practice, *Conservation and Management of Archaeological Sites*, 4 (2), 101-116.

Tversky, A. and Kahneman, D., 2000. *Choices, values and frames*. Cambridge: Cambridge University Press.

UNESCO (United Nations Educational, Scientific and Cultural Organisation), 1954. *Convention for the Protection of Cultural Property in the Event of Armed Conflict*. Retrieved on 20/09/2007 from World Wide Web: http://portal.unesco.org/culture/en/ev.php

UNESCO 1960. *Recommendation concerning the most effective means of rendering museums accessible to everyone*.
Retrieved on 20/09/2007 from World Wide Web: http://portal.unesco.org/en/ev.php

UNESCO 1968. *Recommendation concerning the conservation of cultural property endangered by public or private works*. Retrieved on 20/09/2007 from World Wide Web: http://portal.unesco.org/en/ev.php

Uotila, K., & Sartes, M. 2000. *Medieval Turku: The Lost City. A Project Trying to Reconstruct a Medieval Town in Finland*. BAR INTERNATIONAL SERIES, 843, Oxbow Books: Oxford, 219-224.

Veleni P., 1993. Η τύχη των αρχαιολογικών ιστών στις νέες πόλεις. Το παράδειγμα της Θεσσαλονίκης [the future of archaeological sites in the new developed cities. The example of Thessaloniki.] in *Νέες πόλεις πάνω σε παλιές*[New cities above old one] *Conference at Rhodes, 27-30 September, 1993*. Athens: Eptalofos, 91-101. Ville de Marseille 2007.
Retrieved on 10/02//2006 from World Wide Web www.mairiemarseille.fr/vivre/culture/musée/docks.htm

Vitelli, K.D. and Colwell-Chanthaphonh, C., 2006. *Archaeological ethics*. Lenham, MD:
Oxford: Altamira Press.

Vlassopoulou, H., Eleftheratou, S., Mantis, A., 2000. *Stathmos METRO 'Akropolis': Arhaeologiki periigisi* [*my own translation:* Acropolis METRO Station: Archaeological Tour], Athens: Hellenic Ministry of Culture, 1st Ephorate of Prehistoric and Classical Antiquities, Ministry of Environmental and Public Works, ATTIKO METRO A.E.

von Neumann and Morgenstern, 1947. *Theory of games and economic behaviour*. 2nd edition. Princeton: Princeton University Press.

von Winterfeldt, D., 2001. Decisions with multiple stakeholders and conflicting objectives, in E.U. Weber, J. Baron and G. Loomes (eds), *Conflict and tradeoffs in decision making*. Cambridge: Cambridge University Press, 259-299.

Vroom, V.H. and Yetton, P.W. 1973. *Leadership and decision-making*. Pittsburg: University of Pittsburg Press.

Wainwright, G.J. 1989. 'Saving the Rose', Antiquity, 63 (240), 430-435.

Wallace, P. and Canavan, T. 2005. Interview: Wood Quay Man. *History Ireland*, 49-51.

Walcott, C., Hoppman, P.T. and King, T.D., 1977 . *The role of debate in negotiation*, in D. Druckman (ed), *Negotiations: social psychological perspectives*, Beverley Hills, CA: SAGE: 193-211.

Weber, M., 1918. Politics as a vocation, reproduced in H.H. Gerth and C.W. Mills (eds) *From Max Weber*. New York: Oxford University Press.

Weidhagen-Hallerdt, M., 1993. Från Birger Jarl Till Gustav Vasa. Norstedts Tryckeri AB : Stockholm.

Werner, O. and Schopfle, G.M., 1987. *Systematic fieldwork: Vol. 1, Foundations of ethnography and interviewing*. London: SAGE.

Whitfield, J., 1994. *Conflicts in construction: avoiding, managing, resolving*. Basingstoke, England: Macmillan.

Wilson, D., 1985. Return and Restitution: A museum perspective, in I. McBryde (ed) *Who owns the Past?* Papers from the annual symposium of the Australian of humanities, Melbourne: Oxford University Press: 99-106.

Yalouri, E., 2000. *Global fame, local claim: the Athenian Acropolis of objectification of Greek identity*. Unpublished PhD thesis: University of London.

Yalouri, E., 2001. *The Acropolis: global fame, local claim*. Oxford: Berg.

Zimmerman, L.J., Vitelli, K.D., and Hollowell-Zimmer, J., 2003. *Ethical issues in archaeology*. Walnut Creek, CA: Altamira Press.

Zimmerman, L.J., 2007. *Submission-Dionysiou Aeropagitou St., Athens*. World Archaeological Congress. Retrieved on 20/09/2007 from World Wide Web:
http://www.worldarchaeologicalcongress.org/site/news_pres_15.php Accessed on: 20/09/2007

www.ingramcontent.com/pod-product-compliance
Lightning Source LLC
Chambersburg PA
CBHW061007030426
42334CB00033B/3396